Communications in Computer and Information Science 1849

Rationale

The CCIS series is devoted to the publication of proceedings of computer science conferences. Its aim is to efficiently disseminate original research results in informatics in printed and electronic form. While the focus is on publication of peer-reviewed full papers presenting mature work, inclusion of reviewed short papers reporting on work in progress is welcome, too. Besides globally relevant meetings with internationally representative program committees guaranteeing a strict peer-reviewing and paper selection process, conferences run by societies or of high regional or national relevance are also considered for publication.

Topics

The topical scope of CCIS spans the entire spectrum of informatics ranging from foundational topics in the theory of computing to information and communications science and technology and a broad variety of interdisciplinary application fields.

Information for Volume Editors and Authors

Publication in CCIS is free of charge. No royalties are paid, however, we offer registered conference participants temporary free access to the online version of the conference proceedings on SpringerLink (http://link.springer.com) by means of an http referrer from the conference website and/or a number of complimentary printed copies, as specified in the official acceptance email of the event.

CCIS proceedings can be published in time for distribution at conferences or as post-proceedings, and delivered in the form of printed books and/or electronically as USBs and/or e-content licenses for accessing proceedings at SpringerLink. Furthermore, CCIS proceedings are included in the CCIS electronic book series hosted in the SpringerLink digital library at http://link.springer.com/bookseries/7899. Conferences publishing in CCIS are allowed to use Online Conference Service (OCS) for managing the whole proceedings lifecycle (from submission and reviewing to preparing for publication) free of charge.

Publication process

The language of publication is exclusively English. Authors publishing in CCIS have to sign the Springer CCIS copyright transfer form, however, they are free to use their material published in CCIS for substantially changed, more elaborate subsequent publications elsewhere. For the preparation of the camera-ready papers/files, authors have to strictly adhere to the Springer CCIS Authors' Instructions and are strongly encouraged to use the CCIS LaTeX style files or templates.

Abstracting/Indexing

CCIS is abstracted/indexed in DBLP, Google Scholar, EI-Compendex, Mathematical Reviews, SCImago, Scopus. CCIS volumes are also submitted for the inclusion in ISI Proceedings.

How to start

To start the evaluation of your proposal for inclusion in the CCIS series, please send an e-mail to ccis@springer.com.

Marten Van Sinderen · Fons Wijnhoven ·
Slimane Hammoudi · Pierangela Samarati ·
Sabrina De Capitani di Vimercati
Editors

E-Business and Telecommunications

19th International Conference, ICSBT 2022 Lisbon, Portugal, July 14–16, 2022 and 19th International Conference, SECRYPT 2022 Lisbon, Portugal, July 11–13, 2022 Revised Selected Papers

Editors
Marten Van Sinderen
University of Twente
Enschede, The Netherlands

Fons Wijnhoven
University of Twente
Enschede, The Netherlands

Slimane Hammoudi
ESEO, ERIS
Anger Cedex, France

Pierangela Samarati
University of Milan
Milan, Italy

Sabrina De Capitani di Vimercati
University of Milan
Milan, Italy

ISSN 1865-0929 ISSN 1865-0937 (electronic)
Communications in Computer and Information Science
ISBN 978-3-031-45136-2 ISBN 978-3-031-45137-9 (eBook)
https://doi.org/10.1007/978-3-031-45137-9

This Springer imprint is published by the registered company Springer Nature Switzerland AG
The registered company address is: Gewerbestrasse 11, 6330 Cham, Switzerland

Paper in this product is recyclable.

Preface

The present book includes extended and revised versions of a set of selected papers from the International Conference on Smart Business Technologies – ICSBT 2022 (formerly known as ICE-B - International Conference on e-Business) and the International Conference on Security and Cryptography - SECRYPT 2022.

ICSBT 2022 was held in Lisbon, Portugal, from 14–16 July and SECRYPT 2022 was held in Lisbon, Portugal, from 11–13 July.

ICSBT 2022 received 25 paper submissions from 16 countries and SECRYPT 2022 received 118 paper submissions from 28 countries. This book contains 1 paper from ICSBT 2022 and 6 papers from SECRYPT 2022.

The papers were selected by the event chairs and their selection is based on a number of criteria that include the classifications and comments provided by the program committee members, the session chairs' assessment and also the program chairs' global view of all papers included in the technical program. The authors of selected papers were then invited to submit a revised and extended version of their papers having at least 30% innovative material.

The International Conference on Smart Business Technologies (formerly known as ICE-B - International Conference on e-Business), aims to bring together researchers and practitioners who are interested in e-Business technology and its current applications. The scope of the conference covers low-level technological issues, such as technology platforms, internet of things and web services, but also higher-level issues, such as business processes, business intelligence, value setting and business strategy. Furthermore, it covers different approaches to address these issues and different possible applications with their own specific needs and requirements in the field of technology. These are all areas of theoretical and practical importance within the broad scope of e-Business, whose growing importance can be seen from the increasing interest of the IT research community.

SECRYPT is an annual international conference that focuses on all aspects of security and privacy. The scope of the conference covers novel research on all theoretical and practical aspects of data protection, privacy, security and cryptography, as well as the application of security technology, the implementation of advanced prototypes and techniques, lessons learned and future directions.

The papers selected to be included in this book contribute to the understanding of relevant trends of current research on Smart Business Technologies, Security and Cryptography, including: Big Data, Big Data Management, Machine Learning and AI Security, Applied Cryptography, Intrusion Detection & Prevention, Data Integrity, Security Verification and Validation, Security and Privacy in Pervasive/Ubiquitous Computing, Security and Privacy in Mobile Systems, Security and Privacy in Crowdsourcing, Privacy Enhancing Technologies and Network Security.

We would like to thank all the authors for their contributions and also the reviewers who have helped to ensure the quality of this publication.

July 2022

Marten Van Sinderen
Fons Wijnhoven
Slimane Hammoudi
Pierangela Samarati
Sabrina De Capitani di Vimercati

Organization

ICSBT Conference Chair

Marten van Sinderen	University of Twente, The Netherlands

SECRYPT Conference Chair

Pierangela Samarati	Università degli Studi di Milano, Italy

ICSBT Program Co-chairs

Slimane Hammoudi	ESEO, ERIS, France
Fons Wijnhoven	University of Twente, The Netherlands

SECRYPT Program Chair

Sabrina De Capitani di Vimercati	Università degli Studi di Milano, Italy

ICSBT Program Committee

Andreas Ahrens	Hochschule Wismar, University of Technology, Business and Design, Germany
Saadat M. Alhashmi	University of Sharjah, United Arab Emirates
Salvatore Ammirato	University of Calabria, Italy
Alexandros Bousdekis	National Technical University of Athens, Greece
Chun-Liang Chen	National Taiwan University of Arts, Taiwan, Republic of China
Dickson Chiu	University of Hong Kong, Hong Kong
Ritesh Chugh	Central Queensland University, Australia
Soon A. Chun	City University of New York, USA
Valerio Frascolla	Intel, Germany
Andreas Gadatsch	Hochschule Bonn-Rhein-Sieg, Germany
Francisco García-Sánchez	University of Murcia, Spain
Giulio Di Gravio	Sapienza University of Rome, Italy
Pierre Hadaya	University of Quebec at Montreal, Canada

Ahasanul Haque	International Islamic University Malaysia, Malaysia
Dimitrios G. Katehakis	FORTH, Greece
Peter Loos	German Research Center for Artificial Intelligence, Germany
Samaneh Madanian	Auckland University of Technology, New Zealand
Wilma Penzo	University of Bologna, Italy
Charmaine D. Plessis	University of South Africa, South Africa
Pak-Lok Poon	Central Queensland University, Australia
Ela Pustulka-Hunt	FHNW Olten, Switzerland
Gustavo Rossi	Lifia, Argentina
Jarogniew Rykowski	Poznan University of Economics, Poland
Rong-an Shang	Soochow University, Taiwan, Republic of China
Agostinho S. Sousa Pinto	CEOS.PP, ISCAP, Polytechnic of Porto, Portugal
Vesna Spasojevic Brkic	University of Belgrade, Serbia
Riccardo Spinelli	Università degli Studi di Genova, Italy
Emmanouil Stiakakis	University of Macedonia, Greece
Ben van Lier	University of Applied Science Rotterdam, The Netherlands/Steinbeis University Berlin, Germany
Alfredo Vellido	Universitat Politècnica de Catalunya, Spain

SECRYPT Program Committee

Massimiliano Albanese	George Mason University, USA
Cristina Alcaraz	University of Málaga, Spain
Peter Amthor	Technische Universität Ilmenau, Germany
Muhammad Asghar	University of Auckland, New Zealand
Diogo Barradas	University of Waterloo, Canada
Jonas Böhler	SAP SE, Germany
Francesco Buccafurri	University of Reggio Calabria, Italy
Bogdan Carbunar	Florida International University, USA
Xiaochun Cheng	Middlesex University, UK
Mauro Conti	University of Padua, Italy
Frederic Cuppens	Polytechnique de Montréal, Canada
Nora Cuppens	Polytechnique de Montréal, Canada
Giovanni Di Crescenzo	Peraton Labs, USA
Mario Di Raimondo	University of Catania, Italy
Ruggero Donida Labati	Università degli Studi di Milano, Italy
Mohammed Erradi	ENSIAS, Mohammed V University in Rabat, Morocco
Csilla Farkas	USC, Columbia, USA

Alberto Ferrante	Università della Svizzera Italiana, Switzerland
Anna Lisa Ferrara	University of Molise, Italy
Josep-Lluis Ferrer-Gomila	University of the Balearic Islands, Spain
Sara Foresti	Università degli Studi di Milano, Italy
Steven Furnell	University of Nottingham, UK
Joaquin Garcia-Alfaro	Télécom SudParis, France
Angelo Genovese	Università degli Studi di Milano, Italy
Roberto Gonzalez	NEC Labs Europe, Spain
Dimitris Gritzalis	Athens University of Economics & Business, Greece
Christophe Huygens	KU Leuven, Belgium
Sokratis Katsikas	Norwegian University of Science and Technology, Norway
Shinsaku Kiyomoto	KDDI Research Inc., Japan
Kees Leune	Adelphi University, USA
Albert Levi	Sabancı University, Turkey
Jay Ligatti	University of South Florida, USA
Giovanni Livraga	Università degli Studi di Milano, Italy
Suryadipta Majumdar	Concordia University, Canada
Yunlong Mao	Nanjing University, China
Evangelos Markatos	ICS, Forth, Greece
Fabio Martinelli	Consiglio Nazionale delle Ricerche, Italy
Sjouke Mauw	University of Luxembourg, Luxembourg
David Megias	Universitat Oberta de Catalunya, Spain
Weizhi Meng	Technical University of Denmark, Denmark
Alessio Merlo	University of Genoa, Italy
Guillermo Navarro-Arribas	Universitat Autònoma de Barcelona, Spain
Rolf Oppliger	eSECURITY Technologies, Switzerland
Stefano Paraboschi	University of Bergamo, Italy
Gerardo Pelosi	Politecnico di Milano, Italy
Yunior Ramirez-Cruz	Finquest Luxembourg, Luxembourg
Silvio Ranise	Fondazione Bruno Kessler, Italy
Carsten Rudolph	Monash University, USA
Fabio Scotti	Università degli Studi di Milano, Italy
Pietro Tedeschi	Technology Innovation Institute, UAE
Anselme Tueno	SAP SE, Germany
Lingyu Wang	Concordia University, Canada
Christos Xenakis	University of Piraeus, Greece
Shengzhi Zhang	Boston University, Metropolitan College, USA
Yongjun Zhao	Nanyang Technological University, Singapore

SECRYPT Additional Reviewers

Abdullatif Albaseer	Hamad Bin Khalifa University, Qatar
Zahara Ebadi Ansaroudi	Fondazione Bruno Kessler, Italy
Stefano Berlato	University of Genoa, Italy
Alessandro Budroni	Technology Innovation Institute, UAE
Matteo Cardaioli	University of Padua, Italy
Rosangela Casolare	University of Molise, Italy
El Mostapha Chakir	HENCEFORTH, Morocco
Vincenzo De Angelis	University of Reggio Calabria, Italy
Luca Degani	University of Trento & IIT CNR, Italy
Biniam Fisseha Demissie	Fondazione Bruno Kessler, Italy
Maryam Ehsanpour	University of Padua, Italy
Carles Garrigues-Olivella	Universitat Oberta de Catalunya, Spain
Kyusuk Han	Technology Innovation Institute, UAE
Giacomo Iadarola	IIT-CNR, Italy
Pallavi Kaliyar	Norwegian University of Science and Technology, Norway
Christos Laoudias	University of Cyprus, Cyprus
Sara Lazzaro	Mediterranean University of Reggio Calabria, Italy
Domenico Lofù	Politecnico di Bari, Italy
Hyeran Mun	Korea University, South Korea
Nadir Murru	University of Trento, Italy
Lorenzo Musarella	University of Reggio Calabria, Italy
Gabriele Orazi	University of Padua, Italy
Cristina Romero-Tris	Universitat Oberta de Catalunya, Spain
Amir Sharif	Center for Cybersecurity, FBK, Italy
Chiara Spadafora	University of Trento, Italy
Federico Turrin	University of Padua, Italy

ICSBT Invited Speakers

Henderik A. Proper	Luxembourg Institute of Science and Technology, Luxembourg
Alfredo Cuzzocrea	University of Calabria, Italy
Walid Gaaloul	Télécom SudParis, France

SECRYPT Invited Speakers

Sokratis K. Katsikas	Norwegian University of Science and Technology, Norway
Luca Viganò	King's College London, UK

Contents

SPOT+: Secure and Privacy-Preserving Proximity-Tracing Protocol with Efficient Verification over Multiple Contact Information

Souha Masmoudi[1,2(✉)], Maryline Laurent[1,2], and Nesrine Kaaniche[1,2]

[1] Samovar, Télécom SudParis, Institut Polytechnique de Paris, 91120 Palaiseau, France
souha.masmoudi@telecom-sudparis.eu

[2] Cofounder of the Chair Values and Policies of Personal Information, Institut Mines-Telecom, Paris, France

Abstract. At SECRYPT 2022, Masmoudi *et al.* introduced a group signature scheme that offers an aggregated and batch verification over massive proofs of knowledge, named SEVIL. The performance analysis of the proposed scheme demonstrates its efficiency and its applicability to real world applications. In this paper, we introduce SPOT+, an extension of SEVIL to a concrete use-case referred to as a proximity-tracing protocol. SPOT+ is a secure and privacy-preserving proximity-tracing protocol that ensures data consistency and integrity and preserves the privacy of users who share their contact information with people in proximity. SPOT+ relies on SEVIL to significantly improve the performances of the SPOT framework [*IEEE Access Journal*, 10, 3208697, (2022)] while supporting aggregated and batch verifications over contact information belonging to multiple users. In comparison with SPOT, SPOT+ construction allows to reduce computation complexity by 50% and 99% for verifying data integrity and consistency, respectively, when considering an asymmetric pairing type and a 128-bit security level.

Keywords: Group signatures · Proof of knowledge · Batch verification · Proximity-tracing · Privacy

1 Introduction

With the world-wide adoption of various contact-tracing protocols, several concerns have been raised regarding their practical effectiveness, namely with the increasing number of reported cases. SPOT [14] is one promising solution that permit to detect false injections while preserving users' privacy thanks to the usage of group signatures and non interactive proof of knowledge (PoK). Indeed, group signatures enable any group member, referred to as a signer, to sign a

M. Van Sinderen et al. (Eds.): ICSBT/SECRYPT 2022, CCIS 1849, pp. 1–19, 2023.
https://doi.org/10.1007/978-3-031-45137-9_1

message on behalf of the group, while remaining anonymous. As such, verifiers authenticate the signer as a member of the group, but are not able to identify him. For security reasons, verifiers need to ensure that signers are trustworthy while verifying their signing keys, which compromises signers' privacy. To solve this dilemma and find the trade-off between security and privacy, group signatures might be built upon proof of knowledge (PoK) schemes. That is, the signer proves to verifiers the ownership of the signing key without revealing it, in an interactive or non-interactive session.

Group signatures have been used in several applications namely electronic voting systems [13], privacy-preserving identity management systems [2,10,21], etc. Recently, they have been used to design privacy-preserving proximity-tracing protocols [11,14]. Indeed, in [11] Liu et al. design a proximity-tracing protocol that relies on zero-knowledge proofs and group signatures in order to preserve users' privacy. Users first generate zero-knowledge proofs over their contact information and send them to the doctor in case of infection. Then, after verifying the proofs, the doctor, being a member of a group, generates a group signature over each valid contact information and publishes it in a bulletin board. As such, other users rely on their secret keys to determine their risk score. Later, in the proposal SPOT [14], authors suggested that contact messages generated by users, in a decentralized manner, are first, subject to a real time verification by a centralized computing server and a generation of a partial signature. Then, their integrity is guaranteed thanks to PoK-based group signatures generated by proxies distributed in different geographical areas (i.e., members of the same group). In case of infection, a health authority is responsible for verifying the validity of partial and group signatures. In both solutions, a separate verification (i.e., including the verification of a group signature) should be performed on every contact information.

Giving consideration to the huge number of contact messages and thus, PoK-based group signatures, there is a crucial need to optimize the verification process by verifying multiple contact messages belonging to the same or different users in a single transaction. To this question, Masmoudi *et al.* proposed, in [15], the first group signature scheme, named SEVIL, that offers an efficient, aggregated and batch verification over multiple proofs of knowledge, in particular Groth-Sahai Non-Interactive Witness-Indistinguishable (NIWI) proof scheme [7]. The proposed group signature scheme enables the signer (i.e., member of the group) to preserve his privacy, through the non-disclosure of signing keys, while the verifier still trusts it. The verifier is also able to perform verification over multiple group signatures at once, resulting in performance improvements of up to 50% compared to the naive verification.

In this paper, we present SPOT+, a secure and privacy-preserving proximity-tracing protocol that offers an efficient, aggregated and batch verification over multiple contact information belonging to the same or different users. SPOT+ supports a decentralized certification and a centralized aggregated and batch verification of contact information. Indeed, as in [14], SPOT+ relies on a hybrid architecture that involves:

1. users who share their Ephemeral Bluetooth IDentifiers (EBID) when being in close proximity and who generate a common contact message,
2. a distributed group of proxies that ensure users' anonymity and contact information integrity in a decentralized manner,
3. a centralized server that ensures the correctness of contact information through a real time verification,
4. a centralized health authority that verifies both the integrity and the correctness of multiple contact information provided by one or several infected users.

SPOT+ is designed to support the verification of multiple users' contact information, through the integration and implementation of SEVIL [15]. Indeed, SPOT+ relies on the SEVIL group signature scheme to improve the performances of the verification of contact information integrity and consistency by the health authority. Thus, the contributions of this paper are summarized as follows:

- we design a proximity-tracing protocol that supports efficient batch verification of the correctness and the integrity of contact information without compromising security and users' privacy.
- we evaluate the performances of SPOT+ batch verification and we compare it to the naive verification of each contact information. The comparison demonstrates a gain of up to 50% for contact information integrity verification and 99% of their correctness verification.

The remainder of this paper is organized as follows. Section 2 describes the preliminaries for this work. Section 3 gives an overview of SPOT+ and Sect. 4 details its phases and algorithms. A security discussion is provided in Sect. 5 before evaluating SPOT+ performances in Sect. 6. Section 7 concludes the paper.

2 Preliminaries

In this section, we first, present the batch verification and describe the SEVIL scheme (cf. Sect. 2.1). Second, we give a brief state of the art of proximity tracing protocols in Sect. 2.2. Finally, we summarize the properties and the phases of the SPOT protocol in Sect. 2.3. More details on SEVIL and SPOT can be found in [15] and [14], respectively.

2.1 Batch Verification over Massive Proofs of Knowledge

Regarding the increasing need to verify the integrity of data, on one hand, and resource constraints' problems, on the other hand, batch verification over multiple signatures was introduced by Naccache *et al.* [16] for DSA-type signatures. It allows to perform the verification of multiple signatures in a single transaction, thus to reduce the computation overhead. Batch verification has been applied to many types of digital signatures, namely group signatures. For instance, group signature schemes that offer batch verification have been proposed to solve resource constraints' problems for vehicular ad hoc networks [20] and IoT systems [1,22]. Batch verification schemes [12,15] have been extended to support identification of invalid signatures following the divide-and-conquer approach [17].

Recently, a new group signature offering batch verification over multiple NIWI proofs, called SEVIL has been proposed by Masmoudi *et al.* [15]. SEVIL allows efficient, aggregated and batch verification over Groth-Sahai NIWI proofs, while maintaining a high level of security and privacy. Indeed, verifiers check that signers are trustful without being able to identify them or link several messages signed by the same signer. SEVIL also supports bad signatures identification through the divide-and-conquer approach. In the following, we give a high level description of the original SEVIL scheme through five main algorithms, referred to as Setup, Join, Sign, Batch_Verify and Agg_Verify defined as follows.

- $\mathsf{Setup}() \rightarrow (\mathbf{sk}_g, \mathbf{vk}_g)$ – run by a group manager to set up the group signature parameters. It returns the secret key $\mathbf{sk}_g$ of the group manager, and the group verification key $\mathbf{vk}_g$ that involves the public key of the group manager $\mathbf{pk}_g$ and a common reference string Σ_{NIWI} of a NIWI proof associated with the public key.
- $\mathsf{Join}(\mathbf{sk}_g) \rightarrow (\mathbf{sk}_s, \mathbf{pk}_s, \sigma_k)$ – performed through an interactive session between a group member (i.e., signer) and the group manager. It takes as input the secret key $\mathbf{sk}_g$ of the group manager. The signer generates his pair of private and public keys $(\mathbf{sk}_s, \mathbf{pk}_s)$, and the group manager certifies the signer's public key $\mathbf{pk}_s$ while computing a signature σ_k.
- $\mathsf{Sign}(\mathbf{vk}_g, \mathbf{sk}_s, \mathbf{pk}_s, \sigma_k, m) \rightarrow (\sigma_m, \Pi)$ – run by the signer. It takes as input the group public parameters $\mathbf{vk}_g$, the signer's pair of keys $(\mathbf{sk}_s, \mathbf{pk}_s)$, the signature σ_k over the public key $\mathbf{pk}_s$ and a message m. This algorithm outputs a signature σ_m over the message m and a NIWI proof Π over the two signatures σ_k and σ_m.
- $\mathsf{Batch\_Verify}(\mathbf{vk}_g, \{m_i, \Pi_i\}_{i=1}^N) \rightarrow b$ – performed by any verifier. It takes as input the public parameters $\mathbf{vk}_g$, a list of N messages m_i and the associated proofs Π_i sent by the same or multiple signers. This algorithm returns a bit $b \in \{0,1\}$ stating whether the list of proofs is valid or not.
- $\mathsf{Agg\_Verify}(\mathbf{vk}_{\mathcal{G}}, m, \Pi) \rightarrow b$ – run by any verifier to identify the invalid signature(s), when the Batch_Verify algorithm returns 0 over a list or a sub-list of messages. Given the public parameters $\mathbf{vk}_g$, a message m and the associated proof Π, from an invalid sub-list, the Agg_Verify algorithm returns a bit $b \in \{0,1\}$ stating whether the proof is valid or not.

2.2 Privacy-Preserving Proximity-Tracing Protocols

During the COVID-19 pandemic, several proximity-tracing protocols have been proposed to support centralized [9], decentralized [3,4,11,18,19] or hybrid [5, 8,14] architectures. Relying on the Bluetooth technology, they enable users to broadcast contact information when they are in proximity with other people and to receive alerts when they are at risk of infection.

Centralized solutions ensure that users receive only correct alerts. Indeed, a centralized server is responsible for generating contact tokens to users and to verify the ones of infected users. These roles allow it to track users and identify their contact lists, which undermines their privacy.

Decentralized solutions have been developed to solve privacy issues. They enable users to generate their own contact tokens and share them with users in proximity, such that they remain anonymous. However, users are exposed to false positive alerts as decentralized solutions do not provide means to verify the correctness of contact information. Additionally, most of the proposed solutions [3,4,19] are vulnerable to replay attacks which impacts the reliability of the proximity-tracing application.

Hybrid architecture based solutions have been proposed to leverage the best of both centralized and decentralized architectures, i.e., ensure both security and users' privacy. They rely on a decentralized generation of contact tokens and a centralized verification of infected users' contact information. Indeed, Castelluccia *et al.* proposed Desire [5], a proximity tracing protocol where two users in proximity relies on the Diffie-Hellman key exchange protocol [6] to generate common contact tokens based on their Ephemeral Bluetooth IDentifiers (EBID). As no control and verification are applied on the generated tokens, users are able to collude and merge their contact lists leading to false positive alerts injection. Furthermore, the server responsible for evaluating users' risk scores, is able to de-anonymize users and link their exposure status and risk requests. In [8], contact tokens are also generated in a decentralized way through an interactive session between two users in proximity. However, during the centralized verification, identities of users being in contact with an infected person are revealed to a central server which enables it to track users. In [14], Masmoudi *et al.* proposed a solution, named SPOT, that offers a decentralized generation and certification of users' contact information in order to ensure their integrity and consistency. As a result, malicious users are prevented from injecting false positive alerts. The centralized verification allows to verify the integrity and consistency of infected users' contact information without being able to identify with whom they were contact.

2.3 Secure and Privacy-Preserving ProximiTy Protocol (SPOT)

SPOT is set upon an hybrid architecture that involves four actors, namely a user ($\mathcal{U}$), a server ($\mathcal{S}$), a proxy ($\mathcal{P}$) belonging to a group of proxies, and a health authority ($\mathcal{HA}$). SPOT architecture relies on *(i)* a decentralized proxy-based solution to preserve users' privacy (i.e., anonymity) and ensure the integrity of contact information, and *(ii)* a centralized computing server-based solution to ensure contact information integrity and consistency through real-time verification. In the following, we give a high level description of SPOT three phases.

The first phase, called SYS_INIT, refers to the initialization of the whole system. It includes the generation of the system global parameters and the keys of $\mathcal{S}$ and $\mathcal{HA}$, the setting up of the group of proxies, the joining of proxies to the group and the registration of users at $\mathcal{HA}$. During users' registration, $\mathcal{HA}$

generates, for each user, a unique identifier which is used to generate $\mathcal{U}$'s pair of keys. The user's unique identifier and public key are stored by $\mathcal{HA}$.

The second phase, called GENERATION, refers to the generation of contact information when two users are in close proximity. They exchange their EBIDs in order to compute a common contact message. Each user relays the generated message to the server through the group of the proxies. Indeed, the two users should select two different proxies w.r.t. to a comparison of their EBIDs. The two proxies relay the common contact message to the server. $\mathcal{S}$ performs a real-time verification by checking if he receives the same message from two different proxies. If the verification holds, $\mathcal{S}$ partially signs the message and returns the partial signatures to the two proxies. Each proxy extends the given message with the corresponding user's identifier and signs it on behalf of the group. The resulting message and group signature are sent to the user. They are associated to the common contact message to constitute the contact information stored in the user's contact list for Δ days.

The last phase, called VERIFICATION, refers to the verification of the integrity and consistency of contact information provided by an infected user. For each contact message, $\mathcal{HA}$ performs two verifications. The first one allows to check the validity of the group signature, while the second one allows to verify that the real-time verification over the message has been performed by $\mathcal{S}$. If both verifications hold, the message is added to a set of verified contact messages of infected persons and shared with other users. Otherwise, the message is rejected. As such, SPOT guarantees that users receive only true positive alerts.

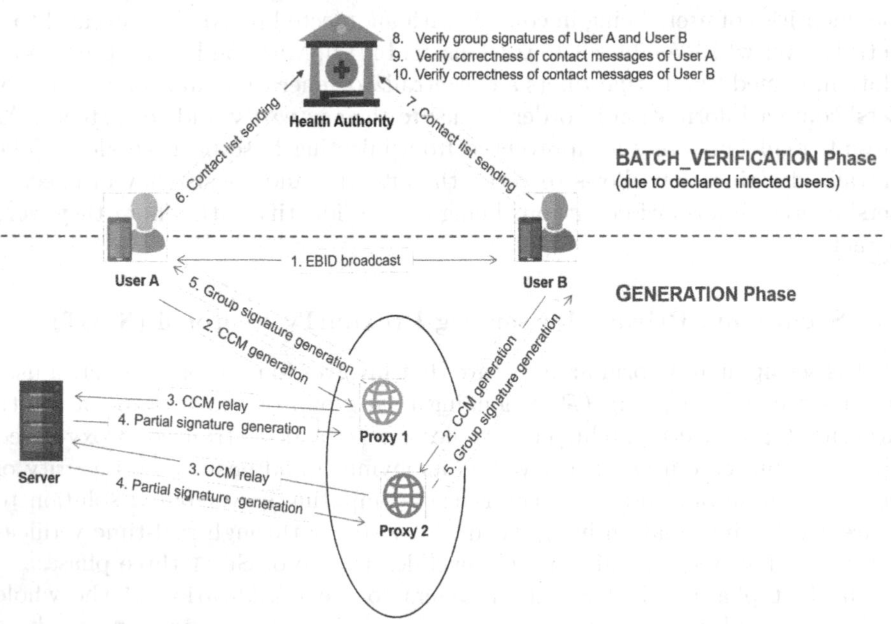

Fig. 1. Overview of the SPOT+ Protocol.

3 SPOT+ Protocol

SPOT+ architecture involves the same entities as SPOT, namely the user $\mathcal{U}$, the server $\mathcal{S}$, the group of proxies $\mathcal{P}$ and the health authority $\mathcal{HA}$, as depicted in Fig. 1. It involves three main phases, referred to as SYS_INIT, GENERATION and BATCH_VERIFICATION. For ease of presentation, we only illustrate GENERATION and BATCH_VERIFICATION phases in Fig. 1 (i.e., we assume that the group of proxies is set up and that users have been already registered at the health authority). SPOT+ includes thirteen PPT algorithms whose chronological sequence is depicted in Fig. 2. Note that, for the sake of clarity, we consider *(i)* only one proxy in the sequence diagram, *(ii)* only one user $\mathcal{U}_A$ for the GENERATION phase, and *(iii)* two infected users $\mathcal{U}_A$ and $\mathcal{U}_B$ for the BATCH_VERIFICATION phase.

3.1 SYS_INIT Phase

The SYS_INIT phase consists of setting up and initializing the whole system, relying on the following seven algorithms.

- $\mathsf{Set\_params}(\lambda) \rightarrow pp$ – run by a trusted authority to set up the system public parameters pp relying on the security parameter λ. Without loss of generality, we assume the system public parameters pp are an implicit input to the rest of the algorithms.
- $\mathsf{j\_keygen}() \rightarrow (\mathtt{sk}_j, \mathtt{pk}_j)$ – run by a trusted authority to generate the pair of keys of both $\mathcal{HA}$ and $\mathcal{S}$ denoted by the couple $(\mathtt{sk}_j, \mathtt{pk}_j)$ where $j = \{\mathcal{HA}, \mathcal{S}\}$.
- $\mathsf{Setup\_ProxyGr}_{\mathcal{GM}}() \rightarrow (\mathtt{sk}_g, \mathtt{vk}_g)$ – performed by the group manager to define the group of proxies and set up the group signature parameters. These parameters include *(i)* public parameters referred to as the proxies' group verification key $\mathtt{vk}_g$ represented by the couple $(\mathtt{pk}_g, \Sigma_{\mathsf{NIWI}})$ (i.e., $\mathtt{pk}_g$ is the group manager public key and Σ_{NIWI} is the Common Reference String CRS of a Groth-Sahai NIWI proof [7]), and *(ii)* secret parameters namely the secret key $\mathtt{sk}_g$ only known by $\mathcal{GM}$.
- $\mathsf{Join\_ProxyGr}_{\mathcal{P}/\mathcal{GM}}(\mathtt{sk}_g) \rightarrow (\mathtt{sk}_p, \mathtt{pk}_p, \sigma_p)$ – run through an interactive session between $\mathcal{P}$ and $\mathcal{GM}$ to enable a proxy to join the group. For this purpose, $\mathcal{P}$ first generates his pair of keys $(\mathtt{sk}_p, \mathtt{pk}_p)$ and shares the public key $\mathtt{pk}_p$ with $\mathcal{GM}$. $\mathcal{GM}$ generates a signature σ_p over $\mathtt{pk}_p$ relying on the secret key $\mathtt{sk}_g$. The signature σ_p is given back to $\mathcal{P}$. The Join_ProxyGr algorithm is performed every time a new proxy joins the group.
- $\mathsf{Set\_UserID}_{\mathcal{HA}}() \rightarrow (t_{\mathcal{U}}, \mathtt{ID}_{\mathcal{U}})$ – performed by $\mathcal{HA}$ when $\mathcal{U}$ installs the proximity-tracing application and asks to be registered. $\mathcal{HA}$ generates a specific secret value $t_{\mathcal{U}}$ and the associated identifier $\mathtt{ID}_{\mathcal{U}}$ for $\mathcal{U}$. Note that $t_{\mathcal{U}}$ is kept secret by $\mathcal{HA}$ and only $\mathtt{ID}_{\mathcal{U}}$ is given back to $\mathcal{U}$.
- $\mathsf{Userkeygen}_{\mathsf{U}}(\mathtt{ID}_{\mathcal{U}}) \rightarrow (\mathtt{sk}_{\mathcal{U}}, \mathtt{pk}_{\mathcal{U}})$ – run by $\mathcal{U}$ to generate his pair of keys $(\mathtt{sk}_{\mathcal{U}}, \mathtt{pk}_{\mathcal{U}})$ relying on his identifier $\mathtt{ID}_{\mathcal{U}}$. Note that the user's public key $\mathtt{pk}_{\mathcal{U}}$ is sent to $\mathcal{HA}$ to be stored in a database DB_{USER}.

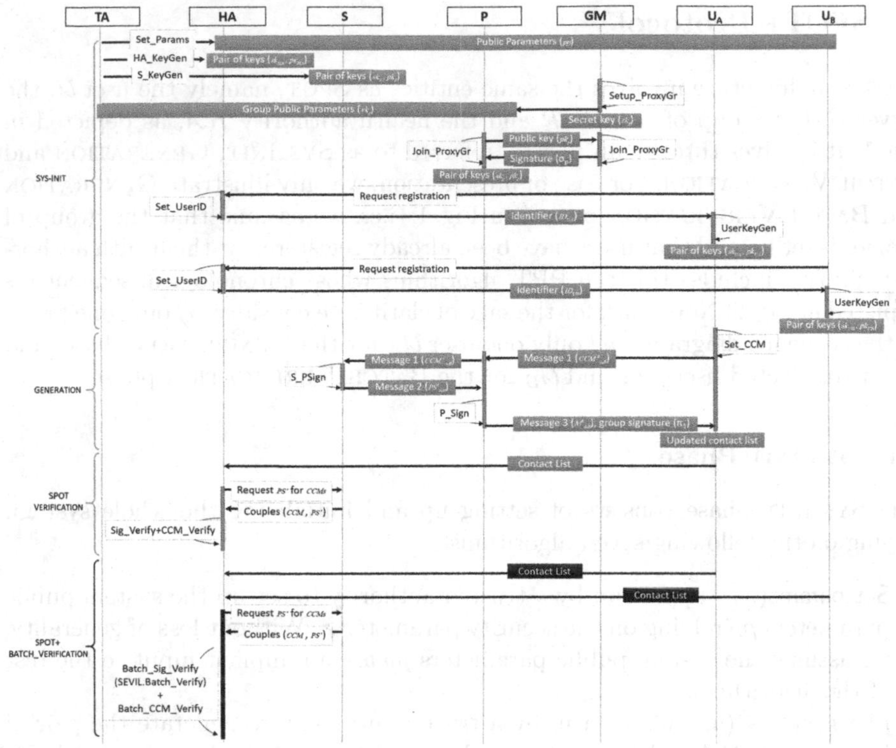

Fig. 2. Workflow of SPOT and SPOT+ Protocols.

Note that the Set_UserID and $\text{Userkeygen}_{\text{U}}$ algorithms are performed every time a new user installs the proximity-tracing application.

3.2 Generation Phase

The Generation phase occurs when two users $\mathcal{U}_A$ and $\mathcal{U}_B$ are in proximity and they exchange random EBIDs denoted by $\mathtt{D}_A^e$ for $\mathcal{U}_A$ and $\mathtt{D}_B^e$ for $\mathcal{U}_B$. Note that e denotes an epoch in which an EBID remains unchanged. These EBIDs are used to generate a contact message relying on the following algorithms.

- $\text{Set\_CCM}_{\mathcal{U}}(\mathtt{D}_A^e, \mathtt{D}_B^e) \rightarrow \mathtt{CCM}_{AB}^e$ – performed by each of two users $\mathcal{U}_A$ and $\mathcal{U}_B$ being in proximity. Each user generates separately a common contact message $\mathtt{CCM}_{AB}^e$ based on EBIDs $\mathtt{D}_A^e$ and $\mathtt{D}_B^e$. Note that $\mathtt{CCM}_{AB}^e$ is relayed to $\mathcal{S}$ via the group of proxies.
- $\text{S\_PSign}_{\mathcal{S}}(\mathtt{CCM}_{AB}^e, \mathtt{sk}_{\mathcal{S}}) \rightarrow (\mathtt{PS}_{AB}^e, \mathtt{PS}_{AB}'^e)$ – run by $\mathcal{S}$ when receiving two copies of the same contact message from two different proxies $\mathcal{P}_1$ and $\mathcal{P}_2$. $\mathcal{S}$ generates a partial signature represented by the couple $(\mathtt{PS}_{AB}^e, \mathtt{PS}_{AB}'^e)$ in order to be stored with the corresponding common contact message $\mathtt{CCM}_{AB}^e$ for Δ days. $\mathcal{S}$ only returns $\mathtt{PS}_{AB}^e$ to $\mathcal{P}_1$ and $\mathcal{P}_2$.

- $\mathsf{P\_Sign}_{\mathcal{P}_1}(\mathtt{vk}_g, \mathtt{sk}_{p_1}, \mathtt{pk}_{p_1}, \sigma_{p_1}, \mathtt{ID}_{\mathcal{U}_A}, \mathtt{PS}^e_{AB}) \rightarrow (\mathtt{M}^e_{AB}, \sigma_m, \pi)$ – performed by each of the two proxies $\mathcal{P}_1$ and $\mathcal{P}_2$ for the corresponding users $\mathcal{U}_A$ and $\mathcal{U}_B$, respectively. For ease of presentation, we consider only the user $\mathcal{U}_A$ and the proxy $\mathcal{P}_1$. Relying on the proxies' group public parameters $\mathtt{vk}_g$, his pair of keys $(\mathtt{sk}_{p_1}, \mathtt{pk}_{p_1})$, the signature σ_{p_1}, the identifier $\mathtt{ID}_{\mathcal{U}_A}$ of $\mathcal{U}_A$ and the message $\mathtt{PS}^e_{AB}$, $\mathcal{P}_1$ generates a new message $\mathtt{M}^e_{AB}$, signs it by computing σ_m, and computes a NIWI proof π over the two signatures σ_p and σ_m. $\mathcal{P}_1$ returns the couple $(\mathtt{M}^e_{AB}, \pi)$ to $\mathcal{U}_A$ that stores it along with the common contact message $\mathtt{CCM}^e_{AB}$ in his contact list $CL_{\mathcal{U}_A}$ for Δ days.

3.3 Batch_Verification Phase

The Batch_Verification phase occurs each period of time t after collecting a list N contact messages from infected users. During this phase, $\mathcal{HA}$ verifies the correctness of the N contact messages, in a single transaction. For this purpose, it performs two verifications relying on the following algorithms.

- $\mathsf{Batch\_Sig\_Verify}_{\mathcal{HA}}(\mathtt{vk}_g, \{\mathtt{M}^e_{A_iB_i}, \Pi_i\}_{i=1}^N) \rightarrow b$ – performed by $\mathcal{HA}$ to check, at once, the validity of multiple group signatures (i.e., NIWI proofs) $\{\Pi_i\}_{i=1}^N$ over messages $\{\mathtt{M}^e_{A_iB_i}\}_{i=1}^N$ belonging to different users. Thus, relying on the group public parameters $\mathtt{vk}_g$, the $\mathsf{Batch\_Verify}_{\mathsf{HA}}$ algorithm returns $b \in \{0,1\}$ stating whether the given list of proofs is valid or not.
- $\mathsf{Agg\_Sig\_Verify}_{\mathcal{HA}}(\mathtt{vk}_g, \mathtt{M}^e_{AB}, \Pi) \rightarrow b$ – run by $\mathcal{HA}$ once the $\mathsf{Batch\_Sig\_Verif}_{\mathcal{HA}}$ algorithm returns 0 over a list or a sub-list of contact messages $\mathtt{M}^e_{AB}$ and the corresponding proof Π. Then, relying on the group public parameters $\mathtt{vk}_g$, the $\mathsf{Agg\_Sig\_Verify}$ algorithm is performed over a single message $\mathtt{M}^e_{AB}$ and the corresponding proof Π, from an invalid sub-list. It returns $b \in \{0,1\}$ stating whether the proof is valid or not.
- $\mathsf{Batch\_CCM\_Verify}_{\mathcal{HA}}(\{\mathtt{M}^e_{AB_i}, \mathtt{PS}'^e_{AB_i}\}_{i=1}^N, \mathtt{pk}_{\mathcal{S}}, t_{\mathcal{U}_A}) \rightarrow b$ – performed by $\mathcal{HA}$ for a user $\mathcal{U}_A$ to verify, in a single transaction, that all the contact messages contained in his contact list, have successfully reached $\mathcal{S}$ and been verified in real time. To this end, $\mathcal{HA}$ retrieves from $\mathcal{S}$, the list $\{\mathtt{PS}'^e_{AB_i}\}_{i=1}^N$ w.r.t. $\mathcal{U}_A$'s list of common contact messages $\{\mathtt{CCM}^e_{AB_i}\}_{i=1}^N$. Then, relying on the public key $\mathtt{pk}_{\mathcal{S}}$ of $\mathcal{S}$ and the secret value $t_{\mathcal{U}_A}$ specific to $\mathcal{U}_A$, it returns $b \in \{0,1\}$ stating whether the list of messages $\{\mathtt{CCM}^e_{AB_i}\}_{i=1}^N$ has been correctly generated or not.

4 SPOT+ Algorithms

This section gives a concrete construction of the different phases and algorithms of Spot+, w.r.t. to the group signature scheme introduced in Sect. 2.1.

4.1 SYS_INIT Phase

- Set_params – this algorithm takes as input the security parameter λ and outputs an asymmetric bilinear group $(q, \mathbb{G}_1, \mathbb{G}_2, \mathbb{G}_3, g_1, g_2, e)$ and a cryptographic hash function $\mathbf{H} : \{0,1\}^* \rightarrow \mathbb{Z}_q$. The system public parameters pp are then represented by the tuple $(q, \mathbb{G}_1, \mathbb{G}_2, \mathbb{G}_3, g_1, g_2, e, \mathbf{H})$.
- HA_keygen – this algorithm takes as input the system public parameters pp, selects a random $x \in \mathbb{Z}_q^*$ and outputs the pair of secret and public keys $(\mathtt{sk}_{\mathcal{HA}}, \mathtt{pk}_{\mathcal{HA}})$ of $\mathcal{HA}$ as

$$\mathtt{sk}_{\mathcal{HA}} = x \quad ; \quad \mathtt{pk}_{\mathcal{HA}} = g_2^x$$

- S_keygen – this algorithm takes as input the system public parameters pp, selects two randoms $y_1, y_2 \in \mathbb{Z}_q^*$ and generates the pair of secret and public keys $(\mathtt{sk}_{\mathcal{S}}, \mathtt{pk}_{\mathcal{S}})$ of $\mathcal{S}$ as

$$\mathtt{sk}_{\mathcal{S}} = (y_1, y_2) \quad ; \quad \mathtt{pk}_{\mathcal{S}} = (Y_1, Y_2) = (g_2^{y_1}, g_2^{y_2})$$

- Setup_ProxyGr$_{\mathcal{GM}}$ – this algorithm takes as input the system public parameters pp and outputs the proxies' group parameters. It is formally defined as follows:

  Setup_ProxyGr$_{\mathcal{GM}}(pp)$:
  $(\mathtt{sk}_g, \mathtt{vk}_g) \leftarrow \mathsf{Setup}(pp)$, where $\mathtt{vk}_g = (\mathtt{pk}_g, \Sigma_{\mathsf{NIWI}})$
  output $(\mathtt{sk}_g, \mathtt{vk}_g)$

- Join_ProxyGr$_{\mathcal{P}/\mathcal{GM}}$ – this algorithm takes as input the system public parameters pp and the secret key of the group manager $\mathtt{sk}_g$. It outputs the pair of keys of a proxy group member $(\mathtt{sk}_p, \mathtt{pk}_p)$ and the signature σ_p over the public key $\mathtt{pk}_p$. The Join_ProxyGr is formally defined as follows:

  Join_ProxyGr$_{\mathcal{P}/\mathcal{GM}}(pp, \mathtt{sk}_g)$:
  $(\mathtt{sk}_p, \mathtt{pk}_p, \sigma_p) \leftarrow \mathsf{Join}(pp, \mathtt{sk}_g)$
  output $(\mathtt{sk}_p, \mathtt{pk}_p, \sigma_p)$

- Set_UserID$_{\mathcal{HA}}$ – this algorithm takes as input the system public parameters pp and selects a secret $t_{\mathcal{U}} \in \mathbb{Z}_q^*$ for a user $\mathcal{U}$. The Set_UserID algorithm outputs the couple $(t_{\mathcal{U}}, \mathtt{ID}_{\mathcal{U}})$, where $\mathtt{ID}_{\mathcal{U}}$ is $\mathcal{U}$'s identifier which is computed as follows:

$$\mathtt{ID}_{\mathcal{U}} = h_{\mathcal{U}} = g_2^{t_{\mathcal{U}}}$$

- Userkeygen$_{\mathcal{U}}$ – this algorithm takes as input the user's identifier $\mathtt{ID}_{\mathcal{U}}$, selects a random $q_{\mathcal{U}} \in \mathbb{Z}_q^*$ and outputs the key pair $(\mathtt{sk}_{\mathcal{U}}, \mathtt{pk}_{\mathcal{U}})$ of $\mathcal{U}$ as:

$$\mathtt{sk}_{\mathcal{U}} = q_{\mathcal{U}} \quad ; \quad \mathtt{pk}_{\mathcal{U}} = h_{\mathcal{U}}^{q_{\mathcal{U}}}$$

4.2 GENERATION Phase

- $\mathsf{Set\_CCM}_{\mathcal{U}}$ – this algorithm takes as input two EBIDs $\mathtt{D}^e_{\mathcal{U}_A}$ and $\mathtt{D}^e_{\mathcal{U}_B}$ belonging to user $\mathcal{U}_A$ and user $\mathcal{U}_B$, respectively, during an epoch e. It returns the corresponding common contact message $\mathtt{CCM}^e_{AB}$ computed as follows:

$$\mathtt{CCM}^e_{AB} = \mathbf{H}(m^e_{AB}) = \mathbf{H}(\mathtt{D}^e_{\mathcal{U}_A} * \mathtt{D}^e_{\mathcal{U}_B})$$

.

- $\mathsf{S\_PSign}_{\mathcal{S}}$ – this algorithm takes as input a common contact message $\mathtt{CCM}^e_{AB}$ and the secret key $\mathtt{sk}_{\mathcal{S}}$ of $\mathcal{S}$, selects a random $r_s \leftarrow \mathbb{Z}^*_q$ and computes the partial signature $(\mathtt{PS}^e_{AB}, \mathtt{PS}'^e_{AB})$ such that:

$$\mathtt{PS}^e_{AB} = \mathtt{CCM}^e_{AB} y_1 r_s + y_2 \quad ; \quad \mathtt{PS}'^e_{AB} = \mathtt{CCM}^e_{AB} r_s$$

- $\mathsf{P\_Sign}_{\mathcal{P}}$ – this algorithm takes as input the proxies' group public parameters $\mathtt{vk}_g$, the secret key $\mathtt{sk}_p$ of $\mathcal{P}$, the signature σ_p over $\mathcal{P}$'s public key, the identifier $\mathtt{ID}_{\mathcal{U}_A}$ of $\mathcal{U}_A$ and the message $\mathtt{PS}^e_{AB}$. It first, computes a new message $\mathtt{M}^e_{AB}$ w.r.t. $\mathtt{ID}_{\mathcal{U}_A}$ and message $\mathtt{PS}^e_{AB}$. It then, generates a signature σ_m over $\mathtt{M}^e_{AB}$ w.r.t. $\mathtt{sk}_p$. Finally, it generates a NIWI proof π over signatures σ_p and σ_m. The $\mathsf{P\_Sign}$ algorithm is formally defined as follows:

$$\frac{\mathsf{P\_Sign}_{\mathcal{P}}(\mathtt{vk}_g, \mathtt{sk}_p, \mathtt{pk}_p, \sigma_p, \mathtt{ID}_{\mathcal{U}_A}, \mathtt{PS}^e_{AB}):}{\begin{array}{l}(\mathtt{M}^e_{AB}, \sigma_m, \pi) \leftarrow \mathsf{Sign}(\mathtt{vk}_g, \mathtt{sk}_p, \mathtt{pk}_p, \sigma_p, \mathtt{ID}_{\mathcal{U}_A}, \mathtt{PS}^e_{AB}) \\ \text{output} \quad (\mathtt{M}^e_{AB}, \sigma_m, \pi)\end{array}}$$

4.3 BATCH_VERIFICATION Phase

- $\mathsf{Batch\_Sig\_Verify}_{\mathcal{HA}}$ – this algorithm takes as input a list of N messages m_i and the corresponding proofs Π_i. Each proof Π_i is composed of six sub-proofs (i.e., two sub-proofs generated over the signature σ_{m_i} w.r.t. the message m_i, and four sub-proofs generated over the signature σ_p w.r.t. the proxy's key $\mathtt{pk}_p$). The list of proofs can be presented as follows:

$$\begin{cases} \{(\vec{\mathcal{A}_{ijm}}, \vec{\mathcal{B}_{ijm}}, \Gamma_{ijm}, t_{ijm})\}_{i,j=1}^{i=N,j=2}, \\ \{(\vec{\mathcal{C}_{ijm}}, \vec{\mathcal{D}_{ijm}}, \pi_{ijm}, \theta_{ijm})\}_{i,j=1}^{i=N,j=2}, \\ \{(\vec{\mathcal{A}_{ilp}}, \vec{\mathcal{B}_{ilp}}, \Gamma_{ilp}, t_{ilp})\}_{i,l=1}^{i=N,l=4}, \\ \{(\vec{\mathcal{C}_{ilp}}, \vec{\mathcal{D}_{ilp}}, \pi_{ilp}, \theta_{ilp})\}_{i,l=1}^{i=N,l=4}. \end{cases}$$

According to the generation of the NIWI proofs over the signatures σ_{m_i} and σ_p, the tuples $\{(\vec{\mathcal{A}_{jm}}, \vec{\mathcal{B}_{jm}}, \Gamma_{jm}, t_{jm})\}_{j=1}^2$ and $\{(\vec{\mathcal{A}_{lp}}, \vec{\mathcal{B}_{lp}}, \Gamma_{lp}, t_{lp})\}_{l=1}^4$ are unchanged for all N proofs and all proxies. Thus, for a the list of N messages, $\mathsf{Batch\_Sig\_Verify}$ returns $b \in \{0,1\}$ stating whether the given list of proofs is valid or not, by checking if Eqs. 1 and 2 hold. Note that the $\mathsf{Batch\_Sig\_Verify}_{\mathcal{HA}}$ algorithm is the same as the $\mathsf{Batch\_Verify}$ algorithm.

$$\prod_i \prod_j \left(e(\vec{\mathcal{C}_{ijm}}, \Gamma_m \vec{\mathcal{D}_{ijm}}) \right) = e(\mathtt{U}, \sum_i \sum_j \pi_{ijm}) e(\sum_i \sum_j \theta_{ijm}, \mathtt{V}) \quad (1)$$

$$\prod_l e(\iota_1(\vec{\mathcal{A}_{lp}}), \sum_i \vec{\mathcal{D}_{ilp}})e(\sum_i \vec{\mathcal{C}_{ilp}}, \iota_2(\vec{\mathcal{B}_{lp}})) \prod_i \prod_l \left(e(\vec{\mathcal{C}_{ilk}}, \Gamma_{lk}\vec{\mathcal{D}_{ilk}})\right) = \left(\prod_l \iota_3(t_{lp})^N\right) e(\mathtt{U}, \sum_i \sum_l \pi_{ilp})e(\sum_i \sum_l \theta_{ilp}, \mathtt{V}) \quad (2)$$

- $\mathsf{Agg\_Sig\_Verify}_{\mathcal{HA}}$ – this algorithm takes as input a message m belonging to an invalid proof-list and its corresponding proof Π. Using the tuples $\{(\vec{\mathcal{A}_{jm}}, \vec{\mathcal{B}_{jm}}, \Gamma_{jm}, t_{jm})\}_{j=1}^{2}$ and $\{(\vec{\mathcal{A}_{lp}}, \vec{\mathcal{B}_{lp}}, \Gamma_{lp}, t_{lp})\}_{l=1}^{4}$ along with the tuples $\{(\vec{\mathcal{C}_{jm}}, \vec{\mathcal{D}_{jm}}, \pi_{jm}, \theta_{jm})\}_{j=1}^{j=2}$ and $\{(\vec{\mathcal{C}_{lp}}, \vec{\mathcal{D}_{lp}}, \pi_{lp}, \theta_{lp})\}_{l=1}^{l=4}$ derived from Π, the $\mathsf{Agg\_Sig\_Verify}$ outputs $b \in \{0, 1\}$ stating whether the proof Π is valid or not, by checking if Eqs. 3 and 4 hold. Note that the $\mathsf{Agg\_Sig\_Verify}_{\mathcal{HA}}$ algorithm is equivalent to the $\mathsf{Agg\_Verify}$ algorithm.

$$\prod_j \left(e(\vec{\mathcal{C}_{jm}}, \Gamma_m \vec{\mathcal{D}_{jm}})\right) = e(\mathtt{U}, \sum_j \pi_{jm})e(\sum_j \theta_{jm}, \mathtt{V}) \quad (3)$$

$$\prod_l e(\iota_1(\vec{\mathcal{A}_{lp}}), \vec{\mathcal{D}_{lp}})e(\vec{\mathcal{C}_{lp}}, \iota_2(\vec{\mathcal{B}_{lp}}))\prod_l \left(e(\vec{\mathcal{C}_{lp}}, \Gamma_{lk}\vec{\mathcal{D}_{lp}})\right) = \left(\prod_l \iota_3(t_{lp})\right) e(\mathtt{U}, \sum_l \pi_{lp})e(\sum_l \theta_{lp}, \mathtt{V}) \quad (4)$$

- $\mathsf{Batch\_CCM\_Verify}_{\mathcal{HA}}$ – this algorithm takes as input the list $\{\mathtt{M}_i\}_{i=1}^{N}$ and the list $\{\mathtt{PS}'_i\}_{i=1}^{N}$ corresponding to the contact messages $\{\mathtt{CCM}_i\}_{i=1}^{N}$ contained in the contact list of user $\mathcal{U}_A$, the server's public key $\mathtt{pk}_{\mathcal{S}}$ and the secret value $t_{\mathcal{U}_A}$ specific to user $\mathcal{U}_A$. The $\mathsf{Batch\_CCM\_Verify}$ algorithm outputs $b \in \{0, 1\}$ stating whether the common contact messages have been correctly verified in real time by $\mathcal{S}$ or not, by checking if Eq. 5 holds:

$$\prod_i \mathtt{M}_i = Y_1{}^{t_{\mathcal{U}_A} \sum_i \mathtt{PS}'_i} Y_2{}^{N t_{\mathcal{U}_A}} \quad (5)$$

5 Security Discussion

This section discusses the security of SPOT+.

Theorem 1. SPOT+ *satisfies unforgeability, unlinkability, anonymity and anti-replay.*

We refer to [14] for formal definitions of the security and privacy properties stated in the theorem. Indeed, unforgeability states that a malicious adversary cannot generate valid contact information without having access to the appropriate keys (i.e., the server and the proxies secret keys). Unlinkability ensures that a curious adversary is not able to link *(i)* two or several common contact messages to the same user during the GENERATION phase and *(ii)* two or several group signatures to the same proxy during the BATCH_VERIFICATION phase. Anonymity means that a curious adversary is not able to identify users involved in a contact list with an infected person. Anti-replay guarantees that a malicious adversary is not able to replay the same contact message in different sessions as a valid contact information. Thus, anti-replay prevents the injection of false positive alerts.

Proof. First, the unforgeability property refers to the unforgeability of both the partial signature generated by the server and the unforgeability of the group signature generated by a proxy. The unforgeability of the partial signature can be inherited from the unforgeability of SPOT. The unforgeability of the proxies' group signature follows from the unforgeability of the new group signature scheme proposed in [15] proven to be negligible according to the soundness of the Groth-Sahai NIWI proof. Thus, SPOT+ is unforgeable.

Second, for unlinkability, the impossibility to link contact messages issued by the same user follows from the *CCM-unlinkability* property of SPOT. The unlinkability of proxies' group signatures derives from the unlinkability of SEVIL which is proven to be satisfied w.r.t. the computational witness-indistinguishability property of Groth-Sahai NIWI proofs. Thus, SPOT+ is unlinkable.

Third, anonymity follows directly from the anonymity property of SPOT which relies on the impossibility to link common contact messages belonging to the same user.

Finally, for anti-replay, if we suppose that the adversary replays a common contact message CCM issued in an epoch e, in another epoch $e' \neq e$, he should be able to produce a new valid partial signature and a corresponding valid group signature over CCM, which contradicts the unforgeability property. Thus, SPOT+ ensures the anti-replay.

6 Performance Evaluation

This section discusses the experimental results, presented in Table 1, and demonstrates the performances' improvements introduced by SPOT+. We, first, describe SPOT test-bed in Sect. 6.1. Then, we analyze, in Sect. 6.2, the computation performances of SPOT+ w.r.t. the batch verification.

6.1 Test-Bed and Methodology

The three phases of SPOT+ including the thirteen algorithms[1] have been implemented and lead to several performance measurements relying on an Ubuntu 18.04.3 machine - with an *Intel* Core *i7*@1.30 GHz processor and 8 GB memory. This machine runs JAVA version 11, and the associated cryptographic library *JPBC*[2].

The SPOT+ prototype is built with six java classes, namely *TrustedAuthority.java*, *GroupManager.java*, *Proxy.java*, *HealthAuthority.java*, *User.java*

[1] The source code is available at https://github.com/soumasmoudi/SPOTv2.
[2] http://gas.dia.unisa.it/projects/jpbc/.

and *Server.java*. The *HealthAuthority.java* class encompasses the verification algorithms of both SPOT and SPOT+ (i.e., Sig_Verify, CCM_Verify, Batch_Sig_Verify, Agg_Sig_Verify and Batch_CCM_Verify algorithms).

For the sake of performances' improvement, a multithreading is applied on algorithms P_Sign, Sig_Verify, Batch_Sig_Verify and Agg_Sig_Verify to allow a simultaneous execution of multiple threads. A preprocessing is also applied on algorithms Sig_Verify, Batch_Sig_Verify and Agg_Sig_Verify to prepare in advance variables used several times when running the algorithm.

The implementation tests rely on two types of bilinear pairings, i.e., a symmetric pairing type called *type A* and an asymmetric pairing called *type F*. For each type of pairing, we consider two levels of security, namely 112-bit and 128-bit security levels.

For accurate measurements of the computation time, each algorithm is run 100 times, while considering a standard deviation of an order 10^{-2}. Thus, each experimental result reflects the mean time of 100 tests.

6.2 Computation Overhead

In this section, we focus on the VERIFICATION and BATCH_VERIFICATION phases of SPOT and SPOT+, respectively. We first, discuss the experimental results of both batch and naive verifications, as depicted in Table 1. Then, we give a comparative analysis of the two verifications. Finally, we evaluate the impact of the messages' number on the computation time for a batch verification.

Table 1. Computation Time in milliseconds of SPOT and SPOT+ Verifications.

Protocol	Verification Algorithm	Computation time (ms)			
		A/112-bits	A/128-bits	F/112-bits	F/128-bits
SPOT	Sig_Verify [a]	6541	15406	31637	36892
	CCM_Verify [a]	174	360	148	190
SPOT+	Batch_Sig_Verify [b]	222989	485233	1018375	1312879
	Agg_Sig_Verify [a]	3096	6916	16065	18834
	Batch_CCM_Verify [b]	139	281	133	175

NOTE: [a] indicates that the algorithm is performed on a single contact message that is generated by the Set_CCM algorithm; [b] indicates that the algorithm is performed on N messages where $N = 100$ for computation times.

Verification Computation Performances. As shown in Table 1, the verification of the correctness of a single contact message, through the Sig_Verify and CCM_Verify algorithms together, requires approximately 7 s (resp. 16 s) for pairing *type A* and 32 s (resp. 37 s) for pairing *type F*. Thus, to verify the correctness of 100 contact messages, the SPOT naive verification requires approximately

12 min (resp. 27 minutes) pairing *type A* and 53 min (resp. more than an hour) for pairing *type F*.

Meanwhile, the Batch_Sig_Verify algorithm that is run to verify 100 messages simultaneously, requires approximately 4 and 8 min for pairing *type A* and 17 and 22 min for pairing *type F*. However, when it is needed to verify a single message, the Agg_Sig_Verify algorithm requires 3 and 7 s for pairing *type A* and 16 and 19 s for pairing *type F*. It is worth noticing that, for a number of messages $N = 100$, the execution of the Batch_Sig_Verify algorithm gives improved computational costs compared to the Agg_Sig_Verify algorithm performed 100 times, separately. Also the Batch_CCM_Verify algorithm gives promising results when verifying 100 messages at once.

Benefit of SPOT+ Batch Verification over SPOT Naive Verification. We consider 100 contact messages partially and fully signed with the S_PSign and P_Sign algorithms, respectively. The resulting proofs (resp. partial signatures) are given as input to both Sig_Verify and Batch_Sig_Verify algorithms (resp. both CCM_Verify and Batch_CCM_Verify algorithms). The Sig_Verify and CCM_Verify algorithms are executed 100 times as they allow to perform verification over a single contact message, while the Batch_Sig_Verify and Batch_CCM_Verify algorithms perform the verification of all the 100 contact messages at once. Thus, we compare the computation time required by the naive and batch verification when being executed over 100 messages.

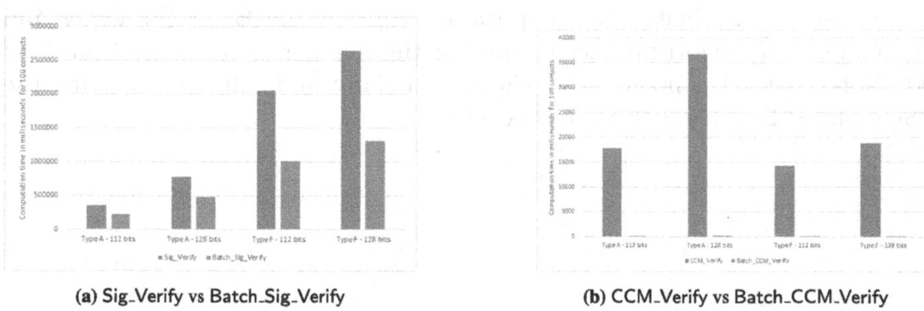

(a) Sig_Verify vs Batch_Sig_Verify

(b) CCM_Verify vs Batch_CCM_Verify

Fig. 3. Computation Time of Batch Verification vs Naive Verification over 100 Messages.

Figure 3 confirms that the batch verification is more efficient than the naive one. On the one hand, as depicted in Sub-Figure 3a, the batch verification of proofs reduces the computation time, for verifying 100 messages, by approximately 37%, for pairing *type A* for the two security levels. Indeed, the processing time moves from 356 s (resp. 777 s) with SPOT naive group signature verification to 223 s (resp. 485 s) with SPOT+ batch group signature verification. For pairing *type F* and the two security levels, the gain of batch verification reaches 50%, since the processing time is moving from 2048 seconds (resp. 2642 s) to 1018 s (resp. 1313 s).

These results are substantiated by the decrease in the number of pairing functions performed during verification. Indeed, to perform verification over N messages, the Sig_Verify algorithm of SPOT requires $30N$ pairing functions, while the Batch_Sig_Verify algorithm of SPOT+ only requires $6N + 9$ pairing functions. These theoretical results expect that the gain reaches approximately 80%, which is higher than the gain obtained through experimentation. This difference can be explained by the number of group elements addition operations introduced while aggregating the verification equations (i.e., $14N$ addition operations). With consideration to the *JPBC* library benchmark[3], it is worth noticing that elementary addition operations are more consuming for pairing *type A* than for pairing *type F*. As a result, the gain is more important for pairing *type F*.

On the other hand, Sub-Figure 3b shows that the batch verification over 100 partial signatures, reduces the computation time by 99% for the two types of pairings with the two different levels of security. Indeed, to verify N partial signatures, the CCM_Verify algorithm requires $2N$ exponentiations, while the Batch_CCM_Verify algorithm requires only two exponentiations and N multiplications.

Impact of Contact List Size on the Verification. Referring to Eqs. 1, 2 and 5, it is worth mentioning that the computation time of both Batch_Sig_Verify and Batch_CCM_Verify algorithms varies according to the number N of contact messages verified. Indeed, as the number of messages grows, the number of pairing functions, exponentiations and multiplications becomes more important. For this purpose, we evaluate the computation time of the Batch_Sig_Verify and Batch_CCM_Verify algorithms when varying the number of messages from 5 to 1000. Note that all contact messages are partially and fully signed with the S_PSign and P_Sign algorithms, respectively.

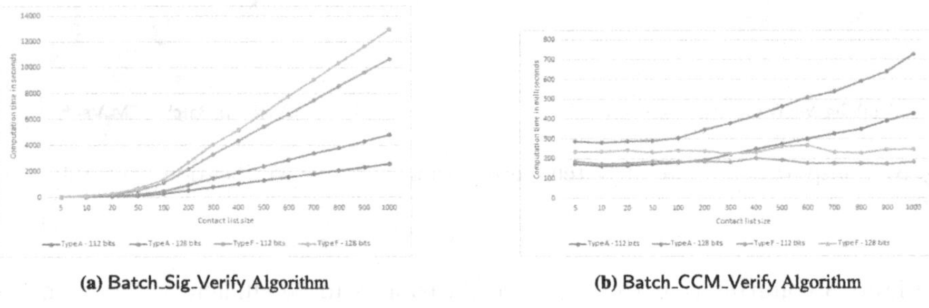

(a) Batch_Sig_Verify Algorithm

(b) Batch_CCM_Verify Algorithm

Fig. 4. Influence of Contact List Size on Batch Verification Computation Time.

Both Figs. 4a and 4b show that the computation time of both Batch_Sig_Verify and Batch_CCM_Verify algorithms increases w.r.t the number of messages, for the two types of pairings and the two security levels.

[3] http://gas.dia.unisa.it/projects/jpbc/benchmark.html.

On the one hand, for the Batch_Sig_Verify algorithm, when varying the size of the contact list from 5 to 1000, the computation time varies from 15 to 2602 seconds (resp. from 26 to 4817) for the pairing *type A* 112-bit (resp. pairing *type A* 128-bit). For pairing *type F*, the computation time varies from 59 to 10677 seconds (resp. 72 to 12978) for the 112-bit security level (resp. the 128-bit security level).

On the other hand, for the Batch_CCM_Verify algorithm, when the size of the contact list varies from 5 to 1000, the computation time, for the pairing *type A*, varies from 174 to 426 milliseconds, for the 112-bit security level (resp. from 287 to 728, for the 128-bit security level). For the pairing *type F*, the computation time is almost constant. The curve slopes are very low compared to those for pairing *type A*. This can be justified by the fact that (i) we have a constant number of exponentiations and (ii) the elementary multiplication operations are more consuming for the pairing *type A* compared to the pairing *type F*.

7 Conclusion

In this paper, we introduce a concrete construction of an efficient, secure and privacy-preserving proximity-tracing protocol, referred to as SPOT+. The proposed protocol offers a batch verification over multiple contact messages, in an effort to improve verification performances of the SPOT protocol [14] w.r.t. the group signature scheme proposed in [15]. Our contribution is proven to satisfy security and privacy requirements of proximity-tracing protocols, namely unforgeability of contact information, non-injection of false positive alerts, unlinkability of users' contact information and anonymity of users being in contact with infected people. Thanks to the implementation of SPOT and SPOT+ algorithms and the comparison of their verification performances, we show that SPOT+ batch verification achieves a gain of up to 50% for verifying the validity of proxies' group signatures. This gain reaches 99% for the verification of the correctness of contact information belonging to the same user.

Acknowledgements. This paper is partly supported by the chair Values and Policies of Personal Information, Institut Mines-Télécom, France.

References

1. Alamer, A.: An efficient group signcryption scheme supporting batch verification for securing transmitted data in the internet of things. Journal of Ambient Intelligence and Humanized Computing (06 2020). DOI: 10.1007/s12652-020-02076-x
2. Camenisch, J., Van Herreweghen, E.: Design and implementation of the idemix anonymous credential system. In: CCS 2002, pp. 21–30. Association for Computing Machinery, New York (2002)
3. Carmela, T., et al.: Decentralized privacy-preserving proximity tracing (2020). https://github.com/DP-3T/documents/blob/master/DP3T%20White%20Paper.pdf

4. Chan, J., et al.: Pact: privacy-sensitive protocols and mechanisms for mobile contact tracing (2020). arXiv:2004.03544
5. Claude, C., et al.: Desire: a third way for a european exposure notification system. https://github.com/3rd-ways-for-EU-exposure-notification/project-DESIRE/blob/master/DESIRE-specification-EN-v1_0.pdf (2020)
6. Diffie, W., Hellman, M.: New directions in cryptography. IEEE Trans. Inf. Theory **22**(6), 644–654 (1976). https://doi.org/10.1109/TIT.1976.1055638
7. Groth, J., Sahai, A.: Efficient non-interactive proof systems for bilinear groups. In: Smart, N. (ed.) EUROCRYPT 2008. LNCS, vol. 4965, pp. 415–432. Springer, Heidelberg (2008). https://doi.org/10.1007/978-3-540-78967-3_24
8. Hoepman, J.H.: Hansel and gretel and the virus: privacy conscious contact tracing (2021). arXiv preprint arXiv:2101.03241
9. Inria, AISEC, F.: Robert: Robust and privacy-preserving proximity tracing (2020). https://github.com/ROBERT-proximity-tracing/documents/blob/master/ROBERT-specification-EN-v1_1.pdf. Accessed June 2022
10. Isshiki, T., Mori, K., Sako, K., Teranishi, I., Yonezawa, S.: Using group signatures for identity management and its implementation. In: DIM 2006 (2006)
11. Joseph, K.L., et al.: Privacy-preserving covid-19 contact tracing app: a zero-knowledge proof approach. IACR Cryptol. ePrint Arch, 2020 (528) (2020)
12. Kim, K., Yie, I., Lim, S., Nyang, D.: Batch verification and finding invalid signatures in a group signature scheme. Int. J. Network Secur. **12**, 229–238 (2011)
13. Malina, L., Smrz, J., Hajny, J., Vrba, K.: Secure electronic voting based on group signatures. In: 2015 38th International Conference on Telecommunications and Signal Processing (TSP), pp. 6–10 (2015)
14. Masmoudi, S., Kaaniche, N., Laurent, M.: spot: secure and privacy-preserving proximity-tracing protocol for e-healthcare systems. IEEE Access **10**, 106400–106414 (2022). https://doi.org/10.1109/ACCESS.2022.3208697
15. Masmoudi., S., Laurent., M., Kaaniche., N.: Sevil: Secure and efficient verification over massive proofs of knowledge. In: Proceedings of the 19th International Conference on Security and Cryptography - SECRYPT, pp. 13–24. INSTICC, SciTePress (2022). https://doi.org/10.5220/0011125800003283
16. Naccache, D., M'Raïhi, D., Vaudenay, S., Raphaeli, D.: Can D.S.A. be improved? — Complexity trade-offs with the digital signature standard —. In: De Santis, A. (ed.) EUROCRYPT 1994. LNCS, vol. 950, pp. 77–85. Springer, Heidelberg (1995). https://doi.org/10.1007/BFb0053426
17. Pastuszak, J., Michałek, D., Pieprzyk, J., Seberry, J.: Identification of bad signatures in batches. In: Public Key Cryptography, pp. 28–45 (03 2004). https://doi.org/10.1007/978-3-540-46588-1_3
18. Pietrzak, K.: Delayed authentication: preventing replay and relay attacks in private contact tracing. In: Bhargavan, K., Oswald, E., Prabhakaran, M. (eds.) INDOCRYPT 2020. LNCS, vol. 12578, pp. 3–15. Springer, Cham (2020). https://doi.org/10.1007/978-3-030-65277-7_1
19. Ronald L., et al.: The pact protocol specification (2020)
20. Wasef, A., Shen, X.: Efficient group signature scheme supporting batch verification for securing vehicular networks. In: 2010 IEEE International Conference on Communications, pp. 1–5 (2010). https://doi.org/10.1109/ICC.2010.5502136

21. Yue, X., Xu, J., Chen, B., He, Y.: A practical group signatures for providing privacy-preserving authentication with revocation. In: Security and Privacy in New Computing Environments, Second EAI International Conference, SPNCE 2019, Tianjin, China, pp. 226–245, June 2019
22. Zhang, A., Zhang, P., Wang, H., Lin, X.: Application-oriented block generation for consortium blockchain-based IoT systems with dynamic device management. IEEE Internet Things J. **8**(10), 7874–7888 (2021). https://doi.org/10.1109/JIOT.2020.3041163

Blind Side Channel Analysis on the Elephant LFSR Extended Version

Julien Maillard[2,3], Awaleh Houssein Meraneh[1], Modou Sarry[1], Christophe Clavier[2], Hélène Le Bouder[1(✉)], and Gaël Thomas[4]

[1] IMT-Atlantique, OCIF, IRISA, Rennes, France
helene.le-bouder@imt-atlantique.fr
[2] Université de Limoges, XLIM-CNRS, Limoges, France
[3] Université de Grenoble Alpes, CEA, LETI MINATEC Campus, 38054 Grenoble, France
[4] DGA Maîtrise de l'Information, Bruz, France

Abstract. The National Institute of Standards and Technology (NIST) started a competition for lightweight cryptography candidates for authenticated encryption. Elephant is one of the ten finalists. Many physical attacks exist on the different traditional cryptographic algorithms. New standard are a new targets for this domain. In this paper, an improvement of the first theoretical blind side channel attack against the authenticated encryption algorithm Elephant is presented. More precisely, we are targeting the LFSR-based counter used internally. LFSRs are classic functions used in symmetric cryptography. In the case of Elephant, retrieving the initial state of the LFSR is equivalent to recovering the encryption key. This paper is an extension of a previous version. So an optimization of our previous theoretical attack is given. In the previous version, in only half of the cases, the attack succeeds in less than two days. In this extended paper, with optimization, the attack succeeds in three quarters of the cases.

Keywords: Blind side channel analysis · Hamming weight · Elephant · LFSR · NIST

1 Introduction

Internet of things (IoT) devices become more and more widespread within our day-to-day life. From military grade to general-purpose hardware, the need for strong security raises. The cryptosystems implemented on those devices must ensure both security and low power consumption overhead. In this context, the *National Institute of Standards and Technology* (NIST) started the competition for lightweight cryptography candidates for authenticated encryption [32]. An authenticated encryption algorithm should ensure confidentiality and integrity of the communications.

The security of authenticated encryption schemes can be supported by several strategies. Various approaches have been considered by the lightweight cryptography competition candidates: cryptographic permutations with sponge or

M. Van Sinderen et al. (Eds.): ICSBT/SECRYPT 2022, CCIS 1849, pp. 20–42, 2023.
https://doi.org/10.1007/978-3-031-45137-9_2

duplex construction [3,16] [15]; block cipher combined with a mode (e.g. AES combined with Galois/Counter Mode) [7,21]; stream cipher paradigms [19].

When discussing about the security of a cryptographic algorithm, numerous tools allow the cryptographers to prove the security of a cipher. Unfortunately, those tools do not consider the interaction of the computing unit with its physical environment. Physical attacks are a real threat, even for cryptographic algorithms proved secure mathematically. Physical attacks are divided in two families: side-channel analysis (SCA) and the fault injection attacks.

Motivation

Many attacks exist on the different traditional cryptographic algorithms, as detailed in the book [33]. Lightweight cryptography, much younger and used in embedded devices and IoT, has been far less studied. For example, attacks on stream ciphers [34] or sponge functions [35] are less common. That is why we chose to study SCA against new authenticated encryptions. The chosen algorithm is the cryptosystem Elephant [7]. More precisely, this paper focuses on its underlying *Linear Feedback Shift Registers* (LFSR), in a block cipher combined with a mode construction. Some attacks exist yet as in [10,11,22–24,34], but this work differs from state-of-the-art attacks by its attacker model. To the best of our knowledge, there is no blind side channel attack on LFSR in the context of authenticated encryption except our previous contribution [20]. This paper is an extension of [20], so motivation is to improve previous results.

Contribution

In this paper, we present a theoretical blind side channel attack targeting the LFSR of the Elephant algorithm. We exploit the usage of intermediate variables that are statistically dependent to the secret (here the secret LFSR initial state) and show that this structure could threaten the security of a cryptosystem's regarding SCA. Also, the study of the influence of the choice of the LFSR is presented. This paper is an extended version of a previous attack [20], so we present a major improvement: an optimization to find the best time, relative to the beginning of encryption, to start the attack is given in Sect. 4.2.

Organization

The paper is organized as follows. In Sect. 2, the context of blind side channel attack and the Elephant are introduced. The theoretical attack is explained in Sect. 3, it is a reminder of the short version of the paper [20]. Details of implementated attack and new improvement are described in Sect. 4. Then, Sect. 5 presents experimental results and discussion about LFSR design. Finally, a conclusion is drawn in Sect. 6.

2 Context

The first section starts by presenting the Elephant cryptosystem. This first part is extracted from the first shorted paper version [20] according the description of the standard [7]. Then, the background contents on blind side channel attacks is introduced. Eventually, a brief state of the art of SCA attacks against LFSRs is presented.

2.1 Elephant

The purpose of an authenticated encryption algorithm is to ensure both confidentiality and integrity. It takes as input different parameters: a plaintext, data

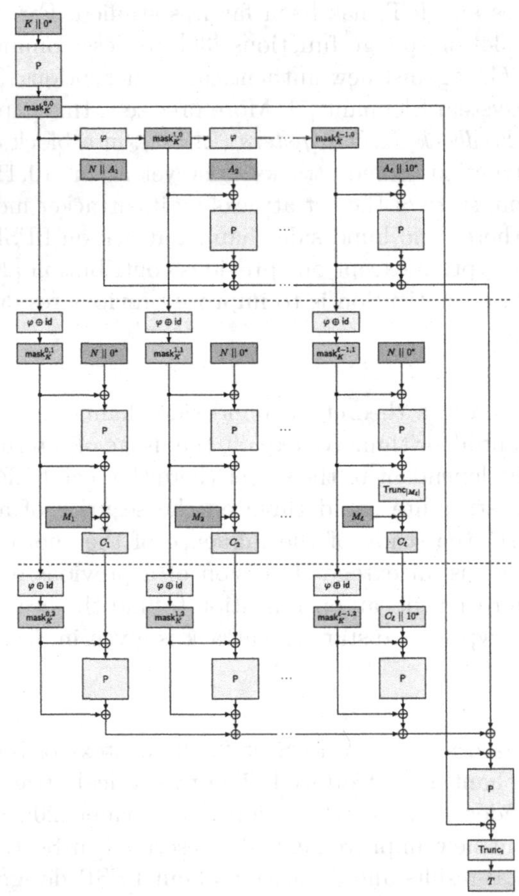

Fig. 1. Elephant associated data authentication (top), plaintext encryption (middle), and ciphertext authentication (bottom). This figure comes from [20] according to the description of Elephant [7].

associated to the plaintext, a secret key, and an initialisation vector, also called a nonce. The nonce is public but must be different for each new plaintext. The algorithm ensures confidentiality of the plaintext and integrity of both the plaintext and the associated data.

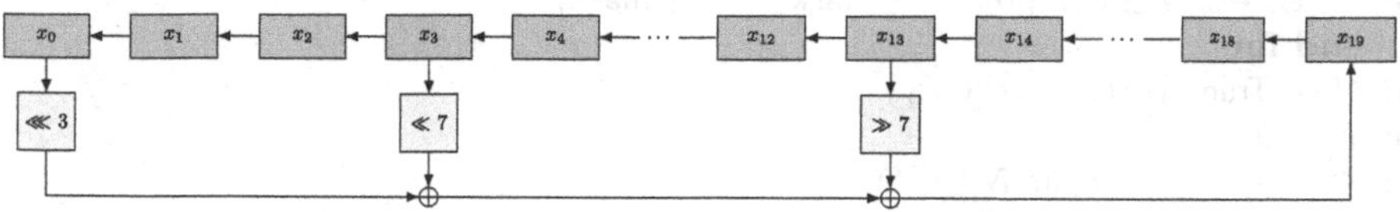

Fig. 2. 160-bit LFSR φ_{Dumbo}. This figure comes from [20] according to the description of Elephant [7].

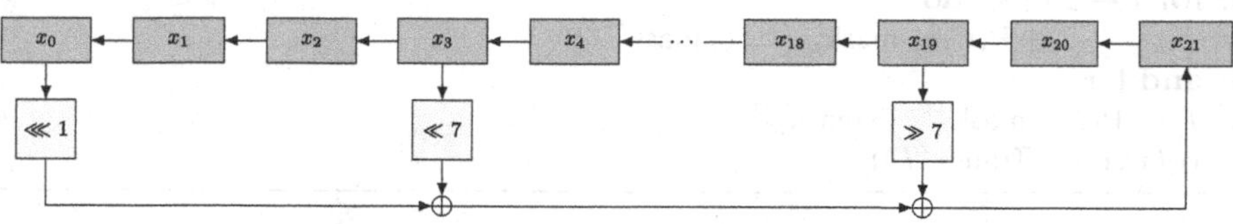

Fig. 3. 176-bit LFSR φ_{Jumbo}. This figure comes from [20] according to the description of Elephant [7].

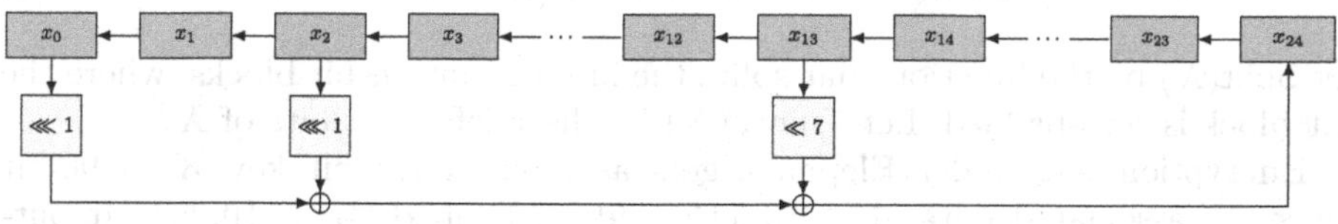

Fig. 4. 200-bit LFSR $\varphi_{\mathsf{Delirium}}$. This figure comes from [20] according to the description of Elephant [7].

$$\varphi_{\mathsf{Dumbo}} : (x_0, \cdots, x_{19}) \mapsto (x_1, \cdots, x_{19}, x_0 \lll 3 \oplus x_3 \ll 7 \oplus x_{13} \gg 7) \qquad (1)$$

$$\varphi_{\mathsf{Jumbo}} : (x_0, \cdots, x_{21}) \mapsto (x_1, \cdots, x_{21}, x_0 \lll 1 \oplus x_3 \ll 7 \oplus x_{19} \gg 7) \qquad (2)$$

$$\varphi_{\mathsf{Delirium}} : (x_0, \cdots, x_{24}) \mapsto (x_1, \cdots, x_{24}, x_0 \lll 1 \oplus x_2 \lll 1 \oplus x_{13} \ll 7) \qquad (3)$$

Elephant [6,7] is a finalist to the NIST lightweight cryptography competition. It is a nonce-based authenticated encryption with associated data (AEAD). Its construction is based on an Encrypt-then-MAC that combines CTR-mode encryption with a variant of the protected counter sum [4,28]. Elephant uses a cryptographic permutation masked with LFSRs in an Even-Mansour-like fashion [17] in place of a blockcipher.

Algorithm 1. Elephant encryption algorithm $\mathtt{enc}$.

Require: $(K, N, A, M) \in \{0,1\}^{128} \times \{0,1\}^{96} \times \{0,1\}^* \times \{0,1\}^*$
Ensure: $(C, T) \in \{0,1\}^{|M|} \times \{0,1\}^t$
$M_1, \cdots, M_{\ell_M} \leftarrow \mathsf{Split}(M)$
for $t \leftarrow 1$ to ℓ_M **do**
  $C_t \leftarrow M_t \oplus \mathsf{P}(N||0^{n-96} \oplus \mathsf{mask}_K^{t-1,1}) \oplus \mathsf{mask}_K^{t-1,1}$
end for
$C \leftarrow \mathsf{Trunc}_{|M|}(C_1|| \cdots ||C_{\ell_M})$
$T \leftarrow 0^n$
$A_1, \cdots, A_{\ell_A} \leftarrow \mathsf{Split}(N||A||1)$
$C_1, \cdots, C_{\ell_C} \leftarrow \mathsf{Split}(C||1)$
$T \leftarrow A_1$
for $t \leftarrow 2$ to ℓ_A **do**
  $T \leftarrow T \oplus \mathsf{P}(A_t \oplus \mathsf{mask}_K^{t-1,0}) \oplus \mathsf{mask}_K^{t-1,0}$
end for
for $t \leftarrow 1$ to ℓ_C **do**
  $T \leftarrow T \oplus \mathsf{P}(C_t \oplus \mathsf{mask}_K^{t-1,2}) \oplus \mathsf{mask}_K^{t-1,2}$
end for
$T \leftarrow \mathsf{P}(T \oplus \mathsf{mask}_K^{0,0}) \oplus \mathsf{mask}_K^{0,0}$
return $(C, \mathsf{Trunc}_\tau(T))$

Let P be an n-bit cryptographic permutation, and φ an n-bit LFSR. Let the function $\mathsf{mask} : \{0,1\}^{128} \times \mathbb{N} \times \{0,1,2\} \rightarrow \{0,1\}^n$ be defined as follows:

$$\mathsf{mask}_K^{t,b} = (\varphi \oplus \mathsf{id})^b \circ \varphi^t \circ \mathsf{P}(K||0^{n-128}) \tag{4}$$

Let $\mathsf{Split}(X)$ be the function that splits the input X into n-bit blocks, where the last block is zero-padded. Let $\mathsf{Trunc}_\tau(X)$ be the τ left-most bits of X.

Encryption $\mathtt{enc}$ under Elephant gets as input a 128-bit key K, a 96-bit nonce N, associated data $A \in \{0,1\}^*$, and a plaintext $M \in \{0,1\}^*$. It outputs a ciphertext C as large as M, and a t-bit tag T. The description $\mathtt{enc}$ is given in **Algorithm** 1 and is depicted on Fig. 1.

Decryption $\mathtt{dec}$ gets as input a 128-bit key K, a 96-bit nonce N, associated data $A \in \{0,1\}^*$, a ciphertext $C \in \{0,1\}^*$, and τ-bit tag T. It outputs a plaintext M as large as C if the tag T is correct, or the symbol $\perp$ otherwise. The description of $\mathtt{dec}$ is analoguous to the one of $\mathtt{enc}$.

Elephant comes in three flavours which differ on the n-bit cryptographic permutation P and the LFSR φ used, as well as the tag size t.

Dumbo uses the 160-bit permutation $\mathsf{Spongent}$-$\pi[160]$ [8], the LFSR φ_{Dumbo} given by Eq. (1) and illustrated on Fig. 2, and has tag size $\tau = 64$ bits.

Jumbo uses the 176-bit permutation $\mathsf{Spongent}$-$\pi[176]$ [8], the LFSR φ_{Jumbo} given by Eq. (2) and illustrated on Fig. 3, and has tag size $\tau = 64$ bits.

$\mathsf{Delirium}$ uses the 200-bit permutation Keccak-$f[200]$ [5,31], the LFSR $\varphi_{\mathsf{Delirium}}$ given by Eq. (3) and illustrated on Fig. 4, and has tag size $\tau = 128$ bits.

2.2 State-of-the-Art

Side Channel Analysis. Even if an algorithm has been proven to be mathematically secure, its implementation can open the gate to physical attacks. SCA are a subcategory of physical attacks. They exploit the fact that some physical states of a device depend on intermediate values of the computation. This is the so-called leakage of information of the circuit. It could be used to retrieve sensitive data, such as secret keys, or to reverse engineer an algorithm. An SCA is often led with a divide-and-conquer approach. Namely, the secret is divided into small pieces that are analysed independently.

Different kinds of leakage sources can be exploited as execution time [18], power consumption [25] or electromagnetic (EM) radiations [36]. In this paper, we consider a power consumption or EM leakage channel. At each instant, the measurement of the intensity of the electric current reflects the activity of the circuit. The power consumption of a device is a combination of the power consumption of each of its logic gates.

Several analysis paradigms have been described in the literature. The *Simple Power Analysis* (SPA) [29] are called simple because they determine directly, from an observation of the power consumption, during a normal execution of an algorithm, information on the calculation performed or the manipulated data. Other attacks like *Correlation Power Analysis* (CPA) [9] use a mathematical model for the leakage. A confrontation between measurement and model is performed. More precisely, a statistic tool called distinguisher gives score to the different targets. Template attacks are statistical categorizations [1] that require no leakage model *a priori*. It is a domain in its own right, as shown different books [30,33].

Blind Side Channel Analysis. The *blind side channel analysis* (BSCA) family is new improvement in SCA. Linge *et al.* has presented the concept in [27]. In parallel, Le Bouder *et al.* published an attack in [26]. Then, these works have been improved by Clavier *et al.* in [13], moreover this contribution introduces for the first time, the term of blind side channel. Now it is a new family of SCA [2,14,20,37].

The main idea is to only perform the attack on the leakage measurements *i.e*, without data such as plaintexts or ciphertexts.

In BSCA, the *Hamming weight* (HW) leakage model have often been used and a strong assumption is made: the attacker is supposed to retrieve a noisy HW from the leakage. In this paper, the considered adversary model is that the HW of all manipulated intermediate variables can be recovered by the attacker. Several techniques, such as signal filtering, trace averaging or templates [12], can be used in order to fulfill this prerequisite.

Overview of SCA Attacks on LFSRs. Linear feedback shift registers (LFSRs) with primitive polynomials are used in many symmetric cryptographic primitives because of their well-defined structure and remarkable properties such as long period, ideal autocorrelation and statistical properties.

The information leakage and the vulnerability of stream ciphers based on Galois LFSRs are studied in [22] and those based on Fibonacci LFSRs are analysed in [10]. In [22], the information leakage of XOR gates is exploited to perform a simple side-channel attack. However, if the leakage from the XOR gates is too low compared to other operations in the cipher, the attack fails. In [11], the attack recovers the initial state of a Galois LFSR by determining the output of the LFSR from the difference in power dissipation values in consecutive clock cycles.

In this paper, a theoretical blind side channel attack targeting the LFSR of the Elephant algorithm is presented. Whereas several attacks on LFSRs have been described in the literature, the specific structure of the Elephant cryptosystem allows us to elaborate a new approach that is depicted in the rest of this paper.

3 Theoretical Attack

This section is a reminder of the first shorted paper version [20].

3.1 Goal

LFSRs are used in different lightweight cryptography candidates, and its initial state often depends on both a key and a nonce. As the nonce needs to be changed for each encryption request, attacks on such schemes are limited to the decryption algorithm. In the case of Elephant, the LFSR only depends on the secret key. Consequently, our attack can be applied in an encryption scenario.

The goal of the presented attack is to retrieve the LFSR secret initial state. One has to remark three important points:

- Retrieving the initial state of the LFSR, which is equal to $\mathsf{mask}_K^{0,0}$, is equivalent to retrieving the secret key. Indeed, the initial state is the result of the known permutation P applied to the key.
- As the retroaction polynomial is publicly known, it is possible to shift the LFSR backwards: an attacker who recover enough consecutive bytes of the secret stream is able to reconstruct the initial state.
- The smaller the LFSR is, the more the attack is able to succeed. As a consequence, the Dumbo instance (see Fig. 2) is the most vulnerable one: the following of this paper is focused on Dumbo.

3.2 Leakage in the LFSR

In this attack, it is assumed that the Hamming weight of every byte of the LFSR can be obtained by an attacker. Let x be a byte: it can take any of the 256 values in $[\![0, 255]\!]$. With the HW of x, the attacker reduces the list of possible values, as shown in Table 1.

Table 1. Number of possible values per Hamming weight value [20,26].

$HW(x)$	0	1	2	3	4	5	6	7	8
$\#x$	1	8	28	56	70	56	28	8	1

Since the LFSR generates a single new byte at each iteration, let $(x_j, \cdots, x_{j+19}) = \mathsf{mask}_K^{j,0}$ be the content of the Dumbo LFSR and x_{j+20} the byte generated at iteration j. Precisely, the attacker has the following relation (L1), according to the Eq. (1).

L1 $x_{j+20} = (x_j \lll 3) \oplus (x_{j+3} \ll 7) \oplus (x_{j+13} \gg 7)$.

The first idea is to use the knowledge of the following Hamming weights: $HW(x_{j+20})$, $HW(x_{j+13})$ and

$$HW(x_j) = HW(x_j \lll 3)\,. \tag{5}$$

So with the two equations (L1) and (5) the attacker has:

$$HW(x_{j+20}) = \begin{cases} HW(x_j) \\ HW(x_j)+1 \\ HW(x_j)-1 \\ HW(x_j)+2 \\ HW(x_j)-2 \end{cases} \tag{6}$$

Looking more precisely at equation (L1), it can be seen that the difference $HW(x_{j+20}) - HW(x_j)$ only depends on four bits. Let $x_j[i]$ denote the i-th least significant bit of byte x_j, these four bits are $\{x_{j+3}[0]; x_{j+13}[7]; x_j[4]; x_j[5]\}$. Table 2 gives the value of observed difference $HW(x_{j+20}) - HW(x_j)$ depending on the values of these four bits. In the worst case, there are only 6 possibilities left, out of 16.

Table 2. Values of $HW(x_{j+20}) - HW(x_j)$ according to $\{x_{j+3}[0]; x_{j+13}[7]; x_j[4]; x_j[5]\}$ [20].

		$(x_{j+3}[0], x_{j+13}[7]) =$			
$HW(x_{j+20}) - HW(x_j)$		$(0,0)$	$(0,1)$	$(1,0)$	$(1,1)$
$(x_j[4], x_j[5]) =$	$(0,0)$	0	+1	+1	+2
	$(1,0)$	0	+1	−1	0
	$(0,1)$	0	−1	+1	0
	$(1,1)$	0	−1	−1	−2

3.3 Link Between the Different Masks

The value $\mathsf{mask}_K^{j,1}$ can be expressed in terms of $\mathsf{mask}_K^{*,0}$ as in (7).

$$\begin{aligned}\mathsf{mask}_K^{j,1} &= (\varphi \oplus \mathsf{id})\left(\mathsf{mask}_K^{j,0}\right)\\ &= \varphi\left(\mathsf{mask}_K^{j,0}\right) \oplus \mathsf{mask}_K^{j,0}\\ &= \mathsf{mask}_K^{j+1,0} \oplus \mathsf{mask}_K^{j,0}.\end{aligned} \tag{7}$$

Likewise, for $\mathsf{mask}_K^{j,2}$, Eq. (8) holds.

$$\begin{aligned}\mathsf{mask}_K^{j,2} &= (\varphi \oplus \mathsf{id})^2\left(\mathsf{mask}_K^{j,0}\right)\\ &= (\varphi^2 \oplus \mathsf{id})\left(\mathsf{mask}_K^{j,0}\right)\\ &= \varphi^2\left(\mathsf{mask}_K^{j,0}\right) \oplus \mathsf{mask}_K^{j,0}\\ &= \mathsf{mask}_K^{j+2,0} \oplus \mathsf{mask}_K^{j,0}\end{aligned} \tag{8}$$

As in the case of $\mathsf{mask}_K^{j,0}$, let y_j denote either the byte j of $\mathsf{mask}_K^{0,1}$ when $0 \leq j \leq 19$, or the new byte obtained after j iterations of the LFSR initialized with $\mathsf{mask}_K^{0,1}$. Likewise, let z_j denote either the byte j of $\mathsf{mask}_K^{0,2}$ when $0 \leq j \leq 19$, or the new byte obtained after j iterations of the LFSR initialized with $\mathsf{mask}_K^{0,2}$.

Eq. (7) then translates to Eq. (9).

$$y_j = x_j \oplus x_{j+1} \tag{9}$$

Likewise, the Eq. 8 translates to (10).

$$z_j = x_j \oplus x_{j+2}. \tag{10}$$

The evolution of the LFSR is analogous to (L1):

$$y_{j+20} = (y_j \lll 3) \oplus (y_{j+3} \ll 7) \oplus (y_{j+13} \gg 7). \tag{11}$$

$$z_{j+20} = (z_j \lll 3) \oplus (z_{j+3} \ll 7) \oplus (z_{j+13} \gg 7). \tag{12}$$

The attacker can thus exploit two attack vectors: on the one hand, equations (L1), (11), and (12) coming from iterating the LFSR, and on the other hand, Eqs. (9) and (10) coming from the different masks used for domain separation.

4 Attack Strategy

For a byte x_j of the Dumbo LFSR with $j \geq 0$, let x'_j denote a guess of its value by the attacker. Given m successive bytes $(x_j, \cdots, x_{j+m-1})$, let $\mathbf{X}_j^m$ denote the set of guesses $(x'_j, \cdots, x'_{j+m-1})$ satisfying the constraints of the Hamming weights of masks x, y and z depicted in Eqs. 9 and 10.

4.1 Algorithm of the Attack

The whole search space corresponding to the initial state of the LFSR is represented as a rooted tree. The nodes at depth j correspond to all the possible values for the bytes x_0 to x_j of the LFSR. The tested candidates are denoted by $(x'_0, \cdots, x'_{19})$. The nodes in the graph of the search space are labelled as follows:

- the nodes at depth j correspond to all the possible values of $(x'_0, \cdots, x'_j)$;
- the children of node $(x'_0, \cdots, x'_j)$, are the nodes labelled: $(x'_0, \cdots, x'_j, x'_{j+1})$ for all values of x'_{j+1}.

In practice, to reduce the number of nodes, only the nodes having the correct Hamming weights are considered. In other words, it suffices to consider nodes with $HW(x'_j) = HW(x_j)$. An example of such a tree is given on Fig. 5.

A backtracking algorithm is used. The tree is traversed in a depth-first manner. For each step, the attacker tests whether the current candidate $(x'_0, \cdots, x'_j)$ satisfies the different conditions given by the observed Hamming weights. This test is given by **Algorithm 2**.

Algorithm 2. isvalid$(x'_0, \cdots, x'_j)$.

Require: Byte-wise partial candidate $(x'_0, \cdots, x'_j)$ of length $1 \leq j+1 \leq 20$
Assumes isvalid$(x'_0, \cdots, x'_{j-1})$ is true.
Ensure: **true** if candidate $(x'_0, \cdots, x'_j)$ is compatible with the observations, **false** otherwise

\# Hamming weights of the xors
if $HW(x'_j) \neq HW(x_j)$ **then**
    return false
end if
if $HW(x'_j \oplus x'_{j-1}) \neq HW(y_{j-1})$ **then**
    return false
end if
if $HW(x'_j \oplus x'_{j-2}) \neq HW(z_{j-2})$ **then**
    return false
end if
\# Hamming weights of the feedbacks
if $|HW(x'_j \lll 3) - HW(x_{j+20})| > 2$ **then**
    return false
end if
if $|HW(x'_{j-3} \lll 3 \oplus x'_j \ll 7) - HW(x_{j+17})| > 1$ **then**
    return false
end if
if $HW(x'_{j-13} \lll 3 \oplus x'_{j-10} \ll 7 \oplus x'_j \gg 7) \neq HW(x_{j+7})$ **then**
    return false
end if
return true

Algorithm 3. Attack.

Require: Observed Hamming weights $HW(x_0), \cdots, HW(x_{19}),\ HW(y_0), \cdots, HW(y_{18})$, and $HW(z_0), \cdots, HW(z_{17})$. For the sake of clarity, they are seen as global variables.

Ensure: S set of keys compatible with the observed Hamming weights

```
(x'_0, ..., x'_19) ← (0, ..., 0)
ℓ ← 0
S ← {}
while true do
    if j < 19 and isvalid(x'_0, ..., x'_j) then
        j ← j + 1
        x'_j ← 0
    else
        if j = 19 and isvalid(x'_0, ..., x'_j) then
            S ← S ∪ {(x'_0, ..., x'_j)}
        end if
        while j ≥ 0 and x'_j = FF do
            j ← j − 1
        end while
        if j ≥ 0 then
            x'_j ← x'_j + 1
        else
            break
        end if
    end if
end while
return S
```

If the test succeeds, the algorithm goes down to the next layer to test the values of the byte x'_{j+1}. If it reaches the bottom of the tree, then a good candidate has been found, and can be saved. The algorithm then iterates upon the next untested node.

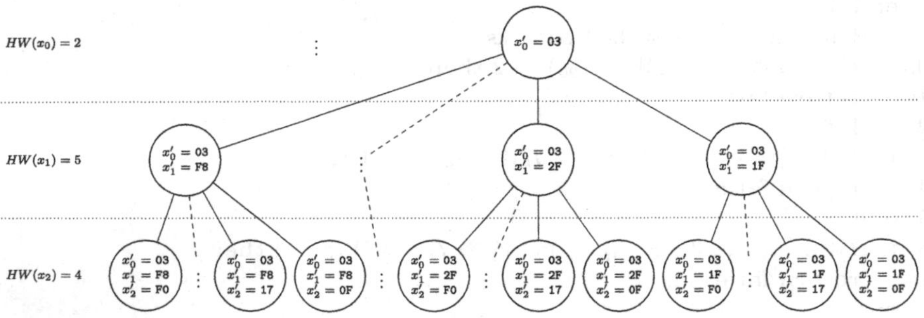

Fig. 5. Example of the tree representation of the LFSR initial state for the Hamming weights given on the left. Only the first three layers of the subtree rooted at $x'_0 = 03$ are shown.

If, at some point, the Hamming weights conditions do not hold for the current (partial) candidate, then no node in the sub-tree rooted at that node can lead to a good candidate. Thus, it can be pruned from the whole tree, saving the cost of browsing it. Finally, the algorithm ends when the whole tree has been explored. A pseudocode of the attack is given by **Algorithm** 3.

4.2 Optimisation of the Attack

Goal of the Optimization. Recall from **Algorithm** 1 that for each new block of data to encrypt, a different mask is used. Therefore the attacker actually can choose which values of index t at lines 2, 10, and 13 of **Algorithm** 1 they would rather attack.

The question raised at this point is: at which time t does the attacker minimize the complexity of the attack? The attacker wants to establish a metric $E(\cdot)$ such that $E(t)$ allows estimating the complexity of an attack at time t. The attacker constructs E such that the computation of $E(t)$:

1. is fast enough to allow exploring a large number of values of t and
2. is accurate enough so that the attacker can accurately select the value of t with minimal attack complexity.

Principle. The general idea for finding the best attack position is to obtain an estimation of the attack complexity at a given time t. For this sake, the LFSR state $(x_t, \cdots, x_{t+19})$ at time t is divided into tuples that can be treated with three different operations. Note that this approach does not exploit the retroaction polynomial of the LFSR. This allows to use it for all the flavours of the Elephant cryptosystem.

1. **Enumerate.** This function takes as an input m indices $(i, \cdots, i+m-1)$ and returns all the candidates $\mathbf{X}_i^m$ for $(x'_i, \cdots, x'_{i+m-1})$ satisfying the constraints of masks x, y and z depicted in Eqs. (9) and (10), based on the knowledge of corresponding $3m-3$ Hamming weights. This operation explores all the possible combinations for each x'_i and only retains the candidates matching the conditions imposed by masks x, y and z. Note that the *enumerate* function quickly becomes computationally intense as m grows. In our experiments, we use this function for $m \in \{1, 2, 3\}$.
2. **Merge.** When m grows, the attacker proceeds with a divide and conquer strategy. Indeed, for $k < m$, the attacker first computes candidates $\mathbf{X}_i^k$ and $\mathbf{X}_{i+k}^{m-k}$ thanks to the *enumerate* function. Then candidates $\mathbf{X}_i^k$ and X_{i+k}^{m-k} are merged into $\mathbf{X}_i^m$ so that each remaining candidate in $\mathbf{X}_i^m$ satisfies the constraints on masks y and z. This approach allows benefiting from the reduced candidate sets $\mathbf{X}_i^k$ and $\mathbf{X}_{i+k}^{m-k}$, allowing to reduce the size of the search space for $\mathbf{X}_i^m$. For a growing m, storing the $\mathbf{X}_i^m$ set in memory can become impractical, hence the *merge* function comes with the *merge_count* variant, that only returns the number $\mid \mathbf{X}_i^m \mid$ of candidates. We emphasize that calling *merge_count* on X_i^m disables calling it for another merge.

3. **Merge Estimator.** The number of candidates $\mid \mathbf{X}_i^m \mid$ can be assessed by applying a reduction factor r on the product of $\mid \mathbf{X}_i^k \mid$ and $\mid \mathbf{X}_{i+k}^{m-k} \mid$. Namely, it is defined as:
$$r = \frac{\mid \mathbf{X}_i^k \mid \times \mid \mathbf{X}_{i+k}^{m-k} \mid}{\mid \mathbf{X}_i^m \mid} \tag{13}$$
Hence, the merging estimation procedure takes as input two indices tuples $(i, \cdots, i+k-1)$ and $(i+k, \cdots, i+m)$, for $k < m$, and their corresponding number of candidates $\mid \mathbf{X}_i^k \mid$ and $\mid \mathbf{X}_{i+k}^{m-k} \mid$. The aim of the estimator is to approximate r based on statistical tools without exploring the entire Cartesian product of $\mathbf{X}_i^k$ and $\mathbf{X}_{i+k}^{m-k}$. The construction of the estimator is discussed in the following.

Gathering Information. The estimator E for the attack complexity can then be defined by applying the previous three functions. The procedure used for the Dumbo LFSR is depicted in Fig. 6.

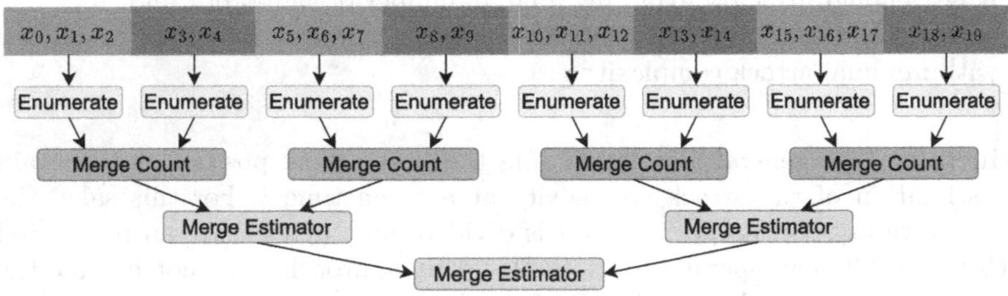

Fig. 6. Gathering information for the Dumbo LFSR.

The 20 LFSR bytes are split into 4 quintuplets. Each quintuplet is itself split into a triplet and a pair of bytes. The attacker gathers the candidates for each triplet and pair with the *enumerate* function, and then call the *merge_count* function on the union of the triplets and pairs to count the exact number of candidates for the quintuplets. Eventually, the attacker applies the *merge estimator* between the first and second, and the third and fourth quintuplets before calling the estimator a last time on the full state.

At this point, it can be seen that the accuracy of the complexity returned by E highly depends on the quality of the *merge_estimator*.

Crafting a Merge Estimator

Naive Estimator

Equations (9) and (10) allow to derive a *reduction triangle* for the merge of two tuples (see Fig. 7).

This reduction triangle can be exploited to obtain a broad estimation on the information gained by a merge, hence, a estimation of the reduction factor of the Cartesian product of $\mathbf{X}_i^k$ and $\mathbf{X}_{i+k}^{m-k}$. Let $\mid \mathbf{X}_{triangle} \mid$ define the number of candidates for the reduction triangle. This corresponds to the product of the number of bytes values that match each three gathered Hamming weights. Then, r_{naive} is defined by:

$$r_{naive} = \frac{\mid \mathbf{X}_{triangle} \mid}{2^{24}} \tag{14}$$

The estimation error of r_{naive} is defined as follows:

$$err_{naive} = r_{naive} - r \tag{15}$$

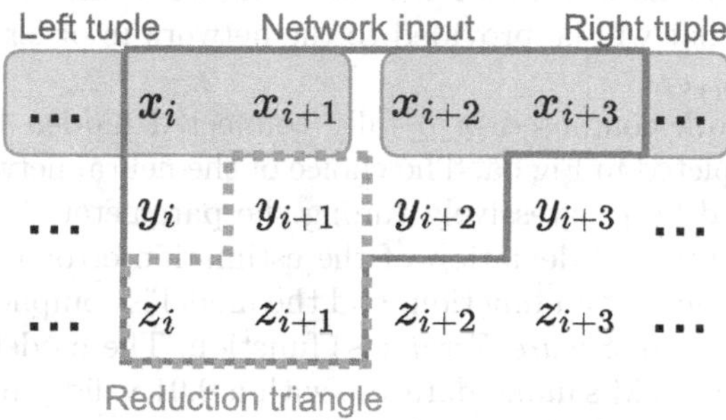

Fig. 7. Necessary data for the naive estimator (reduction triangle) and the neural network based merge estimator.

When $err_{naive} > 0$, reduction factor has been overestimated. This situation raises an issue for the attacker, as the complexity of the attack is falsely underestimated. On the contrary, $err_{naive} < 0$ indicates that the reduction factor has been underestimated. This means that the attacker would probably not consider this step to perform the attack, even if, in reality, the attack complexity would have been much inferior. A distribution of the err_{naive} values is depicted in Fig 8a.

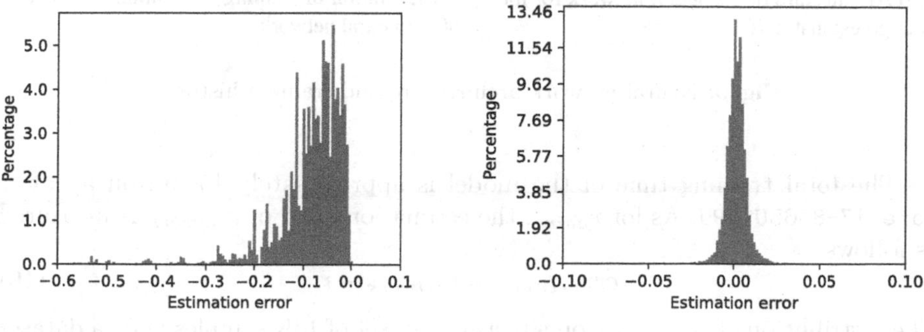

(a) Distribution of err_{naive} for $m = 4$. **(b)** Distribution of $err_{network}$ for $m = 4$.

Fig. 8. Estimation error for the naive and the neural network approach.

The attacker stresses that r_{naive}, despite being fast to compute, has the flaw of not considering all the inter-mask dependencies depicted in Eqs. (9) and (10).

Neural Network Based Estimator

Inter-masks dependencies are difficult to handle as-is for crafting a merge estimator. Luckily, the complex relations that bound these bytes can be exploited thanks to the power of a neural network. Hence, the Hamming weights of the bytes depicted in Fig. 7 can be fed to a neural network in order to predict r.

To do so, we create a dataset by performing 1.3M merges of candidates for two pairs of bytes. Merging pairs allows to quickly compute r, and thus allows building a significant dataset in a reasonable amount of time. We keep the real r values as labels that will be provided to the network in order for it to provide an estimator $r_{network}$.

A neural network composed of 6 fully connected hidden layers is crafted, whose sizes are depicted in Fig 9a. The choice of the neural network architecture has been performed by progressively tuning the parameters in order to reduce the variance and standard deviation of the estimation error for $r_{network}$. Each layer uses the *Relu* activation function, and the model is compiled with the *adam* optimizer and the *Mean-Square-Error* loss function. The model is trained upon 65 epochs upon a 1.287M sample datasets with a 0.01 validation ratio. Training and validation losses are depicted in Fig. 9b.

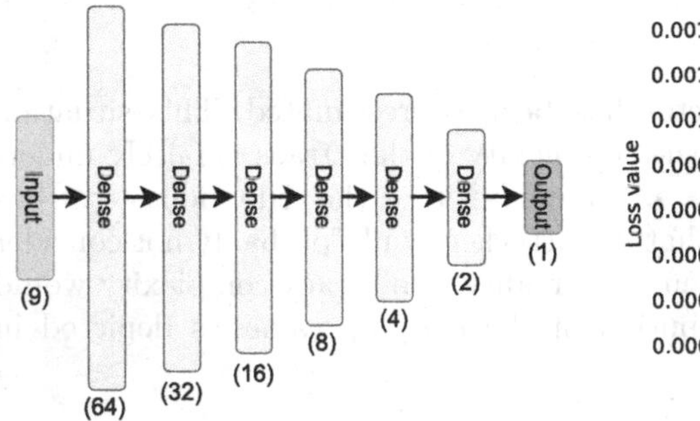

(a) Architecture of the neural network for the merge estimator E.

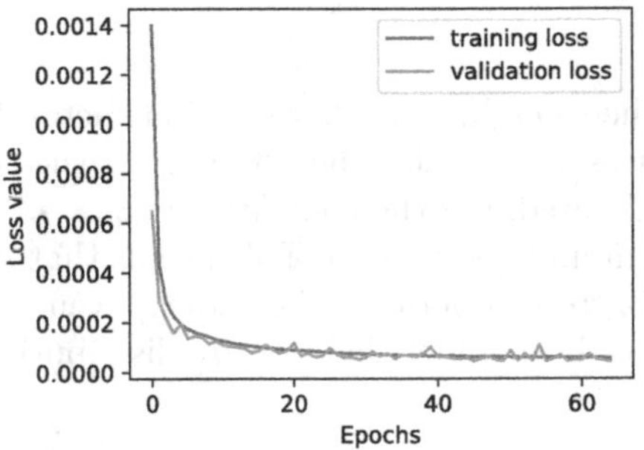

(b) Evolution of training and validation losses of the neural network.

Fig. 9. Neural network architecture and training history.

The total training time of the model is approximately 15 min on a `Intel Core i7-8565U` CPU. As for r_{naive}, the estimation error of $r_{network}$ is measured as follows:

$$err_{network} = r_{network} - r \tag{16}$$

The distribution of $err_{network}$ on a testing dataset of 13K samples (*i.e.*, a dataset that has not been used to train the network) is displayed in Fig. 8b.

Discussion
Figure 8a shows that our naive estimator highly underestimates the reduction factor of a merge between two tuples. Some instances even show more than a 50% delta between r_{naive} and the real reduction factor r. Figure 8b shows that the neural network provides an estimation of r which is more accurate than the naive estimator, as the mean is closer to 0. Moreover, the error variance and standard deviation of the distribution have been reduced compared to the naive estimator. More importantly, the $err_{network}$ distribution does not show outliers (*i.e*, predictions that are far from the mean) unlike err_{naive}. In our experiment, we hence use $r_{network}$ as the reduction factor estimation for the metric E (see Fig. 6).

Estimating the Best Position. The best position for the attack is assessed by applying estimator E in a sliding window fashion upon the iterations of the LFSR. In terms of performance, the computation time is approximately one second per iteration on a `Intel Core i7-8565U CPU`: this enables estimating the attack complexity on several dozens of thousands of steps in less than a day.

Depending on the attacker's computational power, several strategies can be considered. First, the attacker can set up a threshold upon attack complexity. When targeting an encryption stream, the attacker can apply the metric E on the sliding window until it returns an attack complexity that is below this threshold. Another approach is to fix a limit on the sliding window algorithm. Then, when all the attack complexity estimations have been returned, the attacker chooses the lowest one.

Figure 10 illustrates a run of the sliding window algorithm on a Dumbo LFSR with initial state bytes sampled from the uniform distribution. The metric $E(t)$ is computed for $t \in \{0, \cdots, 20000\}$. In this example, minimal estimated attack complexity is approximately $2^{39.30}$ for $t = 10909$. Note that each $E(t)$ can be computed independently: the algorithm can easily be transformed into a parallel version.

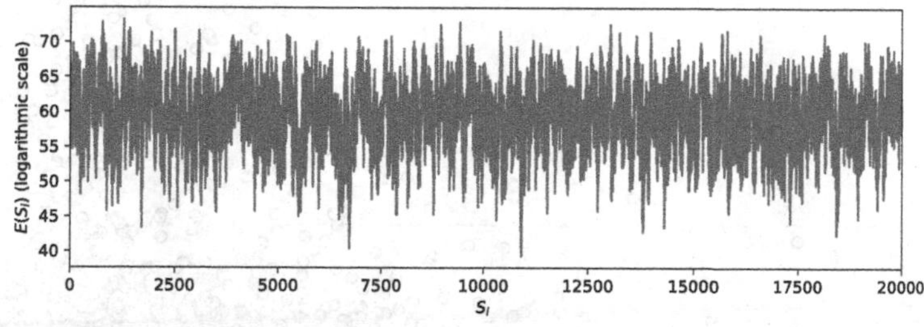

Fig. 10. Example output of the sliding window E estimation algorithm.

5 Results and Discussion

5.1 Elephant Attack

We have simulated the attack on randomly generated Dumbo keys. We selected the lowest 25% of keys with respect to expected complexity given by the estimator E derived in Sect. 4.2. This gave us $N_{runs} = 1275$ keys to test. For each, the number N_{nodes} of nodes effectively traversed in the tree has been counted. This number roughly corresponds to the time complexity of the attack. Among these nodes, we have specifically counted the number N_{keys} of nodes on the last layer; *i.e.* nodes that correspond to plausible guesses that remain to be brute forced to finish the attack.

Only just above three quarters (77.73%) of the runs have ended after two days. This is an improvement (24.16% more) compared to [20] where only 53.57% had finished in the same amount of time. On average, for the runs that finished after two days, the number of nodes traversed is $N_{nodes} = 2^{41.92}$, and the number of remaining keys is $N_{keys} = 2^{36.52}$.

Table 3. Quartiles for estimator and time distributions.

	quartile Q_1	median Q_2	quartile Q_3
estimator E (log_2)	51.62	53.64	55.07
time (hours)	1.61	8.88	37.96

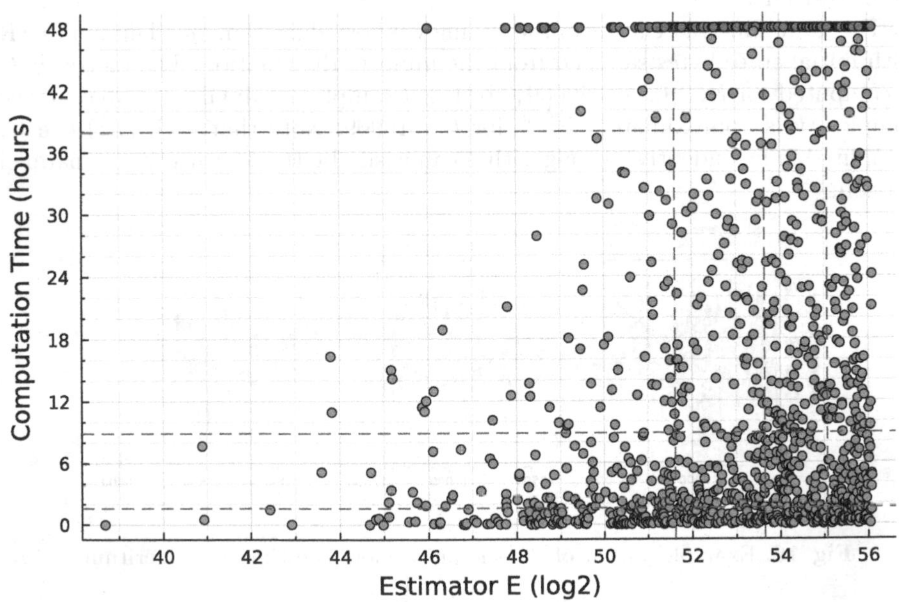

Fig. 11. Estimator E versus actual computation time for finished runs (blue) and unfinished runs (red). Quartiles are represented by dashed lines. (Color figure online)

Figure 11 shows the link between the estimator E and the actual computation time for the differents keys tested. Quartiles for estimator and time distributions are given in Table 3. It should be remembered that data given here only represent the lowest 25% of the estimator distribution and that time is capped at 48h, and therefore do not represent the full distributions.

5.2 Impact of the Generation of Masks

The threat brought by this attack upon the Elephant cryptosystem implies a discussion about mitigations. Apart from using generic countermeasures, like *e.g.* Boolean masking, there seem to be two possibilities for improvement. Indeed, the attacker gains information from two sources:

- from Eqs. (7) and (8) used to derive the masks for domain separation;
- from the LFSR state update equation (L1).

Thus, either the mask derivation or the LFSR can be changed, or both. This section studies the former case.

We ran two experiments, similar to Sect. 5.1 except that the attacker does not gain information from every Hamming weight. In the first experiment, they only know the values of the $HW(x_j)$, and the $HW(y_j)$. In other words, compared to the experiment in the Sect. 5.1, they lost the knowledge of the $HW(z_j)$. Likewise, in the second experiment, they only know the values of the $HW(x_j)$. In both cases, none of the $N_{runs} = 120$ runs done has terminated after a week.

From these experiments, it seems that the combined knowledge of the $HW(x_j)$, $HW(y_j)$, and $HW(z_j)$ contributed heavily on the success of the attack. It would then seem a good idea to tweak the cryptographic mode of operation by finding another way of generating masks for domain separation.

5.3 Studies on Different LFSRs

This section is dedicated to the study of the influence of the choice of the LFSR. We stress that the results shown here are obtained without the optimizations the optimization presented in Sect. 4.2: in practice, an attacker can hope lowering the attack complexity by exploiting the optimization.

To keep the spirit of the original Elephant algorithm, only Fibonacci-like LFSRs, at the byte level, are considered. More specifically, LFSRs considered are: LFSRs where a single new byte is computed from a combination of three bytes using byte-wise shifts and rotations. As usual, the associated feedback polynomial must be primitive to ensure only maximum-length sequences can be generated. Among all possible candidates, different behaviours can be triggered.

In this paper, the *type* of a LFSR is defined as the sequence of the number of bits unknown to the attacker at each depth in the tree where a new feedback occurs.

Looking at equation (L1), it can be seen that:

$$|HW(x_{j+20}) - HW(x_j \lll 3)| \leq 2$$

since there are only 2 bits that are modified by:

$$x_{j+3} \ll 7 \oplus x_{j+13} \gg 7.$$

Thus, if other feedback functions are used, with more bits involved, it can be expected to have an impact on the attack.

Later in the attack, when at depth 3 in the tree, the same idea can be applied to check whether:

$$|HW(x_{j+17}) - HW(x_{j-3} \lll 3 \oplus x_j \ll 7)| \leq 1$$

So since now only the single bit $x_{j+10} \gg 7$ is unknown. Consequently, the type of the Dumbo LFSR is $[2, 1]$.

LFSRs with different types can be a first criterion when testing our attack.

A second criterion is the spacing between the feedback bytes. Indeed, the tighter they are, the faster the attacker can use equation (L1) at its full potential.

In the case of Dumbo, the feedback bytes are at indices 0, 3, and 13. We call 13 the *depth*, this is simply the highest index of the feedback.

We chose LFSRs based on these two criteria. Types is defined from $[2, 1]$ to $[8, 8]$. For types $[2, 1]$, and $[5, *]$, we looked at all the possible LFSRs in order to study the influence of their depth.

The state update function of the different LFSR tested are given by equations (L2) to (L21). Their type and depth are given at the second, respectively third, column of Table 4.

L2 $x_{j+20} \leftarrow x_j \lll 3 \oplus x_{j+1} \ll 7 \oplus x_{j+11} \gg 7$
L3 $x_{j+20} \leftarrow x_j \lll 3 \oplus x_{j+14} \gg 3 \oplus x_{j+17} \gg 7$
L4 $x_{j+20} \leftarrow x_j \lll 1 \oplus x_{j+3} \gg 3 \oplus x_{j+13} \gg 7$
L5 $x_{j+20} \leftarrow x_j \lll 1 \oplus x_{j+9} \ggg 3 \oplus x_{j+15} \gg 7$
L6 $x_{j+20} \leftarrow x_j \lll 3 \oplus x_{j+9} \ll 4 \oplus x_{j+19} \gg 7$
L7 $x_{j+20} \leftarrow x_j \lll 3 \oplus x_{j+1} \ll 5 \oplus x_{j+3} \gg 6$
L8 $x_{j+20} \leftarrow x_j \lll 1 \oplus x_{j+4} \gg 3 \oplus x_{j+19} \gg 5$
L9 $x_{j+20} \leftarrow x_j \lll 1 \oplus x_{j+7} \gg 3 \oplus x_{j+18} \gg 5$
L10 $x_{j+20} \leftarrow x_j \lll 1 \oplus x_{j+3} \gg 3 \oplus x_{j+9} \gg 5$
L11 $x_{j+20} \leftarrow x_j \lll 3 \oplus x_{j+1} \gg 7 \oplus x_{j+17} \ll 4$
L12 $x_{j+20} \leftarrow x_j \lll 3 \oplus x_{j+5} \gg 7 \oplus x_{j+19} \gg 3$
L13 $x_{j+20} \leftarrow x_j \lll 1 \oplus x_{j+5} \ll 7 \oplus x_{j+16} \ll 3$
L14 $x_{j+20} \leftarrow x_j \lll 1 \oplus x_{j+1} \gg 7 \oplus x_{j+9} \gg 3$
L15 $x_{j+20} \leftarrow x_j \lll 1 \oplus x_{j+13} \ll 5 \oplus x_{j+19} \ll 3$
L16 $x_{j+20} \leftarrow x_j \lll 3 \oplus x_{j+14} \gg 7 \oplus x_{j+17} \gg 3$
L17 $x_{j+20} \leftarrow x_j \lll 3 \oplus x_{j+4} \ll 1 \oplus x_{j+5} \gg 6$
L18 $x_{j+20} \leftarrow x_j \lll 1 \oplus x_{j+3} \gg 1 \oplus x_{j+9} \ll 1$
L19 $x_{j+20} \leftarrow x_j \lll 1 \oplus x_{j+4} \gg 1 \oplus x_{j+5} \ll 1$
L20 $x_{j+20} \leftarrow x_j \lll 3 \oplus x_{j+1} \gg 1 \oplus x_{j+8} \lll 7$
L21 $x_{j+20} \leftarrow x_j \lll 3 \oplus x_{j+3} \ll 5 \oplus x_{j+4} \lll 5$

Table 4. Type, depth, proportion of runs finished after two days of computations, the average number of nodes traversed, and the number of remaining keys for Dumbo (L1), and LFSRs (L2) to (L21) [20].

LFSR	type	depth	finished	N_{nodes}	N_{keys}
(L1)	[2, 1]	13	53.57%	$2^{41.82}$	$2^{36.59}$
(L2)	[2, 1]	11	82.5%	$2^{41.23}$	$2^{36.39}$
(L3)	[5, 1]	17	0.83%	$2^{42.89}$	$2^{34.68}$
(L4)	[5, 1]	13	94.17%	$2^{39.68}$	$2^{33.68}$
(L5)	[5, 1]	15	28.33%	$2^{42.13}$	$2^{35.25}$
(L6)	[5, 1]	19	11.67%	$2^{42.38}$	$2^{36.77}$
(L7)	[5, 2]	3	100.0%	$2^{30.93}$	$2^{24.93}$
(L8)	[5, 3]	19	0.83%	$2^{43.99}$	$2^{37.59}$
(L9)	[5, 3]	18	0.0%	–	–
(L10)	[5, 3]	9	95.83%	$2^{40.32}$	$2^{34.0}$
(L11)	[5, 4]	17	0.83%	$2^{43.58}$	$2^{35.6}$
(L12)	[5, 5]	19	0.0%	–	–
(L13)	[5, 5]	16	0.0%	–	–
(L14)	[5, 5]	9	82.5%	$2^{41.43}$	$2^{34.95}$
(L15)	[5, 5]	19	0.0%	–	–
(L16)	[5, 5]	17	0.0%	–	–
(L17)	[8, 2]	5	100.0%	$2^{35.53}$	$2^{29.17}$
(L18)	[8, 7]	9	78.75%	$2^{41.56}$	$2^{34.79}$
(L19)	[8, 7]	5	100.0%	$2^{35.41}$	$2^{29.42}$
(L20)	[8, 8]	8	79.17%	$2^{41.59}$	$2^{35.78}$
(L21)	[8, 8]	4	100.0%	$2^{34.76}$	$2^{29.29}$

We ran the same experience as in Sect. 5.1 for every considered LFSR with $N_{tests} = 120$. For each LFSR, we noted the proportion of runs finished after two days of computations, the average number of nodes effectively traversed in the tree, and the average number of remaining keys. Results are summarized in Table 4.

From these experiments, it seems that the depth has a much more relevant impact than the type. Yet, this seems to be quite tailored to our particular attack. Changing the generation of the different masks is generally more impactful, since it can cut down in three the amount of information given to the attacker.

6 Conclusion

In this paper and its previous version, theoretical and simulated practical blind side-channel attack targeting the LFSR of the Elephant algorithm have been presented. Elephant is a pertinent target. First, Elephant is a finalist for the (NIST) competition for lightweight cryptography candidates for authenticated encryption. Moreover, Elephant is an interesting target because the internal LFSR only depends on the secret key. In other words, in the use case of Elephant, retrieving the initial state of the LFSR is equivalent to recovering the encryption key.

Different tweaking options have been considered. Going from the most impactful to the least, they are changing the mask derivation for domain separation, and modifying the LFSR, looking at the importance of depth and type.

Our attack is based on the fact that an attacker can retrieve the Hamming weights of the different bytes in the LFSR. The Elephant design, where there exist relations between the different masks of the LFSR, is an added vulnerability to our attack. In the previous version, in half the cases, the key is retrieved in less than two days. In this paper, an important improvement is made. The result is that in three quarters of the cases, the key is retrieved in less than two days. To have this new result the main idea has been that the attacker can wait and decide when to begin the attack. In other words the attacker has to find the best attack position in the LFSR computation progress.

Future works may consider the inclusion of noise in the simulations. To succeed we need a new tool able to treat errors resulting noisy measurement Hamming weight. An idea is to use a belief propagation as in [26]. Ultimate future work can be performing the attack on an actual implementation.

Acknowledgments. This research is part of the chair CyberCNI.fr with support of the FEDER development fund of the Brittany region and with APCIL project fund of the Brittany region too.

References

1. Archambeau, C., Peeters, E., Standaert, F.-X., Quisquater, J.-J.: Template attacks in principal subspaces. In: Goubin, L., Matsui, M. (eds.) CHES 2006. LNCS, vol. 4249, pp. 1–14. Springer, Heidelberg (2006). https://doi.org/10.1007/11894063_1
2. Azouaoui, M., Papagiannopoulos, K., Zürner, D.: Blind side-channel SIFA. In: 2021 Design, Automation & Test in Europe Conference & Exhibition (DATE). IEEE (2021)
3. Beierle, C., et al.: Schwaemm and ESCH: lightweight authenticated encryption and hashing using the sparkle permutation family. NIST round 2 (2019)
4. Bernstein, D.J.: How to stretch random functions: the security of protected counter sums. J. Cryptol. **12**, 185–192 (1999). https://doi.org/10.1007/s001459900051
5. Bertoni, G., Daemen, J., Peeters, M., van Assche, G.: The Keccak reference (2011)
6. Beyne, T., Chen, Y.L., Dobraunig, C., Mennink, B.: Dumbo, Jumbo, and Delirium: parallel authenticated encryption for the lightweight circus. IACR Trans. Symmetr. Cryptol. **2020**, 5–30 (2020)
7. Beyne, T., Chen, Y.L., Dobraunig, C., Mennink, B.: Elephant v2. NIST lightweight competition (2021)
8. Bogdanov, A., Knežević, M., Leander, G., Toz, D., Varıcı, K., Verbauwhede, I.: Spongent: a lightweight hash function. In: Preneel, B., Takagi, T. (eds.) CHES

2011. LNCS, vol. 6917, pp. 312–325. Springer, Heidelberg (2011). https://doi.org/10.1007/978-3-642-23951-9_21
9. Brier, E., Clavier, C., Olivier, F.: Correlation power analysis with a leakage model. In: Joye, M., Quisquater, J.-J. (eds.) CHES 2004. LNCS, vol. 3156, pp. 16–29. Springer, Heidelberg (2004). https://doi.org/10.1007/978-3-540-28632-5_2
10. Burman, S., Mukhopadhyay, D., Veezhinathan, K.: LFSR based stream ciphers are vulnerable to power attacks. In: Srinathan, K., Rangan, C.P., Yung, M. (eds.) INDOCRYPT 2007. LNCS, vol. 4859, pp. 384–392. Springer, Heidelberg (2007). https://doi.org/10.1007/978-3-540-77026-8_30
11. Chakraborty, A., Mazumdar, B., Mukhopadhyay, D.: Fibonacci LFSR vs. Galois LFSR: which is more vulnerable to power attacks? In: Chakraborty, R.S., Matyas, V., Schaumont, P. (eds.) SPACE 2014. LNCS, vol. 8804, pp. 14–27. Springer, Cham (2014). https://doi.org/10.1007/978-3-319-12060-7_2
12. Chari, S., Rao, J.R., Rohatgi, P.: Template attacks. In: Kaliski, B.S., Koç, K., Paar, C. (eds.) CHES 2002. LNCS, vol. 2523, pp. 13–28. Springer, Heidelberg (2002). https://doi.org/10.1007/3-540-36400-5_3
13. Clavier, C., Reynaud, L.: Improved blind side-channel analysis by exploitation of joint distributions of leakages. In: Fischer, W., Homma, N. (eds.) CHES 2017. LNCS, vol. 10529, pp. 24–44. Springer, Cham (2017). https://doi.org/10.1007/978-3-319-66787-4_2
14. Clavier, C., Reynaud, L., Wurcker, A.: Quadrivariate improved blind side-channel analysis on Boolean masked AES. In: Fan, J., Gierlichs, B. (eds.) COSADE 2018. LNCS, vol. 10815, pp. 153–167. Springer, Cham (2018). https://doi.org/10.1007/978-3-319-89641-0_9
15. Daemen, J., Hoffert, S., Peeters, M., Assche, G.V., Keer, R.V.: Xoodyak, a lightweight cryptographic scheme (2020)
16. Dobraunig, C., Eichlseder, M., Mendel, F., Schläffer, M.: Ascon. Submission to the CAESAR competition (2014)
17. Granger, R., Jovanovic, P., Mennink, B., Neves, S.: Improved masking for tweakable Blockciphers with applications to authenticated encryption. In: Fischlin, M., Coron, J.-S. (eds.) EUROCRYPT 2016. LNCS, vol. 9665, pp. 263–293. Springer, Heidelberg (2016). https://doi.org/10.1007/978-3-662-49890-3_11
18. Handschuh, H., Heys, H.M.: A timing attack on RC5. In: Tavares, S., Meijer, H. (eds.) SAC 1998. LNCS, vol. 1556, pp. 306–318. Springer, Heidelberg (1999). https://doi.org/10.1007/3-540-48892-8_24
19. Hell, M., Johansson, T., Maximov, A., Meier, W., Yoshida, H.: Grain-128aead, round 3 tweak and motivation (2021)
20. Houssein Meraneh, A., Clavier, C., Le Bouder, H., Maillard, J., Thomas, G.: Blind side channel on the elephant LFSR. In: SECRYPT (2022)
21. Iwata, T., Khairallah, M., Minematsu, K., Peyrin, T.: Duel of the titans: the Romulus and Remus families of lightweight AEAD algorithms. IACR Trans. Symm. Cryptol. **2019**, 992 (2020)
22. Joux, A., Delaunay, P.: Galois LFSR, embedded devices and side channel weaknesses. In: Barua, R., Lange, T. (eds.) INDOCRYPT 2006. LNCS, vol. 4329, pp. 436–451. Springer, Heidelberg (2006). https://doi.org/10.1007/11941378_31
23. Jurecek, M., Bucek, J., Lórencz, R.: Side-channel attack on the a5/1 stream cipher. In: Euromicro Conference on Digital System Design (DSD). IEEE (2019)
24. Kazmi, A.R., Afzal, M., Amjad, M.F., Abbas, H., Yang, X.: Algebraic side channel attack on trivium and grain ciphers. IEEE Access (2017)

25. Kocher, P., Jaffe, J., Jun, B.: Differential power analysis. In: Wiener, M. (ed.) CRYPTO 1999. LNCS, vol. 1666, pp. 388–397. Springer, Heidelberg (1999). https://doi.org/10.1007/3-540-48405-1_25
26. Le Bouder, H., Lashermes, R., Linge, Y., Thomas, G., Zie, J.-Y.: A multi-round side channel attack on AES using belief propagation. In: Cuppens, F., Wang, L., Cuppens-Boulahia, N., Tawbi, N., Garcia-Alfaro, J. (eds.) FPS 2016. LNCS, vol. 10128, pp. 199–213. Springer, Cham (2017). https://doi.org/10.1007/978-3-319-51966-1_13
27. Linge, Y., Dumas, C., Lambert-Lacroix, S.: Using the joint distributions of a cryptographic function in side channel analysis. In: Prouff, E. (ed.) COSADE 2014. LNCS, vol. 8622, pp. 199–213. Springer, Cham (2014). https://doi.org/10.1007/978-3-319-10175-0_14
28. Luykx, A., Preneel, B., Tischhauser, E., Yasuda, K.: A MAC mode for lightweight block ciphers. In: Peyrin, T. (ed.) FSE 2016. LNCS, vol. 9783, pp. 43–59. Springer, Heidelberg (2016). https://doi.org/10.1007/978-3-662-52993-5_3
29. Mangard, S.: A simple power-analysis (spa) attack on implementations of the AES key expansion. In: Lee, P.J., Lim, C.H. (eds.) ICISC 2002. LNCS, vol. 2587, pp. 343–358. Springer, Heidelberg (2003). https://doi.org/10.1007/3-540-36552-4_24
30. Mangard, S., Oswald, E., Popp, T.: Power Analysis Attacks. Springer, Boston, MA (2008). https://doi.org/10.1007/978-0-387-38162-6
31. NIST: SHA-3 standard: permutation-based hash and extendable-output functions. FIPS 202 (2015)
32. NIST: Lightweight Cryptography Standardization Process (2018)
33. Ouladj, M., Guilley, S.: Side-Channel Analysis of Embedded Systems. Springer, Cham (2021). https://doi.org/10.1007/978-3-030-77222-2
34. Rechberger, C., Oswald, E.: Stream ciphers and side-channel analysis. In: ECRYPT Workshop, SASC-The State of the Art of Stream Ciphers. CiteSeer (2004)
35. Samwel, N., Daemen, J.: DPA on hardware implementations of Ascon and Keyak. In: Proceedings of the Computing Frontiers Conference. ACM (2017)
36. Standaert, F.X.: Introduction to side-channel attacks. In: Verbauwhede, I. (ed.) Secure Integrated Circuits and Systems. Integrated Circuits and Systems. Springer, Boston, MA (2010). https://doi.org/10.1007/978-0-387-71829-3_2
37. Yli-Mäyry, V., et al.: Diffusional side-channel leakage from unrolled lightweight block ciphers: a case study of power analysis on prince. IEEE Trans. Inf. Forensics Secur. **PP**, 3033441 (2020)

Stacked Ensemble Models Evaluation on DL Based SCA

Anh Tuan Hoang(✉), Neil Hanley, Ayesha Khalid, Dur-e-Shahwar Kundi, and Maire O'Neill

Centre for Secure Information Technologies (CSIT), ECIT, Queen's University Belfast, Belfast, UK
{at.hoang,n.hanley,a.khalid,d.kundi}@qub.ac.uk, m.oneill@ecit.qub.ac.uk

Abstract. Side-channel analysis (SCA) has proved its effectiveness in attacking the cryptographic implementations for high security algorithms like Advanced Encryption Standard (AES). The improvement of machine learning (ML) in general and deep learning (DL) in particular in SCA shows that DL is a big threat in hardware security, in which the secret key of SCA countermeasure AES can be revealed with only 40 traces [17]. Combination of multiple DL can improve the effectiveness of SCA more. However, how to combine those models together is still a question. This paper applied stacked ensemble ML to combine the predictions from a number of inputs and sub-models together to enhance the power of DL in attacking AES implementation with SCA countermeasures. We train not only the output probabilities of sub-models but also their maximum likelihood score (MLS) in a stacked ensemble model to improve the performance of convolutional neural network (CNN)-based models. Further more, output probabilities from multiple trace inputs to the same sub-model are also utilized for our stack ensemble model training. A two step training procedure is required, one is for each sub-model and the other is for the stacked ensemble model, which takes inputs as the output probabilities of the above trained sub-models. This paper evaluate the effectiveness of various stacked ensemble models in terms of the number of input traces and the number of sub-models used for the first training stage. Our best model generates state-of-the art results when attacking the ASCAD variable-key database, which has a restricted number of training traces per key, recovering the key within 20 attack traces [15] in comparison to 40 traces as required by the original CNN with Plaintext feature extension (CNNP)-based model.

Keywords: SCA · AES · Deep learning · CNN · CNNP · Stacked ensemble · Key reveal · Masking

1 Introduction

Since SCA was introduced in 1996 [20] based on the difference in the power consumption of bit transitions, much research has been conducted on efficient methods to both break and protect cryptographic implementations. Common attack

M. Van Sinderen et al. (Eds.): ICSBT/SECRYPT 2022, CCIS 1849, pp. 43–68, 2023.
https://doi.org/10.1007/978-3-031-45137-9_3

methods such as differential power analysis (DPA) [21], correlation power analysis (CPA) [5], or differential frequency-based analysis (DFA) [10], allow divide and conquer strategies to significantly reduce the computational complexity of key recovery when additional power (or electromagnetic) information is available. For example, in the case of the AES-128, it is reduced from $\mathcal{O}\left(2^{128}\right)$ to $\mathcal{O}\left(16 \times 2^{8}\right)$. In order to protect against such attacks a number of countermeasures have been proposed, many of which are now standard in commercial security products such as credit cards *etc.* At the hardware layer techniques such as dual-rail logic [6,16,31,40,41] attempt to equalise the power consumption of the underlying algorithm regardless of the data being processed, while at the algorithmic layer techniques such as masking [7,12,18,28,33] introduce fresh randomness to reduce the useful leakage available to an attacker. Both these techniques, as well as all other countermeasures, come with various trade-offs for the level of protection provided in terms of execution time, randomness required, silicon (or memory) size *etc.*

While statistical and ML have a long history, recent progress in DL in particular, has led to such techniques being applied in the SCA context for key recovery in the presence of countermeasures. These attacks fall under the profiling adversarial model, where it is assumed that the attacker has a similar (or identical) training device(s) to measure a large quantity of traces in order to build an accurate power model, which then allows key recovery from the target device in relatively few traces. Among the DL approaches, CNN based models seem most promising [17,23,30,39,44] due to their effectiveness when training with raw data, with the *convolutional* layer acting as a filter to pick out the relevant features for classification.

1.1 Related Work

There are a large number of available ML and DL algorithms and models, as well as more general statistical learning techniques that can be applied to SCA. Some initial DL based SCA attacks have been proposed by [11,24,25]. However, these attacks are based on an assumption that the number of masks are either very limited, or an adversary is able to fully access the internal values of the target devices when profiling, including the values of the random masks, which is generally not feasible in practice.

In efforts to increase the effectiveness of DL performance in the context of SCA, an in-depth analysis in [22,32] noted that the size of filter in a CNN model is an important factor as its length should cover the most interesting points of interest (PoI) to enable the combination of the corresponding leakage, however it is also easily defeated if a designer inserts fake computational operations into the design.

A non-profiled DL attack approach was proposed in [39]. The secret key is revealed by combining key guesses with an analysis of DL accuracy/loss metrics, with the intuition that these will be highest/lowest, for the correct key. While this method requires training a DL model for each hypothesis key hence is computationally intense, it was successful in attacking sensitive data protected by multiple masks.

State of the art efforts seen to include SCA domain knowledge into DL architectures as proposed by [14,17], in which the plaintext was given as an additional input to increase the accuracy when directly training on the key value.

Our proposed model shares the same idea with [15], where the outputs of trace(s) from CNN-based model with Plaintext feature extension (CNNP) model(s) are combined in a following stacked ensemble model to increase the accuracy while reducing the number of traces. Inputs for the stacked ensemble model is not only the probabilities of the hypothesis keys but also their MLS. Hence, our model combines strength of multiple models, CNNP and MLS. In comparison with [15], this paper includes more evaluations with other stacked ensemble convolutional neural network with Plaintext feature extension (SECNNP) models. They include SECNNP model with single trace and multiple CNN-based model with Plaintext feature extension (CNNP) sub-models, SECNNP model with multiple traces and single CNNP sub-model and SECNNP model with multiple traces and multiple CNNP sub-models.

The main finding of the proposed research are as follows:

- The use of multiple sub-models and trace combination in a stacked ensemble model increases the accuracy of a ML model rather than simply summing up outputs of sub-models using the MLS method.
- MLS is an efficient method for models and trace combination and should be included in the ensemble model.
- Stacked ensemble model shows the best results with single trace input to multiple CNNP sub-models.

1.2 Our Contributions

This paper shows the limitations of applying MLS when combining sub-models for an ensemble model in the field of SCA (based on traces from a protected AES implementation). We propose stacked ensemble models developed from CNN models with Plaintext extension (CNNP at [17]) that looks to enhance DL from a side-channel aspect, taking the strength of number of models [29] and MLS into consideration. Our proposed models allow key recovery when targeting an AES implementation protected with multiple masking scheme.
Our main contributions include:

1. Demonstrating the advantage of using the stacked ensemble model as a method for combining multiple models and traces over the ordinary MLS and MLS-based ensemble method.
2. Evaluation and verification of the robustness of our proposed stacked ensemble model with plaintext extension on the ASCAD database.
3. Introduction of a new SECNNP model architecture for SCA. While the ASCAD masked AES design is an example target of the architecture, it can be applied to any AES implementation.

4. Reducing the requirements of applying DL in SCA, particularly when attacking implementations with countermeasures, in which thousands of traces can be required to break protected AES implementations using DL. This work allows for key recovery with around 20 traces.
5. Discussion on the optimal number of sub-models and traces required in the stacked ensemble model.
6. Discussion about the trade-off between accuracy and training time for single and multiple *convolutional* filter kernel size models.

2 Background

2.1 Side-Channel Analysis and Countermeasures

SCA Approaches, Leakage Models and Problems. Side channel attacks work on the principal that the power consumed by a device is dependent on the operation being performed and the data being processed. This allows an adversary to estimate what the power consumption should be for some intermediate value that is a function of some known data (*e.g.* a plaintext or ciphertext byte), and some unknown data (*e.g* a secret key byte). In a non-profiled attack, a statistical distinguisher (*e.g.* students t-test) can then be used between the actual power traces, and the estimated traces in order to determine if the secret key hypotheses is correct. In order to improve the effectiveness of the distinguisher, a leakage model is generally first applied to the intermediate value. For a profiled attack, as in this paper, it is assumed that an attacker has a similar or identical device on which they can record a large number of acquisitions, allowing an accurate profiling of the actual power leakage of the device.

Leakage models can be Hamming weight (HW) or Identity (ID). In this paper, we use the ID leakage model, where an intermediate value of the cipher is considered as the leakage. This simply considers that different values consume different amounts of power. Hence, the traces are labelled by some intermediate value for training, making a broader range of features are learnt at different points in time. The number of labels for classification is $2^8 = 265$ for an 8-bit word sub-key. It requires a small number of traces, *e.g.* less than 100 for attacking a secret key.

SCA Countermeasures. While a number of SCA countermeasures in both hardware and software have been proposed in the literature (such as dual-rail logic, dummy operations, threshold implementations *etc.*), here we focus on masking as this is the countermeasure that is applied to the traces under consideration. Masking (including higher-order variants) applies one or several random masks to the sensitive data such as to the input of the S-Box or the S-Box itself, respectively forming 1st-order or higher-order masking schemes [33]. Masking methods can be divided into 2 types: additive and multiplicative, and the sensitive data can be protected with one or several independent random or fixed masks. There is a trade-off to be determined in relation to the level of protection required against the additional processing and randomness requirements of the masking scheme. It is relatively straightforward to mask data for linear operations, however non-linear functions can be trickier to implement securely.

A number of masking techniques to protect AES have been proposed, with a rotating masking scheme introduced in [28] which frequently changes the masked S-Box among 16 pre-computed ones. [18] introduces an algorithm for masking a lookup table of a block-cipher at any order, which refreshes the random masks between every successive shift of the input for new look up table generation. [12] introduces a secret sharing scheme that is compatible with 4th order boolean masking, in which each part of the data is shared and computed among different partners. Different from additive masking, multiplicative masking schemes such as [2] multiply the sensitive data with a random mask. This is used to mask data for multiplication operations such as multiplicative inversion in $GF\left(2^8\right)$ for AES S-Box computation. This method can face difficulties for zero-val ue inputs as they are not effectively masked by the multiplicative mask [7]. [7] also proposed a solution based on random embedding of $GF(2^8)$ to a larger structure so that zero values are mapped onto another compatible set of values as shown in [26]. The two masking types can be combined into an adaptive masking scheme, resulting in a number of masked AES countermeasures dth-order [1,4,9,13,27,34,42]. Multi masking for AES implementations can be seen as masking of the plaintext by:

$$\overline{p_i} = p_i \oplus m_i \tag{1}$$

and masking the S-Box for value $i \in [0 \ldots 255]$, which can be prepared in advance:

$$\overline{\text{S-Box}\,(x)} = \text{S-Box}\,(x \oplus m_{i,in}) \oplus m_{i,out} \tag{2}$$

in which, p and m are the plaintext and mask, respectively in Eq. 1 and x is the masked input for the S-Box, $\oplus m_{i,in}$ and $\oplus m_{i,out}$ are the masks used to unmask the input and mask the output of S-Box in Eq. 2.

Equation 1 ensures that the linear AddRoundKey operation which follows the S-Box works as expected on the masked data, but no unmasked data is processed. Equation 2 ensures that the non-linear S-Box operation will be masked by unknown pair values $m_{i,in}$ and $m_{i,out}$ so that on every execution different data will be processed regardless of the input value. In our experiment, the target implementation has a higher-order masking scheme as described in [32], in which the plaintext and SBox are masked by two independent masks as shown in Eqs. 1 and 2.

2.2 Convolutional Neural Networks with Plaintext Feature Extension

CNNs are a DL architecture that incorporates several different types of layers for detecting features for classification. Our work relies on *convolutional*, *Max-Pooling*, *dropout*, *dense* (or *fully-connected*) and *softmax* layers, and the use of non-linear activation functions (*ReLu* and *Softmax*) [8,19,36,38].

It is clearly shown in [17] that the plaintext (or ciphertext) is an important factor in building leakage models as it is XORed with the key prior to the S-Box in the first round. The output of this operation can be used for labelling traces when training DL models.

$$y = \text{S-Box}\,(p_i \oplus k_i) \tag{3}$$

in which, p and k are the plaintext and key, respectively.

Regardless of the countermeasure utilised, the designer needs to modify the plaintext in some way in order to hide the sensitive value input to the S-Box.

The plaintext will be directly used with the key where no countermeasure is implemented, or masked by one or several masks via XOR to hide the sensitive data, breaking the relationship between the sensitive data in the S-Box computation and the attackers ability to hypothesis on power consumption. Whatever the designers do to protect the sensitive data from side-channel leakage, they will need to modify some signal or variable related to plaintext, and this processing will leave either first or higher-order leakage. The model for Convolutional Neural Network with Plaintext input (CNNP) with a single *convolutional* filter kernel size can be given by the following formula:

$$s \circ [\lambda^3] \circ \beta \circ [\lambda^2] \circ [P_{ext} \circ [\delta \circ [\alpha \circ \gamma_x]]^3] \tag{4}$$

in which, s, λ, β, P_{ext}, δ, α, and γ are the *softmax*, *fully-connected*, *dropout*, *plaintext feature extension*, *MaxPooling*, *activation*, and *convolutional* layers respectively. γ_x is a *convolutional* layer with filter kernel size of 3. CNNP with one-hot encoding [17] is used as sub-models in our Stacked Ensemble CNNP (SECNNP) and is shown in Fig. 1

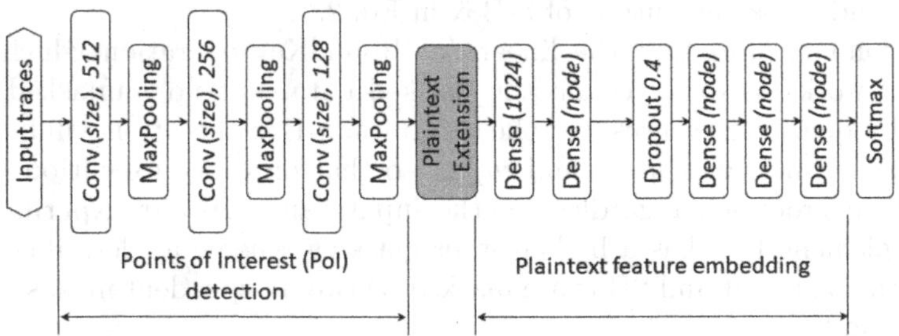

Fig. 1. CNNP sub-models [17].

Maximum Likelihood Scores. Maximum likelihood scores (MLS) can be used for combining results of attacks from multiple different traces [37] and/or different models [29] with the same key. It estimates the *likelihood* of each hypothesis key by multiplying the classification probability given by independent traces and/or models to create a *scores vector*. Values in this *scores vector* are then sorted according to probability for ranking. Accuracy is considered as the location of the correct key in the ranked *scores vector*. The closer the rank of the correct key is to 1, the higher the accuracy of the evaluated model.

In the stacked ensemble model, the MLS of multiple models and traces can be used as an additional input to increase the accuracy.

3 ASCAD Database and Reference ML Models

An open-source database of side-channel traces, along with profiling attack models is available at [32]. The traces are acquired from an ATMega embedded device running AES with boolean masking and hiding implemented, with details of the algorithm given in [32]. The database also provides a number of reference attack models include Template Attack (template attack (TA)), Multilayer Perceptron (multilayer perceptrons (MLPs)) and pre-trained CNN. A new ASCAD-v2 implementation is provided with affine masking with shuffling on an ARM Cortext-M4 architecture at [35]. However, this paper aims to ASCAD-v1 due to the availability of dataset and reference models like CNNP [17], TA, MLP and ASCAD-CNN (VGG16 like) models [32,35]

3.1 ASCAD Database (v1)

The ASCAD database v1 targets a software protected AES implementation running on an 8-bit AVR ATMega8515. The software is implemented using assembly for maximum control over register usage. The linear section of the AES algorithm is protected by 16 different random masks, while the non-linear S-Box is protected by a pair of input and output masks. The side-channel information is recorded via the electromagnetic radiation emitted by the device, and is sampled at $2GSs^{-1}$. The target S-Box is the third S-Box operation in the first round as data for that S-Box is provided for both test and training traces. Two datasets with fixed and variable key are provided, each split into training and test sets. The test set for both datasets contains a fixed key, while one training set has a fixed key for all traces, while the other training set has a variable key which is randomly generated for each trace. The measurements for the variable key dataset also differ in relation to signal quality and the number of PoI provided [3]. As shown in [17], CNNP can break the fixed key dataset without taking traces as inputs due to the bijection of $S[(.) \oplus K]$ into fixed K, we will not take the ASCAD fixed key dataset into our consideration.

The ASCAD variable-key dataset has a set of 200,000 traces for training and 100,000 traces for testing. The training traces have random variable keys, as well as random plaintext and mask values. The 100,000 testing traces have the same key with random plaintext and mask values. Each trace has 1,400 features and is again labelled by the output of the 3rd S-Box in the first round, giving ≈ 781 traces per label. The variable-key database has 3 transforms, $\text{ASCAD}_{sync}^{variable}$, which is the original, $\text{ASCAD}^{variable}_{desync50}$, and $\text{ASCAD}^{variable}_{desync100}$, in which the traces are randomly shifted for a number of points in a range of 50 and 100, respectively. We evaluate our proposed SECNNP model on the $\text{ASCAD}^{variable}_{sync}$ dataset.

3.2 Reference Comparison Models

Even though a number for reference models of TA, MLP, and CNN are provided as part of the ASCAD database [32], CNNP [17] shows its advanced performance in attacking the database, in that it needs just 60 traces to achieve rank 3. We utilize CNNP as sub-models in building our proposed SECNNP model. Detail of the CNNP model and how multiple traces are combined using MLS is discussed in Subsect. 2.2.

4 Stacked Ensemble Models for DL Based SCA

4.1 Ensemble Methods Development

Deep learning relies on minimizing some loss function in a given environment, and so, the algorithm will decide the type of patterns it can learn. Hence, for given traces, different algorithms (or different models) will be able to capture different SCA leakage and in many cases, their predictive power complement each other, making a model fails to find the good features in a trace but another succeeds. Ensemble models learn the optimal combination of the base model predictions to increase accuracy.

As an development from [15], this paper present various stacked ensemble models using CNNP sub-models. They will be evaluated on AES implementations based on recovering the unmasked value of the S-Box output (even where that value is masked) and allow key recovery given knowledge of the plaintext. The trained CNNP models from [17] then are used as sub-models in the SECNNP model, in which the same labelling is used but the inputs are the hypothesis key probabilities predicted by those sub-models. Hence, our model requires two training steps.

- The first training step is the training of a number of general machine learning models, in which a number of CNNP [17] instances are trained. The accuracy of those instances must be diverse [43], and so different numbers of epochs, hyperparameters and *dropout* layers are used in the CNNP sub-models training.
- The use of a second training step is proposed in this paper, in which a number of traces with the same class (from the same plaintext in other words) are provided to the model(s) trained in the first step for their probability of hypothesis key outputs. The MLS of the same trace on multiple models, the MLS of multiple traces on each model and the MLS of all traces on all models are calculated. The output probabilities of each hypothesis key by each sub-model, together with the MLSs calculated above are grouped together as inputs to a MLP. The MLP is trained by the corresponding class given by the

trace(s) at the first step. Even though, there is no limitation on the number of traces and models involved in the MLP, we limit the number of models and traces to 3 and 6 due to the computational complexity.

Since the MLSs of traces and models received from the first step are used as an additional input for the MLP, they will be called inner-MLS. The proposed stacked ensemble model will need either multiple traces or multiple sub-models or both for the availability of the inner-MLS. Depending on the number of traces and sub-models, there are three kinds of stacked ensemble models: single sub-model with multiple traces, multiple sub-models with a single trace and multiple sub-models with multiple traces as described in Subsects. 4.3, 4.2, and 4.4. Due to the limitation in the number of traces and sub-models given above, an outer-MLS is used to combine the attacking results from more traces than a input together. Differing from the first and second training step, where the traces are from the same classes, traces in this MLS combination can come from different classes. Hence, we have two kinds of attack: a single plaintext attack, where all traces come from the same plaintext in the SECNNP model and the final MLS and a multiple plaintext attack, where all traces in the SECNNP model come from the same plaintext, but different plaintexts are used in the final MLS.

4.2 Single Trace Multiple CNNP Sub-models Stacked Ensemble Model

This model utilizes multiple CNNP sub-models for hypothesis key probability calculation independently. Since multiple independent hypothesis key probabilities are obtained from different CNNP instances, the MLS for the second stage input can be calculated from those outputs and single input trace is required for the structure.

Figure 2 shows the proposed SECNNP with one input trace and m CNNP sub-models. The number of CNNP sub-models can change within the limitation of available computational power. Equation 5 shows the function of the first *fully-connected* layer of the proposed structure with the hypothesis key probabilities as input and the MLS from one input trace.

In the SECNNP with one input trace and m CNNP sub-models, each output is the probability of the hypothesis keys, and so, the input to the first *Dense (1024)* ($\text{Dense}_1(1024)$ in Fig. 2) after the Hypothesis key probabilities combination module are $m \times 256$ values in m groups of 256. The formula for the *fully-connected* layer with m CNNP sub-models and M nodes is now:

$$Dense_1 1024[j] = \sum_{p=1}^{m} \sum_{i=1}^{256} (b[j] + prob[p][i] \times w[j][p][i]); \qquad j \in [1..M] \tag{5}$$

in which $Dense_1 1024[j]$ is the jth output of the *fully-connected* layer, $prob[p][i]$ and $w[j][p][i]$ are the probability and corresponding weight of the hypothesis key i of the input trace predicted by the CNNP sub-model p.

The formula for the *MLS* module is the multiplication of the probability of each hypothesis key generated by each CNNP sub-model. The MLS of each hypothesis i ($MLS[i]$) among 256 key possibilities is calculated by:

$$MLS[i] = \prod_{p=1}^{m}(prob[p][i]); \qquad i \in [0..255] \tag{6}$$

The formula for node j of the *fully-connected* layer after the MLS and hypothesis key probabilities combination module ($\text{Dense}_2(1024)$) is:

$$\begin{aligned} Dense_2 1024[j] = &\sum_{i=1}^{256}(b[j] + MLS[i] \times w_{mls}[j][i]) + \\ &\sum_{i=1}^{256}(b[j] + prob[i] \times w_{prob}[j][i]); \qquad j \in [1..M] \end{aligned} \tag{7}$$

in which $Dense_2 1024[j]$ is the jth output of the *fully-connected* layer, $MLS[i]$ is the output for hypothesis key i from the *MLS* module, w_{mls} is the weight for the MLS variables, $prob[i]$ is the output probability of hypothesis key i from the $Softmax_1$ module and w_{prob} is the weight for the probability for those hypothesis key.

4.3 Multi-trace Single CNNP Sub-model Stacked Ensemble Model

This model utilizes only one sub-model for hypothesis key probability calculation. Consequently, multiple traces from the same plaintext are required for the MLS calculation before becoming an additional input to the second training stage of the MLP structure.

Figure 3 shows the proposed (SECNNP) model with m input traces and a single CNNP sub-model. The number of input traces can change within the limitation of computational power. Modules $\text{Dense}_1(1024)$, MLS and $\text{Dense}_2(1024)$ in Fig. 3 share the same Eqs. 5, 6 and 7 above except that $prob[l][i]$ is the probability of the hypothesis key i of the input trace l predicted by CNNP model.

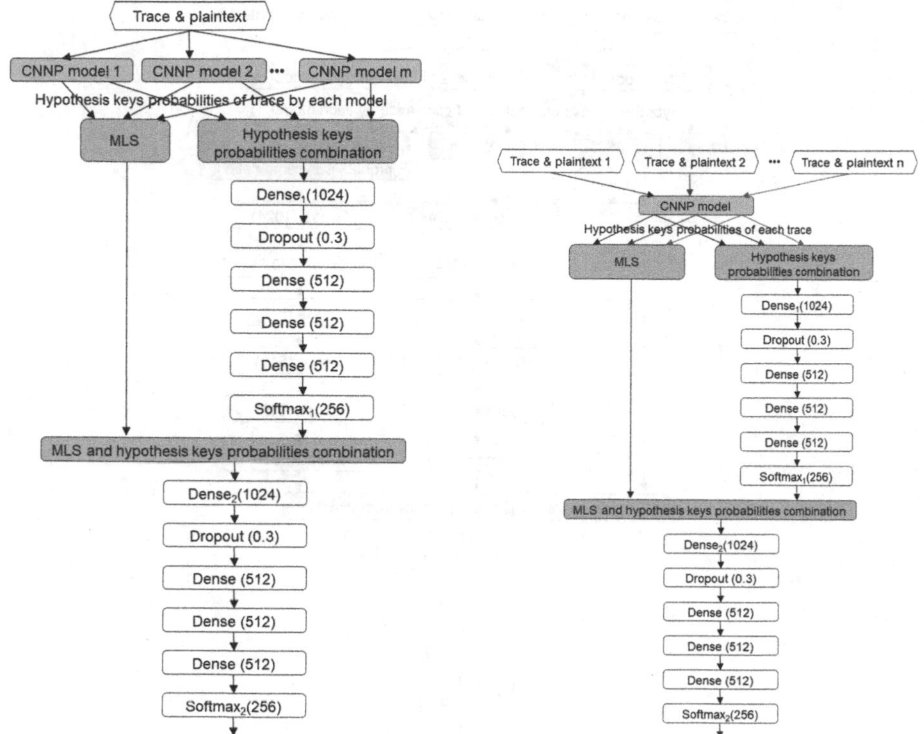

Fig. 2. SECNNP model with single trace and multiple CNNP sub-models.

Fig. 3. SECNNP model with multiple traces and single CNNP sub-model.

4.4 Multi-trace Multiple CNNP Sub-models Stacked Ensemble Model

This model is the combination of the two models above, and utilizes multiple traces and multiple CNNP sub-models for calculation of the hypothesis keys probabilities independently. Since two independent hypothesis key probability outputs are given from different CNNP instances and different traces, two inner MLSs are used as additional inputs for the SECNNP model. One is the MLS from multiple traces predicted by each CNNP sub-model and the other is the MLS of all traces and all sub-models.

Figure 4 shows the proposed SECNNP model with n input traces and m CNNP sub-models. The number of CNNP sub-models and traces can change within the limitation of computational power.

Similar to the SECNNP model with multiple inputs and a single CNNP sub-model, the first MLS (MLS_1) is used to combine the probabilities of the hypothesis keys predicted by each CNNP sub-model. The computation of the

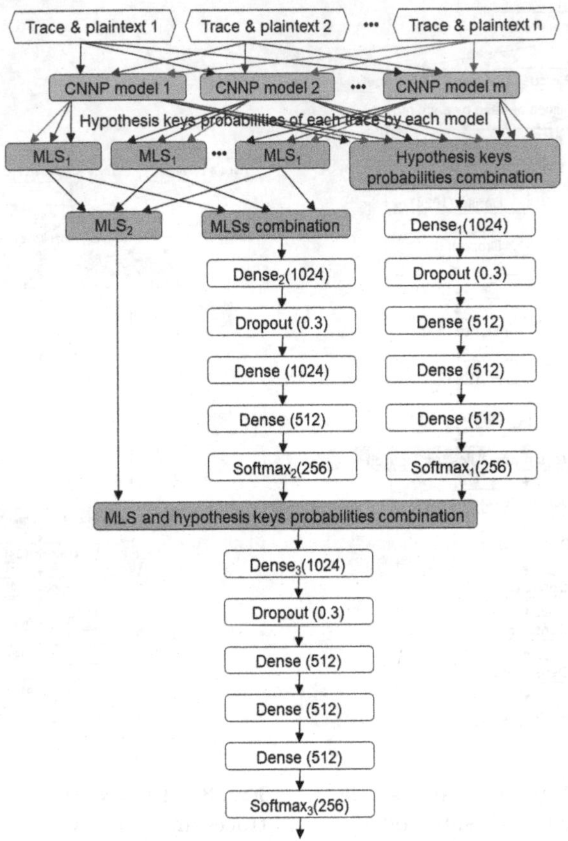

Fig. 4. SECNNP model with multiple traces and multiple CNNP sub-models [15].

MLS for each CNNP sub-model with n input traces is given by:

$$MLS_1[i] = \prod_{l=1}^{n}(prob[l][i]); \qquad i \in [0..255] \tag{8}$$

in which, l is the input trace number to a specific CNNP model and i is the hypothesis key. $prob[l][i]$ is the probability of the hypothesis key i of the trace l predicted by the related CNNP sub-model.

The second MLS (MLS_2) layer is used to combine the prediction of all n traces predicted by all *CNNP* sub-models. The formula for MLS_2 for a hypothesis key i is given by:

$$\begin{aligned} MLS_2[i] &= \prod_{p=1}^{m}(MLS_1[p][i]) \\ &= \prod_{p=1}^{m}\prod_{l=1}^{n}(prob[p][l][i]); \qquad i \in [0..255] \end{aligned} \tag{9}$$

in which, l is the input trace number, p is the CNNP model number, i is the hypothesis key, and so, $prob[p][l][i]$ is the probability of hypothesis key i of the input trace l predicted by the CNNP sub-model p.

The *fully-connected* layer with m CNNP sub-models and n traces receives $m \times n$ probability inputs. The formula for that layer with M nodes is now:

$$Dense_1 1024[j] = \sum_{p=1}^{m}\sum_{l=1}^{n}\sum_{i=1}^{256}(b[j] + prob[p][l][i] \times w[j][p][l][i]); \qquad j \in [1..M] \tag{10}$$

in which $Dense_1 1024[j]$ is the jth output of the *fully-connected* layer, $prob[p][l][i]$ and $w[j][p][l][i]$ are the probability and corresponding weight of the hypothesis key i of the input trace l predicted by the CNNP sub-model p.

The *fully-connected* layer $Dense_2$ (1024) receives m inputs, which are the MLS of the CNNP sub-models (MLS_1). The formula of that layer with M nodes is now:

$$Dense_2 1024[j] = \sum_{p=1}^{m}\sum_{i=1}^{256}(b[j] + MLS[p][i] \times w[j][p][i]); \qquad j \in [1..M] \tag{11}$$

in which $Dense_2 1024[j]$ is the jth output of the *fully-connected* layer, $MLS[p][i]$ and $w[j][p][i]$ are the probability and corresponding weight of the hypothesis key i of all n input traces predicted by the CNNP sub-model p and combined by MLS_1.

The *fully-connected* layer $Dense_3$(1024) receives 3 inputs, which are the three 256 hypothesis keys probabilities given by $Softmax_1$, $Softmax_2$ and the combined MLS_2 of all n traces predicted by all m CNNP sub-models (MLS_2). The formula of that layer with M nodes is now:

$$\begin{aligned} Dense_3 1024[j] = &\sum_{i=1}^{256}(b[j] + MLS_2[i] \times w_{MLS_2}[j][i]) + \\ &\sum_{i=1}^{256}(b[j] + prob_{Softmax_2}[i] \times w_{Softmax_2}[j][i]) + \\ &\sum_{i=1}^{256}(b[j] + prob_{Softmax_1}[i] \times w_{Softmax_1}[j][i]); \qquad j \in [1..M] \end{aligned} \tag{12}$$

in which $Dense_3 1024[j]$ is the jth output of the *fully-connected* layer *$Dense_3$ (1024)*, $MLS_2[i]$ is the output probability of hypothesis key i from module MLS_2 and $w_{MLS_2}[j][i]$ is the weight of the corresponding input $MLS_2[i]$ for the node j. Similarly, $prob_{Softmax_1}[i]$, $w_{Softmax_1}[j][i]$, $prob_{Softmax_2}[i]$ and $w_{Softmax_2}[j][i]$ are the output probability of hypothesis key i and its weight from the $Softmax_1$ and $Softmax_2$ modules.

5 SECNNP Structures Evaluation

Even though [32] provides a number of reference models such as TA, MLPs and a pre-trained CNN, the CNNP models are used for benchmarking and as sub-models for the proposed SECNNP model due to their better performance.

While a number of variants of the SECNNP architecture with different hyper-parameter (number of traces, number of sub-models, number of layers and number of nodes) were tested, in the following we present results from five SECNNP models with the architectures shown in Figs. 2, 3 and 4. The number of traces is in the range of [1..6] and the number of CNNP sub-models is in the range of [1..3]. Four SECNNP models use CNNP with single *convolutional* filter kernel size of 3. The other SECNNP model is built with a single trace and three CNNP sub-models with *convolutional* filter kernel sizes of 3 and 5. The models are trained and evaluated using the ASCAD v1 database traces on a variable-key dataset. Training is performed on a VMware virtual machine, with access to virtual NVIDIA GRID M60-8Q and M40-4Q GPUs with 8 GB and 4 GB memory respectively.

In the experiments using the ASCAD database, the number of training epochs and time for each model, together with the rank of the correct key are reported. Our comparison method is straightforward, in that we train the CNNP models with the *training dataset* group. The hyperparameters are taken from [17], in which, we focus on the CNNP models with *convolutional* filter kernel size of 3 and the transfer learning CNNP model with *convolutional* filter kernel sizes of 3 and 5. Three models with different epochs are selected as sub-models for the SECNNP structure in Figs. 2, 3 and 4. The SECNNP structures are then retrained on the same *training dataset* group for the final SECNNP models. We evaluate the trained models on the separate *test dataset* group provided in the ASCAD database. The evaluation is carried out for both a single (or chosen) *plaintext* and multiple *plaintexts*.

- In the single (or chosen) *plaintext* evaluation, traces in the *test dataset* group are sorted by the *plaintext*. Those that belong to the same *plaintext* are then grouped by [1..6] depending on the number of traces required by the SECNNP model. Multiple groups of traces with the same *plaintext* are used if more traces (*e.g.* 42) are required.
- In the multiple *plaintext* evaluation, traces in the *test dataset* group are sorted by the *plaintext*. Those belonging to the same *plaintext* are then grouped by [1..6] depending on the number of traces required by the SECNNP model as it is in the single *plaintext* evaluation method. Multiple groups of traces with different *plaintexts* are used if more traces (*e.g.* 42) are required.

At each *run*, a number of trace groups are randomly selected with the same or different *plaintext(s)* from the test dataset for the attack phase, with the maximum likelihood score (MLS) of each hypothesis key calculated as a function of the number of traces. These maximum likelihood scores are then sorted after each run and the rank of the correct key is recorded. N runs are evaluated and the mean of the correct key rank is computed. We evaluate our models using 100,000 traces from the test dataset. Depending on how fast the key rank converges, the number of traces for each run is different.

On average, there are 390 traces for each *plaintext* in the 100,000-trace database. We set the number of traces in one run to 42 and N to 8 runs so that the total number of traces with the same selected *plaintext* will not exceed the available 390 ones. The better performing models are the ones that have a lower key rank with similar or less traces required.

In the evaluation with multiple *plaintexts*, we set the number of traces to 42 to identify with the evaluation with a single *plaintext*. The number of runs N is set to 50 for average rank calculation.

In our experiments, we consider the number of traces required for a model be able to attack the key as the number where the correct sub-byte key achieves rank 3 or below because a brute force key search for the entire key should then take at least $3^{16} = 43,046,721$ loops, an acceptable computational for modern computers.

5.1 SECNNP Evaluation with Single *Convolutional* Filter Kernel Size

SECNNP Evaluation with Single *Convolutional* Filter Kernel Size for Single Selected Plaintext. In this section, we will compare the accuracy in attacking traces that come from the same *plaintext* using the SECNNP models with single *convolutional* filter kernel size, the CNNP sub-models (reference) and the MLS of those sub-models. Three CNNP models are used as reference models and as sub-models for the SECNNP model generation. In the case of SECNNP with a single CNNP sub-model, the CNNP model with *convolutional* filter kernel size of 3 and epoch as in [17] is used. In the case of SECNNP with multiple CNNP sub-models, the models with the same structure but with underfit, overfit and the epoch in [17] are used. The input traces for training and attacking can be in the range of [1..6]. Depending on the selected *plaintext*, the results differ. In the majority of cases, the new SECNNP model achieves a better correct key rank or equivalent compared with the reference models (CNNP sub-models and their MLS [17]). In a few cases, the new SECNNP model achieves a worse correct key rank compared with the reference models (CNNP sub-models and their MLS). On average, a better correct key rank is achieved by the SECNNP models.

Figure 5 provides a comparison between a typical case from the SECNNP models, and the CNNP reference models and their MLS for a single selected *plaintext*. For most selected *plaintexts*, the SECNNP model with three CNNP sub-models and a single trace input shows the best results (dashed blue line), in which the correct key achieves key rank 2 or 3 after just 12 traces. This result improves upon the results predicted by the reference models and the result combined by MLS (black lines), in which the correct key achieves rank 10 with 36 traces.

Figure 6 shows another typical case, in which the SECNNP model with three CNNP sub-models and single trace input achieves the best prediction result

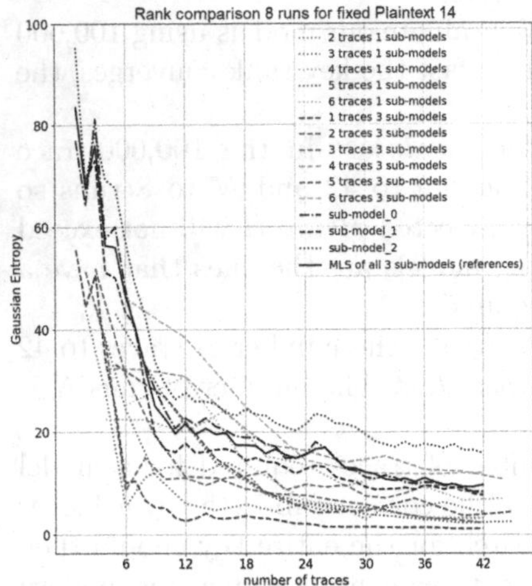

Fig. 5. SECNNP models with single *convolutional* filter kernel size prediction on single selected *plaintext* with better rank than the reference models.

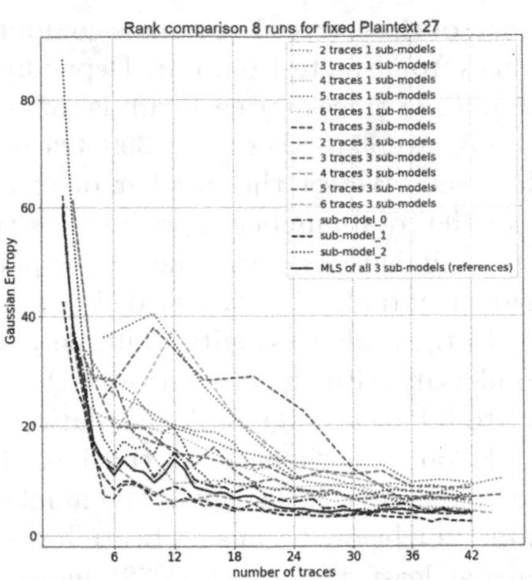

Fig. 6. SECNNP models with single *convolutional* filter kernel size prediction on single selected *plaintext* with comparable rank compared with the reference models.

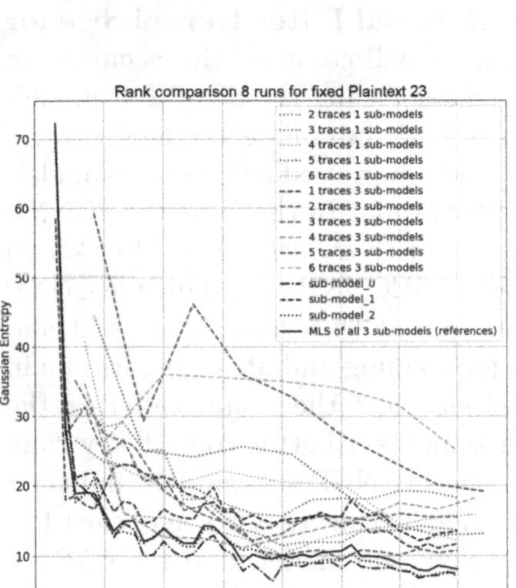

Fig. 7. SECNNP models with single *convolutional* filter kernel size prediction on single selected *plaintext* with worse rank than the reference models.

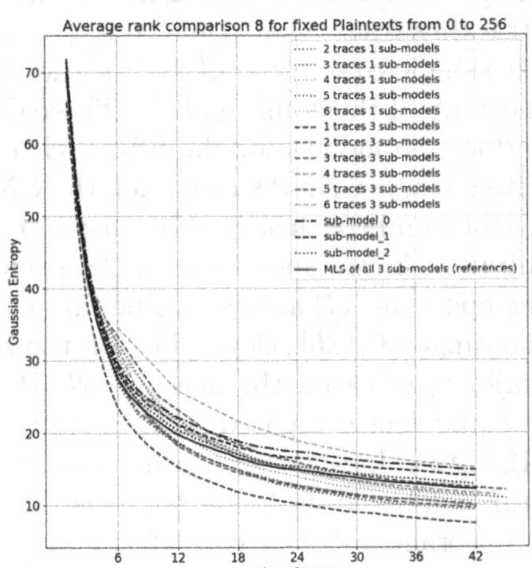

Fig. 8. Average rank comparison of the SECNNP models with single *convolutional* filter kernel size.

among the proposed SECNNP models and is comparable with the reference models and their MLS, in which the correct key rank 4 can be achieved with 36 traces.

The worst and least common case is shown in Fig. 7, in which the correct key predicted by the CNNP reference models and their MLS achieve higher rank than that of the proposed SECNNP models. None of the models performs well for the selected *plaintext*.

On average for all 256 selected *plaintexts*, the proposed SECNNP model built from three CNNP sub-models with a single trace achieves the best performance for correct key rank, as shown in Fig. 8. The other SECNNP models that perform well are built from three CNNP sub-models with 2 and 3 input traces. Even though the MLS of the reference CNNP models shows improvement in accuracy compared with those reference models, it still achieves less accuracy than that of the SECNNP. The average rank of the correct key predicted by the best SECNNP model with selected *plaintexts* achieves 10 with 24 traces and 6 with 42 traces (blue line) while the correct key predicted by the MLS of the reference models can achieve rank 13 with 42 traces (black continuous line). The average correct key rank gets worse when the number of input traces increases. The worst performance is the SECNNP model with a 6-input trace. This is due to of less diversity among the traces belonging to the same *plaintext* group.

SECNNP Evaluation with Single *Convolutional* Filter Kernel Size for Multiple Plaintexts. In this section, we will compare the accuracy in attacking traces that come from different *plaintexts* using the SECNNP models with single *convolutional* filter kernel size, with the CNNP sub-models (reference models) and the MLS of those sub-models.

Figure 9 shows the average rank of the correct key for 50 *runs*, 42 traces each.

The evaluation has been done for the SECNNP models with *convolutional* filter kernel size 3 on traces belonging to multiple *plaintexts* groups, in which trace groups are randomly selected. Consequently, models with the same number of input traces (*e.g.* the SECNNP model built from 1 sub-model and 2 input traces and the SECNNP model built from 3 sub-models and 2 input traces *etc.*) are evaluated on the same traces. Hence, the reference models (the CNNP sub-models and their MLS) can be compared with the SECNNP model with 3 CNNP sub-models and 1 input trace because they are evaluated on the same traces. As can be seen in Fig. 9, the proposed SECNNP model with 1 input trace and 3 CNNP sub-models reduces the required number of traces for attacking the sub-byte key 3 to a half compared with the reference models, in which the MLS of the reference models required 42 traces to achieve key rank 3 while the proposed SECNNP needs just 24 to achieve the same key rank.

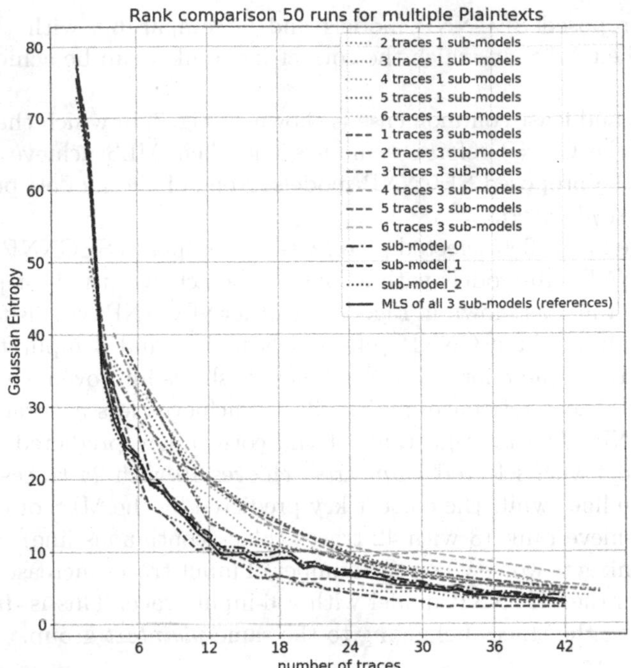

Fig. 9. Key rank comparison between proposed SECNNP models with single *convolutional* filter kernel size and reference models and their MLS for multiple *plaintexts* [15].

5.2 SECNNP Evaluation with Multiple *Convolutional* Filter Kernel Sizes

Due to the better accuracy achieved with the SECNNP model with multiple CNNP sub-models and a single trace input (Fig. 2), in this section, we evaluate a different SECNNP model with the same structure but three 2-*convolutional*-filter-kernel-size CNNP sub-models are used. The proposed model utilizes the CNNP model with *convolutional* filter kernel sizes of 3 and 5 as detailed in [17] as the sub-models. Similar to the evaluation in Subsect. 5.1, 42 traces are used in one run, 8 runs for each selected *plaintext* and 50 runs for multiple *plaintexts*.

SECNNP Evaluation with Multiple *Convolutional* Filter Kernel Sizes on Single Selected Plaintext. In this subsection, we evaluate the SECNNP model with two *convolutional* filter kernel sizes on different selected *plaintexts*. The evaluation results differ for the different *plaintexts* but in most situations, the SECNNP model achieves better or equivalent key rank compared to the CNNP models with two *convolutional* filter kernel sizes that are used to build it. Figures 10 and 11 show examples of the typical cases for a selected *plaintext*, in which the rank of the correct key predicted by the SECNNP model is better (Fig. 10) or equal (Fig. 11) to that of the reference models and the MLS calculated from them.

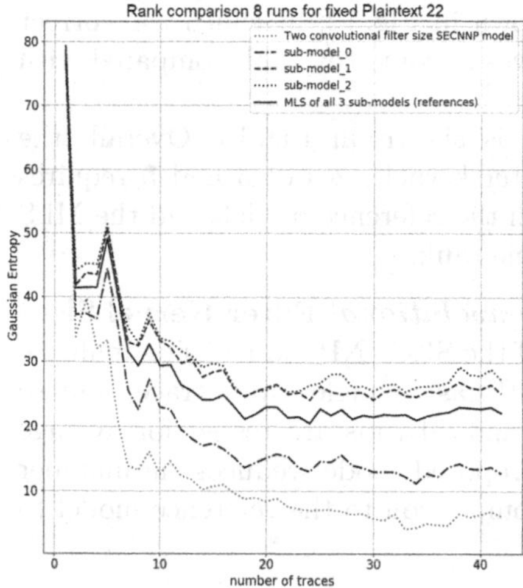

Fig. 10. SECNNP models with two *convolutional* filter kernel sizes prediction on single selected *plaintext* with better rank than the reference models.

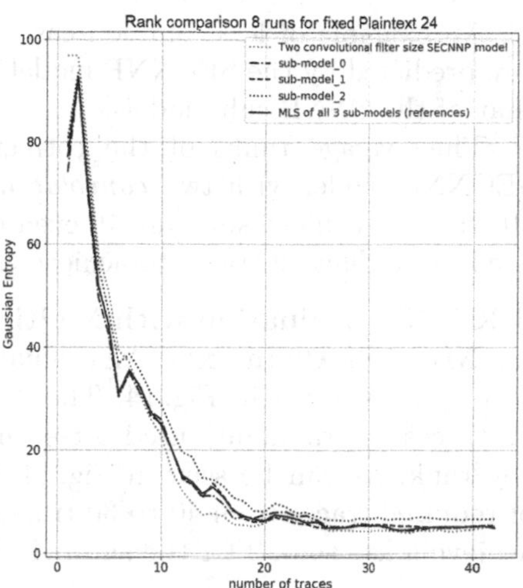

Fig. 11. SECNNP models with two *convolutional* filter kernel size prediction on single selected *plaintext* with the equivalent rank with the reference models.

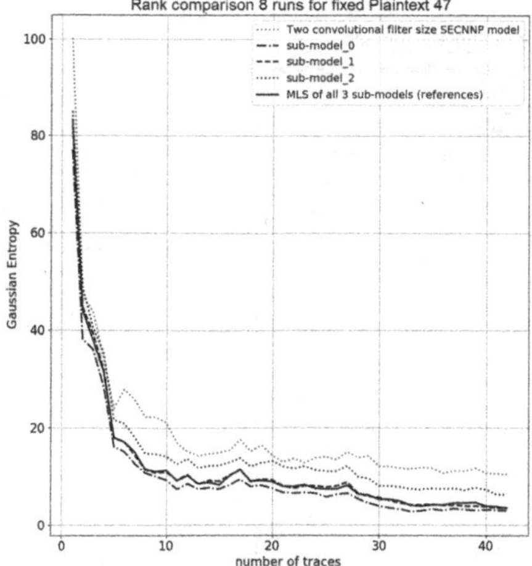

Fig. 12. SECNNP models with two *convolutional* filter kernel size prediction on single selected *plaintext* with worse rank compared with the reference models.

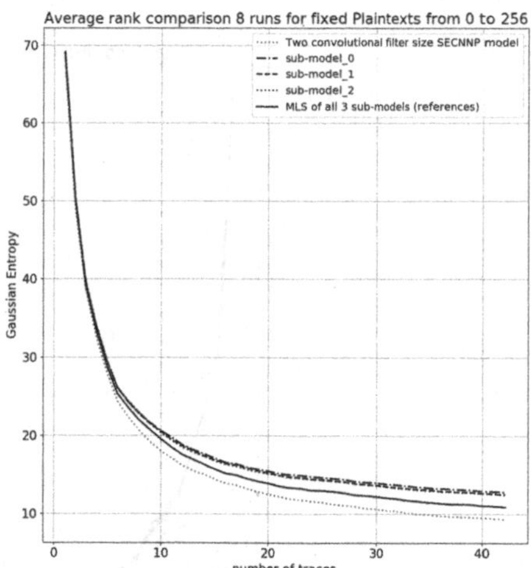

Fig. 13. Average key rank comparison between proposed SECNNP models with single *convolutional* filter kernel size and reference models and their MLS on selected *plaintext.*

An example of less common cases is shown in Fig. 12, in which the correct key predicted by the SECNNP model achieves a worse key rank compared with that of the CNNP sub-models.

The average ranks of the correct key is shown in Fig. 13. Overall, the SECNNP model with two *convolutional* filter kernel sizes of 3 and 5 requires 30 traces to achieve key rank 10 even though the reference models and the MLS need more than 42 traces to achieve the same rank.

SECNNP Evaluation with Multiple *Convolutional* Filter Kernel Sizes for Multiple Plaintexts. An evaluation of the SECNNP model using multiple *plaintexts* is given in Fig. 14. The SECNNP has a single input trace, and so 42 traces are randomly used for each run and 50 runs are tested for average key rank. As can be seen in Fig. 14, the proposed model reduces the number of required traces from 40 to 30 traces in comparison to the reference model to achieve a key rank 2 for the sub-byte key.

5.3 Comparison of SECNNP Models with Multiple and Single *Convolutional* Filter Kernel Sizes

As can be seen in Fig. 9, the SECNNP model with one input trace and three CNNP sub-models shows the best accuracy, we will evaluate the same SECNNP model in this section with different number of *convolutional* filter kernel sizes in

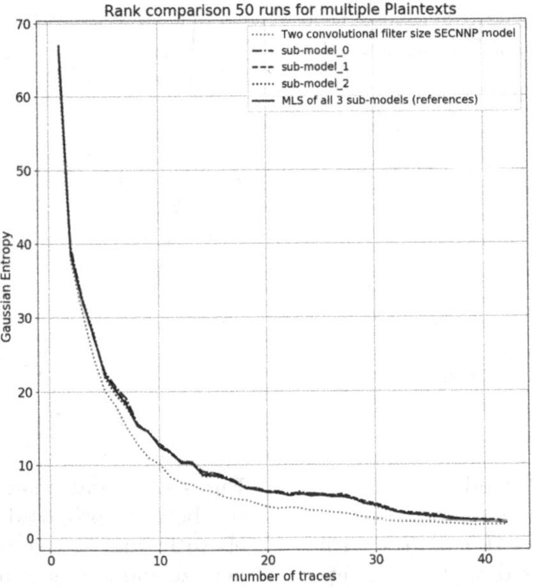

Fig. 14. Key rank comparison between proposed SECNNP models with two *convolutional* filter kernel size and reference models and their MLS for traces belong to multiple *plaintext* groups.

the CNNP sub-models. Figure 15 shows the correct key rank comparison between the SECNNP model developed from a CNNP model with two *convolutional* filter kernel size (in red) and a CNNP model with one *convolutional* filter kernel size (in green). The black lines are the CNNP reference models that are used to build these two SECNNP models. The SECNNP model has one input trace with three CNNP sub-models. Results from multiple plaintexts are combined using MLS. Figure 15 shows that the SECNNP models with two *convolutional* filter kernel sizes of 3 and 5 (shown in red) is slightly better than that of the SECNNP with single *convolutional* filter kernel size of 3 (shown in green) in attacking multiple *plaintexts*. Both reduce the number of required traces to a half to achieve the correct key rank 2 compared with their corresponding CNNP sub-models (shown in black).

6 Discussion

The evaluation of the proposed SECNNP models revealed the following:

- Re-training from the mistakes of the classifiers (sub-models) improves the accuracy. The proposed SECNNP is re-trained from the same dataset with the probability of each hypothesis key. This training gives the model a chance to learn from its mistakes by looking at the relationship between the probabilities of the correct and incorrect hypothesis keys. Diversity among the sub-models [43] is considered as a factor for the improvement in key rank.

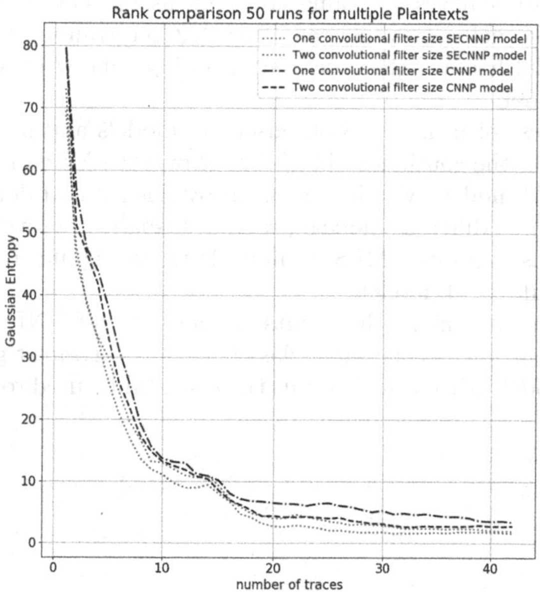

Fig. 15. Two versus one *convolutional* filter kernel sizes SECNNP models on multiple *plaintexts* [15].

- A deeper structure which combines models with different input data improves the accuracy. Even though a deeper CNNP on its own does not improve the accuracy, making the model deeper together with changing the input data from traces to hypothesis key probabilities and combining models can increase the accuracy of the SECNNP model. It reduces the number of required traces to a half, from 40 to 20 making a brute force attack possible.
- It is not necessary to have combination of many different CNN structures to achieve higher accuracy. Instead, the same structure trained with a different number of epochs so that they show diversity in attacking traces are good to combine in an stacked ensembles model. Diversity among the sub-models plays a key role in making the ensemble approach beneficial when the individual models are less than perfect. If there is no diversity between the sub-models in an ensemble, it will not improve accuracy [43]. Diversity can be achieved if the epochs are not overfitted ones.
- A trade-off in time and accuracy. In our experiment, the SECNNP model with a single *convolutional* kernel size requires double the training time compared with the equivalent CNNP model. Consequently, training the SECNNP model with two *convolutional* filter kernel size requires double the efforts compared with that of the single *convolutional* filter kernel size SECNNP model. Both need 20 traces to achieve a sub-byte key rank 2 and 3, respectively which are acceptable to allow a brute force attack to achieve all the sub-byte keys. Hence, the single *convolutional* kernel filter size SECNNP model is better in time and accuracy than that of the two *convolutional* kernel filter size SECNNP model. In addition, the SECNNP model with single *convolutional* filter kernel size achieves the same key rank as the CNNP model with two *convolutional* kernel sizes while requiring 2/3 the training time. Attack the SECNNP model has a higher accuracy training time trade-off than that of the CNNP model.
- The effectiveness of using MLS on ensemble models and multiple traces. In Fig. 5 to Fig. 14, the continuous black line shows the MLS or the ensemble of different CNNP models, which are shown by dashed and dotted black lines. The MLS of these different models provides a slight improvement in the key rank. In contrast, applying MLS to multiple traces significantly improves the correct key rank for all models.
- Due to less diversity among the results predicted by a CNNP model on multiple traces that belong to the same class (the same *plaintext* group), multiple CNNP sub-models with a single input trace should be used to build SECNNP model.

7 Conclusion

This paper has introduced, verified and proved the stacked ensemble approach for enhancing the power of CNNP in profiling SCAs. New network structures re-train output probabilities of the CNNP sub-models and their MLS in an additional DL model to improved results over the state-of-the-art CNNP model. The paper also introduces a new MLS layer which combines the Maximum likelihood scores of multiple models and multiple traces in supporting for SECNNP model development. Three models of single input trace multiple CNNP sub-models, multiple input traces single CNNP sub-model and multiple input traces multiple CNNP sub-models are evaluated. The best attack result came from the single trace three-CNNP-sub-model SECNNP model, which requires only 20 traces to recover the secret sub-key of the SCA countermeasure AES implementation. This improvement also shows a new way in building deeper structures and again proves the power of DL based SCA.

Acknowledgements. We would like to thank the people and organizations who support the research and helped improve the paper: The UK Research Institute in Secure Hardware and Embedded Systems (RISE) and The EPSRC Quantum Communications Hub (EP/T001011/1).

References

1. Ahn, S., Choi, D.: An improved masking scheme for s-box software implementations. In: Revised Selected Papers of the 16th International Workshop on Information Security Applications - Volume 9503, WISA 2015, pages 200–212. Springer-Verlag, New York Inc., New York (2016)
2. Akkar, M.-L., Giraud, C.: An implementation of DES and AES, secure against some attacks. In: Koç, Ç.K., Naccache, D., Paar, C. (eds.) CHES 2001. LNCS, vol. 2162, pp. 309–318. Springer, Heidelberg (2001). https://doi.org/10.1007/3-540-44709-1_26
3. Benadjila, R., Cagli, E., Dumas, C., Prouff, E., Strullu, R., Thillard, A.: The atmega8515 sca traces databases (2017). https://github.com/ANSSI-FR/ASCAD/tree/master/ATMEGA_AES_v1. Accessed 15 Oct 2019
4. Bilgin, B., Gierlichs, B., Nikova, S., Nikov, V., Rijmen, V.: A more efficient AES threshold implementation. In: Pointcheval, D., Vergnaud, D. (eds.) AFRICACRYPT 2014. LNCS, vol. 8469, pp. 267–284. Springer, Cham (2014). https://doi.org/10.1007/978-3-319-06734-6_17
5. Brier, E., Clavier, C.: Olivier, F. Correlation power analysis with a leakage model. **3156**, 16–29 (2004)
6. Chen, Z., Zhou, Y.: Dual-rail random switching logic: a countermeasure to reduce side channel leakage. In: Goubin, L., Matsui, M. (eds.) CHES 2006. LNCS, vol. 4249, pp. 242–254. Springer, Heidelberg (2006). https://doi.org/10.1007/11894063_20
7. D, J. and Tymen, C.: Multiplicative masking and power analysis of aes. IACR Cryptology ePrint Archive 2002, p. 91 (2002)
8. Das, S.: CNN Architectures: lenet, alexnet, vgg, googlenet, resnet and more.. (2017). https://medium.com/analytics-vidhya/cnns-architectures-lenet-alexnet-vgg-googlenet-resnet-and-more-666091488df5. Accessed 15 Oct 2019

9. De Cnudde, T., Reparaz, O., Bilgin, B., Nikova, S., Nikov, V., Rijmen, V.: Masking aes with d+1 shares in hardware. In: Proceedings of the 2016 ACM Workshop on Theory of Implementation Security, TIS 2016, pp. 43–43. ACM, New York (2016)
10. Gebotys, C.H., Ho, S., Tiu, C.C.: EM analysis of Rijndael and ECC on a wireless java-based PDA. In: Rao, J.R., Sunar, B. (eds.) CHES 2005. LNCS, vol. 3659, pp. 250–264. Springer, Heidelberg (2005). https://doi.org/10.1007/11545262_19
11. Gilmore, R., Hanley, N., O'Neill, M.: Neural network based attack on a masked implementation of AES. In: 2015 IEEE International Symposium on Hardware Oriented Security and Trust (HOST), pp. 106–111 (2015)
12. Goubin, L., Martinelli, A.: Protecting AES with Shamir's secret sharing scheme. In: Preneel, B., Takagi, T. (eds.) CHES 2011. LNCS, vol. 6917, pp. 79–94. Springer, Heidelberg (2011). https://doi.org/10.1007/978-3-642-23951-9_6
13. Gross, H., Mangard, S., Korak, T.: An efficient side-channel protected AES implementation with arbitrary protection order. In: Handschuh, H. (ed.) CT-RSA 2017. LNCS, vol. 10159, pp. 95–112. Springer, Cham (2017). https://doi.org/10.1007/978-3-319-52153-4_6
14. Hettwer, B., Gehrer, S., Güneysu, T.: Profiled power analysis attacks using convolutional neural networks with domain knowledge. In: Cid, C. and Jr., M. J. J., SAC 2018. LNCS, vol. 11349, pp. 479–498. Springer, Cham (2018). https://doi.org/10.1007/978-3-030-10970-7_22
15. Hoang, A., Hanley, N., Khalid, A., Kundi, D., O'Neill, M.: Stacked ensemble model for enhancing the DL based SCA. In: di Vimercati, S.D.C., Samarati, P. (eds.) Proceedings of the 19th International Conf. on Security and Cryptography, SECRYPT 2022, Lisbon, Portugal, July 11–13, 2022, pp. 59–68. SCITEPRESS (2022)
16. Hoang, A.-T., Fujino, T.: Intra-masking dual-rail memory on lut implementation for sca-resistant aes on fpga. ACM Trans. Reconfigurable Technol. Syst. **7**(2),10:1–10:19 (2014)
17. Hoang, A.-T., Hanley, N., O'Neill, M.: Plaintext: A missing feature for enhancing the power of deep learning in side-channel analysis? breaking multiple layers of side-channel countermeasures. IACR Trans. Cryptographic Hardware Embedded Syst. **2020**(4), 49–85 (2020)
18. JS, C.: Higher Order Masking of Look-Up Tables. Springer, Heidelberg (2014)
19. Karpathy, A.: Stanford cs231n - convolutional neural networks for visual recognition (2019). http://cs231n.github.io/convolutional-networks/. Accessed 14 Oct 2019
20. Kocher, P.C.: Timing attacks on implementations of Diffie-Hellman, RSA, DSS, and other systems. In: Proceedings of the 16th Annual International Cryptology Conference on Advances in Cryptology, CRYPTO '96, pp. 104–113. Springer, London (1996)
21. Kocher, P., Jaffe, J., Jun, B.: Differential power analysis. In: Wiener, M. (ed.) CRYPTO 1999. LNCS, vol. 1666, pp. 388–397. Springer, Heidelberg (1999). https://doi.org/10.1007/3-540-48405-1_25
22. Maghrebi, H.: Deep learning based side channel attacks in practice. IACR Cryptology ePrint Archive **2019**, 578 (2019)
23. Maghrebi, H., Portigliatti, T., Prouff, E.: Breaking cryptographic implementations using deep learning techniques. IACR Cryptology ePrint Archive **2016**, 921 (2016)
24. Markowitch, O., Medeiros, S., Bontempi, G., Lerman, L.: A machine learning approach against a masked AES, vol. 5 (2013)
25. Martinasek, Z., Dzurenda, P., Malina, L.: Profiling power analysis attack based on MLP in DPA contest v4.2. In: 2016 39th International Conference on Telecommunications and Signal Processing (TSP), pp. 223–226 (2016)

26. Meyer, L.D., Reparaz, O., Bilgin, B.: Multiplicative masking for AES in hardware. IACR Trans. Cryptogr. Hardw. Embed. Syst. **2018**(3), 431–468 (2018)
27. Moradi, A., Poschmann, A., Ling, S., Paar, C., Wang, H.: Pushing the limits: a very compact and a threshold implementation of AES. In: Paterson, K.G. (ed.) EUROCRYPT 2011. LNCS, vol. 6632, pp. 69–88. Springer, Heidelberg (2011). https://doi.org/10.1007/978-3-642-20465-4_6
28. Nassar, M., Souissi, Y., Guilley, S., Danger, J.-L.: Rsm: a small and fast countermeasure for AES, secure against 1st and 2nd-order zero-offset SCAS. In: Proceedings of the Conference on Design, Automation and Test in Europe, DATE 2012, pp. 1173–1178. EDA Consortium, San Jose (2012)
29. Perin, G., Chmielewski, Å., Picek, S.: Strength in numbers: Improving generalization with ensembles in machine learning-based profiled side-channel analysis. IACR Trans. Cryptographic Hardware Embedded Syst. **2020**(4), 337–364 (2020)
30. Picek, S., Samiotis, I. P., Kim, J., Heuser, A., Bhasin, S., Legay, A.: On the performance of convolutional neural networks for side-channel analysis. In: SPACE (2018)
31. Popp, T., Mangard, S.: Masked dual-rail pre-charge logic: DPA-resistance without routing constraints. In: Rao, J.R., Sunar, B. (eds.) CHES 2005. LNCS, vol. 3659, pp. 172–186. Springer, Heidelberg (2005). https://doi.org/10.1007/11545262_13
32. Prouff, E., Strullu, R., Benadjila, R., Cagli, E., Dumas, C.: Study of deep learning techniques for side-channel analysis and introduction to ascad database. Cryptology ePrint Archive, Report 2018/053 (2018). https://eprint.iacr.org/2018/053
33. Reparaz, O., Bilgin, B., Nikova, S., Gierlichs, B., Verbauwhede, I.: Consolidating masking schemes. In: CRYPTO (2015)
34. Rivain, M., Prou, E., Doget, J.: Higher-order masking and shuing for software implementations of block ciphers - extended version? (2019)
35. Benadjila, R., Louiza Khati, E.P., Thillard, A.: Hardened library for aes-128 encryption/decryption on arm cortex m4 achitecture (2019). https://github.com/ANSSI-FR/SecAESSTM32. Accessed 12 May 2021
36. Saha, S.: A comprehensive guide to convolutional neural networks - the eli5 way (2018). https://towardsdatascience.com/a-comprehensive-guide-to-convolutional-neural-networks-the-eli5-way-3bd2b1164a53. Accessed 14 Oct 2019
37. Standaert, F.-X., Malkin, T.G., Yung, M.: A unified framework for the analysis of side-channel key recovery attacks. In: Joux, A. (ed.) EUROCRYPT 2009. LNCS, vol. 5479, pp. 443–461. Springer, Heidelberg (2009). https://doi.org/10.1007/978-3-642-01001-9_26
38. Szegedy, C., et al.: Going deeper with convolutions. CoRR, abs/1409.4842 (2014)
39. Timon, B.: Non-profiled deep learning-based side-channel attacks with sensitivity analysis. IACR Trans. Cryptographic Hardware Embedded Syst. **2019**(2), 107–131 (2019)
40. Tiri, K., Akmal, M., Verbauwhede, I.: A dynamic and differential cmos logic with signal independent power consumption to withstand differential power analysis on smartcards, pp. 403–406 (2002)
41. Tiri, K., Verbauwhede, I.: A Logic Level Design Methodology for a secure dpa resistant asic or Fpga Implementation. In: Proceedings of the Conference on Design, Automation and Test in Europe - Volume 1, DATE '04, p. 10246. IEEE Computer Society, Washington, DC (2004)
42. Ueno, R., Homma, N., Aoki, T.: Toward more efficient dpa-resistant aes hardware architecture based on threshold implementation, pp. 50–64 (2017)

43. Wang, W.: Some fundamental issues in ensemble methods. In: 2008 IEEE International Joint Conference on Neural Networks (IEEE World Congress on Computational Intelligence), pp. 2243–2250 (2008)
44. Weissbart, L., Picek, S., Batina, L.: One trace is all it takes: Machine learning-based side-channel attack on eddsa. Cryptology ePrint Archive, Report 2019/358 (2019). https://eprint.iacr.org/2019/358

Explaining the Use of Cryptographic API in Android Malware

Adam Janovsky[1(✉)], Davide Maiorca[2], Dominik Macko[1], Vashek Matyas[1], and Giorgio Giacinto[2]

[1] Masaryk University, Brno, Czech Republic
adamjanovsky@mail.muni.cz
[2] University of Cagliari, Cagliari, Italy
{davide.maiorca,giacinto}@unica.it

Abstract. Cryptography allows for guaranteeing secure communications, concealing critical data from reverse engineering, or ensuring mobile users' privacy. Android malware developers extensively leveraged cryptographic libraries to obfuscate and hide malicious behavior. Various system-based and third-party libraries provide cryptographic functionalities for Android, and their use and misuse by application developers have already been documented. This paper analyzes the use of cryptographic APIs in Android malware by comparing them to benign Android applications. In particular, Android applications released between 2012 and 2020 have been analyzed, and more than 1 million cryptographic API expressions have been gathered. We created a processing pipeline to produce a report to reveal trends and insights on how and why cryptography is employed in Android malware. Results showed that the usage of cryptographic APIs in malware differs from that made in benign applications. The different patterns in the use of cryptographic APIs in malware and benign applications have been further analyzed through the explanations of Android malware detectors based on machine learning approaches, showing how crypto-related features can improve detection performances. We observed that the transition to more robust cryptographic techniques is slower in Android malware than in benign applications.

Keywords: Cryptography · Android · Malware

1 Introduction

The increased number of Android operating system users during the last decade, reaching almost 3 billion in 2021 [7], is one of the key motivations of the increase of security threats targeting Android showed [27]. The use of Smartphones to store an increasing number of personal and business-related information, including health, finance, and access tokens, made it one of the targets of cyber attacks. Cryptographic primitives are employed to conceal critical information

M. Van Sinderen et al. (Eds.): ICSBT/SECRYPT 2022, CCIS 1849, pp. 69–97, 2023.
https://doi.org/10.1007/978-3-031-45137-9_4

and securely carry out communication with internal components, applications, and web services. At the same time, it is natural to imagine malware authors leveraging cryptography in many artful ways to serve their malevolent objectives. For instance, cryptography equips attackers with the ability to fingerprint the parameters of an infected device, encrypt users' media files, establish a secure connection with a command-and-control server, or manage ransom payments carried out by victims infected by, e.g., ransomware.

Previous research conveyed a significant effort in analyzing cryptography in benign applications. The focus was mainly on the misuse of cryptographic application programming interface (API) in benign Android applications, i.e., finding and eliminating vulnerabilities in the employed crypto-routines that may allow attackers to obtain sensitive information [8,11,31,39].

To the best of our knowledge, however, no study explored how cryptography is currently employed in *malicious* applications, the only example being a previous work from the authors of this contribution [18]. That paper was focused on providing details on the cryptographic API used in Android malware, its evolution over time, and the potential contribution that such a study can provide for improving malware detectors.

Notably, this paper is an extended version of a conference paper published in SECRYPT 2022 [18]. In this extended work, we aim to make a step forward by focusing on machine-learning techniques for Android malware detection. In particular, we aim at assessing the effectiveness of considering the information on cryptographic API as additional features in the design of Android malware detectors.

We can summarise the aim of this paper as the answer to the following research questions related to cryptography and Android malware:

1. **RQ.1:** Are there significant differences in how cryptography is employed in benign and malicious applications?
2. **RQ.2:** How do features related to cryptography affect the performances of Android malware detectors?

We believe that answering these questions will shed more light on the mechanisms of Android malware, providing new insights for its analysis, characterization, and detection. To this end, in this paper, we propose two main contributions. First, we deliver a comprehensive comparison of how cryptography is employed in 603 937 malicious and benign applications released in the last decade. Such a comparison is carried out with an open-source[1], scalable approach that inspects (among others) the usage of hash functions, symmetric and public-key encryption, PRNGs, etc. In total, we inspect over 10^6 of cryptographic API expressions.

Second, we show that cryptographic features demonstrate their discriminant power in distinguishing malicious and benign applications by employing techniques inherited from the interpretation of learning models. This allows us to

[1] The code is accessible from github.com/adamjanovsky/AndroidMalwareCrypto.

point out possible connections between cryptographic API and malicious actions and augment state-of-the-art malware detectors' performances.

The attained results show many intriguing and surprising trends. For example, unlike benign applications, malware authors do not typically resort to strong cryptography to perform their actions. We show that malware often favors the use of cryptographically defeated primitives, e.g., weak hash functions MD5 [43] or SHA-1 [41], or symmetric encryption scheme DES [6]. These insights can also be especially useful to learning-based models, which can leverage these cryptographic trends to improve the detection rate of malware. We believe the results presented in this work can constitute a seminal step to foster additional research on the relationship between cryptography and Android malware.

The paper is organized as follows: Sect. 2 provides all the necessary technical background. The proposed methodologies are reported in Sects. 3 and 4, where the processing pipeline and the machine-learning approaches are described, respectively. Reported results on the statistics of crypto usage and in-depth analysis for various crypto functions are reported in Sect. 6. Section 7 shows how explaining machine learning-based Android malware detectors can provide useful information for threat analysis. Moreover, crypto-related features can be essential in detecting some malware samples. The limitations of the present study are discussed in Sect. 8 while Sect. 9 provides a thorough analysis of the related research works. Conclusions are reported in Sect. 10.

2 Technical Background

This section provides the basic technical elements that will be used in the rest of the paper. We first describe the structure of Android applications. Then, we provide an overview of the techniques used to analyze Android applications. Finally, we describe the prominent functionalities of the cryptographic APIs that can be employed in Android applications.

2.1 Background on Android

Android applications can be represented as zipped `.apk` (Android application package - APK) archives comprising: *(i)* The `AndroidManifest.xml` file, which provides the application package name, the name of the app basic components, and the permissions that are required for specific operations; *(ii)* One or more `classes.dex` files, which represent the application executable(s), and which contain all the implemented classes and methods executed by the app. This file can be disassembled to a simplified format called `smali`; *(iii)* Various `.xml` files that characterize the application layout; *(iv)* External resources that include images and native libraries.

Although Android applications are typically written in `Java`, they are compiled to an intermediate bytecode format called `Dalvik`, whose instructions are contained in the `classes.dex` file. This file is parsed at install time and converted to a native ARM code executed by the Android RunTime (ART). The use of ART allows speeding up the execution in comparison to the previous runtime (`dalvikvm`, available till Android 4.4), where applications were executed with a just-in-time approach: during installation, the `classes.dex` file was only slightly optimized, but not converted to native code.

2.2 Analysis Techniques for Android Applications

Android applications, like any other application written for different platforms, can be analyzed either statically or dynamically. Static analysis can be performed in two different ways. The Dalvik bytecode's instructions are disassembled, or the executable is decompiled to its Java source. Typical analysis techniques involve, among others, program slicing, data flow and taint analysis and the extraction of the application call graphs. Dynamic analysis can be performed by tracing the execution of the instructions, as well as the changes in memory during the execution of the applications.

Both approaches feature their limitations, and a comprehensive analysis requires the exploitation of the complementarities. Static analysis can be evaded by obfuscation techniques, such as renaming user-implemented functions, modifying the call graph, and using reflection or encryption API [16,25]. Dynamic analysis can be especially challenging due to the so-called *path-explosion* problem, where the application should be stimulated to take different execution branches. This operation is particularly complex in Android apps, as there are numerous ways to interact with them. As applications are typically executed in emulated environments, a malicious application can first check whether the application is being debugged or not. Finally, dynamic analysis can be resource- and time-consuming.

The choice of the right technique explicitly depends on the analysis goals. Static analysis is typically recommended for large-scale analyses, as it is much faster to carry out, and its scalability outweighs its limitations over many samples.

2.3 Cryptography in Android

Android developers typically have several means to implement cryptographic functionality for their applications: *(i)* Using Java Cryptographic Architecture (JCA) via Android API; *(ii)* Using third-party Java cryptographic libraries; *(iii)* Using third-party native cryptographic libraries; *(iv)* Designing and/or employing their cryptographic functions. Note that the last method is widely discouraged by the cryptographic community and is unfeasible to be reliably employed, as it has no well-grounded fingerprint. We also stress that, in most cases, developers do not need to develop their cryptographic functions because they can more easily and reliably employ readily available tools. For these reasons, we will not discuss the *(iv)* case in the rest of the section.

Android API cryptographic functionalities are delivered via JCA. JCA provides a stable set of classes and functions that can be called from two main packages, `javax.crypto` and `java.security` [14,35]. These packages contain more than 100 classes covering the majority of cryptographic primitives and protocols, such as hash functions, symmetric encryption schemes, digital signature algorithms, and so forth. Although the Android documentation explicitly recommends using specific primitives[2], many weak and insecure cryptographic primitives (such as the MD5 hashing function or the symmetric cipher DES) can be chosen. Apart from providing the API, the JCA introduces an abstraction layer of the so-called Cryptographic Service Providers. Such providers register themselves at the JCA and are responsible for implementing any subset of the API. Different Android versions suggest using different providers, such as `BouncyCastle` [21] and `Conscrypt` [15], which are among the most popular ones. While these providers differ in their internals, they must comply with the API and expose identical function names and argument ranges.

Apart from the Android API, practically any cryptographic functionality can be supplied by some third-party library. Still, there is no curated list of either Java or native cryptographic libraries for the Android platform to our best knowledge. During our study, we noticed libraries specifically focusing on a subset of cryptographic functions, such as providing functionality only for AES encryption. We also noticed libraries exposing various cryptographic primitives and protocols, such as the OpenSSL library. These full-fledged libraries can provide functionalities similar to the Android API.

3 Methodology

This section describes the methodology employed to extract and analyze the cryptographic API embedded in Android applications. We start by formalizing the problem and properly defining its domain and constraints. We then show how we implemented this formalism by discussing our developed analysis framework. Our findings are based on the static analysis of the Java source code obtained by decompiling the Android executables.

3.1 Problem Formalization

We organize the problem formalization in two parts: part one treats the definition of the crypto-routines of interest for our analysis, and part two describes the process of locating those routines in the application source code.

I. Definition of Crypto-Routines. Given a set of Android applications, we denote the set of all possible functions $\mathbb{F}$ contained in their source code as:

$$\mathbb{F} = \mathbb{U} \cup \mathbb{S} \cup \mathbb{T} = \mathbb{C} \cup \mathbb{C}^c,$$

where $\mathbb{U}$ represents the set of functions defined by the user, $\mathbb{S}$ is the set of system-related functions contained in the Android SDK, and $\mathbb{T}$ is the set of functions

[2] AES-256 in CBC or GCM mode, SHA-2 for hash functions, SHA-2 HMAC for MACs and SHA-2 ECDSA for signatures as of early 2020 [14].

belonging to third-party libraries. Given a set of known crypto-related functions $\mathbb{C}$, our goal is to study the intersection of $\mathbb{C}$ and $\mathbb{S}$, denoted as $\mathbb{F}_{cs}$. In other words, $\mathbb{F}_{cs}$ is the set of cryptography-related functions that are defined in the system package (in Android, represented by JCA functions). In this analysis, we discard custom cryptographic functions that users or third parties may implement. The automatic detection of such functions would be a complex task in a large-scale analysis, which may lead to false positives (or negatives) without further manual inspection. In our study, we solely aim to answer what functions from $\mathbb{F}_{cs}$ the malware authors favor.

From the cryptographical perspective, the functions contained in $\mathbb{F}_{cs}$ can be divided into the following categories: *(i) Hash functions.* Cryptographic hash functions such as MD5, SHA-1, or SHA-2; *(ii) Symmetric encryption.* Symmetric cipher primitives such as AES, DES, or RC4; *(iii) Public-key encryption.* Asymmetric primitives, in Android represented by the RSA cryptosystem; *(iv) Digital signature algorithms.* Primitives that empower digital signatures, e.g., ECDSA; *(v) MAC algorithms.* Primitives that construct Message Authentication Codes, also called MACs; *(vi) PRNG.* Functions to run pseudo-random number generators (PRNG); *(vii) Key agreement protocols.* Algorithms for key exchange, in JCA represented by Diffie-Hellman protocol; *(viii) Others.* Functions that do not fall into any of the previous categories.

II. Locating Cryptographic API. All functions in $\mathbb{F}_{cs}$ are available through two Java packages in Android API: `javax.crypto` and `java.security`. Our research goal is to reveal *which cryptographic functions have been chosen and directly employed by the authors.* Notably, Android applications typically contain third-party packages that invoke crypto functions. We aim to exclude those packages from our analysis as the application authors did not contribute to them.

Thus, for each Android sample, we are interested in extracting the cryptographic API $\mathbb{F}_a \subseteq \mathbb{F}_{cs}$ that is invoked from user-defined functions $\mathbb{U}$. To obtain the functions belonging to $\mathbb{F}_a$, we developed the following two-steps procedure: *(i)* We automatically detect the classes that belong to third-party or system libraries, and we exclude them from the set of classes that should be explored. By doing so, we establish the list of *user-implemented functions* $\mathbb{U}$; *(ii)* We extract all references to crypto-related functions $\mathbb{F}_{cs}$ that are invoked directly from $\mathbb{U}$.

The first step is motivated by the discovery [42] that more than 60% of Android APK[3] code (on average) originates from third-party packages. To study user-authored code, it is therefore critical to differentiate, with reasonable certainty, whether a class belongs to a third-party library or not. This task can be extremely challenging and was extensively studied, e.g., by [4,24,42]. It does not suffice to merely search for the `import` clauses in the decompiled source code since non-system packages could be renamed. This scenario is especially frequent in malicious applications, as the authors aim to defend against forensic investigation techniques. Inspired by the systematic review of third-party package

[3] Android Application Package, an archive that encapsulates the whole Android application.

detectors [44], we opted to tackle this task with LibRadar, a popular third-party library detection tool that uses clustering techniques and complex signatures to recognize such libraries [24]. The results reported in the review paper show that LibRadar achieved the highest precision and second-highest recall while it took approx. 5 s to evaluate an APK on average. The runner-up requires over 80 s per APK, which would be unsuitable for large-scale analysis. LibRadar was trained on a large dataset of Android applications and can reliably fingerprint more than 29 000 third-party libraries without relying on package names. Consequently, LibRadar can identify obfuscated packages. Using LibRadar[4], we filter the identified third-party packages of an APK from subsequent cryptographic API analysis.

3.2 Crypto API Extraction Pipeline

Given a dataset containing Android APKs, our system generates a comprehensive report of the embedded cryptographic API. Our system requires configuration files for the to-be-conducted experiment. Apart from other choices, the files contain a list of APKs that can be loaded from a disk or downloaded from the Internet.

The APKs are then processed in parallel, and each sample traverses the following pipeline:

1. **Pre-Processor.** This module decompiles the APKs to obtain their Java source code. Then, the third-party packages of the APKs are identified, and the whole Java source code of the APKs is extracted.
2. **Crypto-Extractor.** This module extracts and analyzes the cryptographic function call sites in the application source code. Their filtering is achieved by matching pre-defined regular expressions. Additionally, the crypto-extractor also detects both Java and native third-party cryptographic libraries.
3. **Evaluator.** This module stores, organizes, and aggregates the information retrieved by the analyzed APKs to a JSON record.

The evaluator outputs a report of the cryptographic usage for each APK. We designed the system in a modular fashion to allow for the addition of other modules for extracting further valuable insights from the APKs.

4 Cryptography and Machine Learning

To accurately detect malicious applications through machine learning approaches, multiple features are typically extracted. Among these features, cryptographic usage statistics are undoubtedly helpful in pointing out differences

[4] Since LibRadar requires a large Redis database to run (preventing parallelization), we actually leveraged its lightweight version LiteRadar. Before doing so, we compared the output of both tools on a small subset to find out that this decision has a negligible effect on the number of detected libraries.

between benign and malicious applications. In this paper, we also aim to explore *whether the statistics on the usage of cryptographic functions can be useful to recognize malicious samples from benign ones effectively.* To answer this question, we propose three approaches that employ machine learning techniques, described in the following.

4.1 Cryptographic Learning Model

The first technique consists of defining a learning-based system whose structure is inspired by other popular detection systems [9,10,26]. In particular, the proposed system performs the following steps: *(i)* it takes as an input an Android application and extracts its cryptographic API usage with the pipeline described in Sect. 3.2; *(ii)* it encodes this statistics into a vector of *features*; *(iii)* it trains a machine-learning classifier to predict a benign/malicious label.

The feature vector includes features that can be categorized into the following three sets:

- **Set A:** flags indicating the use of third-party cryptographic libraries (both Java and native).
- **Set B:** frequencies of specific cryptographic API constructors and imports of crypto-related classes, e.g., number of DES constructors in a sample.
- **Set C:** aggregated statistics of call sites and imports related to categories of cryptographic primitives: hash functions, symmetric encryption schemes, and so forth. For example: how many distinct hash functions a sample uses.

By joining these sets, we obtain 300 potentially informative features. These features are further filtered with the following feature selection process. The dataset with candidate features is split in a 9:1 ratio into training/test sets. First, we examine all possible pairs of features. If a pair exhibits Pearson's correlation coefficient higher than 0.95, we drop a random feature of such a pair. Second, we remove the features deemed uninformative by Boruta [20]. Boruta is a supervised algorithm that iteratively replicates features, randomly permutates their values, trains a random forest, and removes redundant features based on the z-score. This feature selection process yields 189 features on the dataset used in this study, whose details are reported in Sect. 6.1.

To choose the classifier best suited for our study, we resorted to a preliminary experiment on a dataset similar to the one used in this study. The following machine learning approaches have been considered: Naive Bayes, Logistic Regression, Support Vector Machines with linear kernel, Random Forest, Gradient Boosted Decision Trees (GBDT), and Multilayer Perceptron (MLP). The classifiers' hyperparameters have been tuned using 10-fold cross-validation on the training dataset, optimizing for the F1 score. The best classifier, according to the performances on the F1 score, was selected as the candidate model for carrying out the explanation analysis, followed by experiments aimed at showing the capability of crypto-related features to enhance the performances of Android malware detectors. The selected classifier turned out to be the Random Forest (which works as a majority-voting ensemble of decision trees trained on different subsets of the data) with an F1 score of 57.07%. In this preliminary study, GBDT and MLP had an F1 score of 56.89% and 56.41%, respectively, while the other classifiers provided significantly smaller performances.

4.2 Explaining the Learning Model

To further advance the understanding of cryptographic API in Android detection, we extracted *explainations* from the predictions of the cryptographic classifier. Explanation techniques allow understanding of the learning process results through the analysis of the training samples' features that influence the classifiers' decisions. In this paper, we used both *global* and *local* feature importances as reported in previous work dealing with the explanation of Android malware detectors [28,29]. The global analysis evaluates the impact of the features averaged over the whole dataset, while the local analysis evaluates the impact of the features on specific samples.

To interpret the classifier's predictions, we used Shapley additive explanations (SHAP) [22] that are successfully used outside the computer science field. SHAP can consistently explain both local predictions and global feature importance by measuring each feature's contribution to the prediction. This method uses Shapley values [38] from coalitional game theory. Each player is a feature or a coalition of features, and the game (payout) is the prediction. Shapley values are considered optimal because they satisfy the properties of efficiency, symmetry, and additivity.

4.3 Enhancing Existing Malware Classifiers

The third approach consists of taking a well-established malware classifier for Android as a baseline and measuring its performance when enhanced with features related exclusively to cryptographic API. To this end, we chose `R-PackDroid` [26], an available learning-based classifier (trained on random forests) based on static features, and we expand its feature set by adding the cryptographic features described above. There are multiple reasons for which this system was chosen as a baseline: (i) It was initially designed to detect ransomware; (ii) It harvests a relatively small number of features; (iii) It features a high detection rate (the original paper documents over 97% F1 score).

Considering the characteristics described above, it would normally be challenging to improve the already strong performance of the system by adding more features. To keep some space for improvement when enhancing the classifier with cryptographic features, we decreased the number of `R-PackDroid` features from 211 to 10 in a controlled manner, leading to an F1 score of 76%. To measure the effect of cryptographic API features on the model, we replicated the following procedure 1000 times: *(i)* We sample 10 random features from `R-PackDroid`[5]; *(ii)* We build a random forest classifier and measure its F1 score; *(iii)* We enhance

[5] The tuples were sampled in advance to avoid repetition.

the 10 R-PackDroid features with all 189 cryptographic API features chosen by feature selection; *(iv)* We use the expanded feature set to build another random forest classifier and measure its performance gain over the baseline classifier.

With the three strategies described above, we unveil the role of cryptographic API for malware detection, as will be shown in Sect. 7.

5 Implementation of the Processing Pipeline

We now provide a more detailed description of each module, as well as the technical challenges that we had to face during the development of our system. Our tool is implemented in Python 3.8 and is provided as an open-source repository for further collaboration.

5.1 Pre-processor

The first task of the pre-processor is to obtain the decompiled Java source code of the input APKs. To get object-oriented access to the source code, we instrumented the open-source tool Androguard [3]. As Androguard supports multiple decompilers, we made preliminary tests with various decompilers to verify that applications would be correctly parsed. The attained results showed that JADX decompiler [40] is capable of the most mature recovery of the Java code, and hence was used in this study. For each APK, all .java classes in its .dex files were recovered. In some samples, a small fraction (<1%) of classes did not survive the decompilation process. These classes were ignored from further processing.

The second task of the pre-processor is to craft a list of third-party packages residing in the scrutinized APK. As mentioned in the previous section, this task is handled with the help of LiteRadar that was trained on a large dataset of Android applications, and can reliably fingerprint more than 29 000 third-party libraries. It should be stressed that the LiteRadar does not rely on package names, and can thus identify obfuscated packages as well. Using LiteRadar, we check every APK for the presence of third-party packages. Each package identified as a third party is then excluded from the cryptographic API analysis.

5.2 Crypto-Extractor

The crypto-extractor component executes two sub-tasks. The first objective is to gather a list of third-party *cryptographic* libraries imported from the APK. For this scenario, we discriminate between *(i)* Java cryptographic libraries and *(ii)* native cryptographic libraries. In total, we searched for 23 distinct libraries. Their names, together with the reasons behind choosing them, can be found in Sect. 6.

The candidate list of native cryptographic libraries is then matched inside any of the following three import statements that load a native library directly from the source code: ReLinker.loadLibrary, System.loadLibrary, and Native.loadLibrary. The candidate list of Java cryptographic libraries is compared with the list of third-party packages identified earlier by LiteRadar. If any package appears in both lists, we note down the usage of the respective cryptographic library.

The second goal of the crypto-extractor is to collect comprehensive data about cryptographic API usage. Although the packages `javax.crypto` and `java.security` contain more than 100 classes and interfaces, only some of those can reveal insights about the diversity of cryptography usage in the malware. We analyzed all classes in these packages and discarded out-of-scope instances to obtain 86 classes for our analysis. Most of the diversity in the cryptographic API landscape can be explained by the study of *object constructors*, and of their parameters. Whatever the developers' aim concerning cryptography is, they must first create a suitable object to address it. To give an example, when developers want to hash a file, they must first obtain the hash object by calling the constructor `MessageDigest.getInstance()`. When this constructor is called, e.g., with a string parameter `"SHA-256"`, this reveals the probable usage of the SHA-256 hash function in the APK. We specified 333 constructors and parameters and recorded all occurrences of these in the source code[6]. Specifically, we performed a line-by-line search of each of the user-defined classes. If the searched line contained any of the constructors, we note down its usage. By doing so, we collected a rough landscape of cryptography usage in the whole source code. This data was further refined and processed to draw conclusions.

Notably, constructors parameters can be obfuscated (and thus missed by our analysis - e.g., `MessageDigest.getInstance(a)`, where `a` is some variable). In this case, our system cannot properly parse such constructors. However, we argue that this limitation could only partially be statically solved, as even more advanced techniques (such as program slicing) can be easily defeated by more advanced obfuscation [16,25]. Moreover, in large-scale scenarios, the problems introduced by the presence of some obfuscation are significantly outweighed by the dataset size. Nevertheless, for the sake of a fair analysis, we computed the exact fraction of obfuscated constructors for each of the cryptographic primitives we analyzed.

6 Trends in Cryptography

In this section, we answer RQ.1: *Are there significant differences in how cryptography is employed in benign and malicious applications?* We report the most significant statistics we obtained with the API extraction methodology presented in Sect. 3.2. First, we discuss the general prevalence of cryptographic API that can be extracted with static analysis by discussing the effects of obfuscation, the incidence of third-party packages, and the overall differences between benign and malicious applications. Then, we provide a more detailed focus on the distribution of cryptographic API in malicious applications.

---

[6] While having the capability to capture such diverse landscape, in Sect. 6 we present results only for 220 constructor variants from 8 classes, since the rest is used very rarely. No conclusions can be drawn from such rare events.

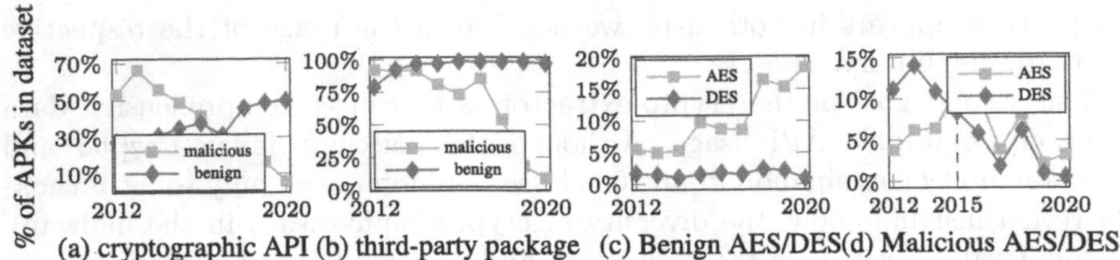

Fig. 1. Time evolution of important dataset characteristics. The y-axis shows the percentage of APKs exhibiting a given feature, whereas the x-axis represents the time in years. In subplot (a) we see the ratio of APKs in which we detected *any* cryptographic API. Subplot (b) shows APKs for which we detect any third-party package. These are the main artifacts of increasing obfuscation. Subplots (c), (d) document the usage of AES vs. DES in benign, and malicious samples respectively. AES has been the most prevailing cipher suite in benign applications since 2012. On the contrary, DES was more popular in malware in previous years, only in 2015 being outrun by AES [18].

6.1 Dataset

To gain an all-around view of the cryptographic API landscape in Android applications, we leverage the Androzoo dataset [1]. Currently, Androzoo is the largest available dataset of Android applications, containing more than 15 million of APKs. We sampled 302 039 benign applications and 301 898 malicious applications from Androzoo released in the years 2012–2020. We strived for uniform distribution of samples in the studied timeline. Yet, for years 2018 and 2020 we could only collect a limited number of malicious samples – 19 305 and 10 039, respectively. To speed up the computation, we only gathered APKs smaller than 20 MB (approximately 89% of malicious APKs in the Androzoo fulfill this criterion).

To accurately discriminate malicious files, we consider an APK as malicious if it was flagged malicious by at least five antivirus scanners from the VirusTotal service[7], which should reliably eliminate benign files deemed malicious, as reported by Salem [37]. Our samples are predominantly originating from 3 distinct sources: Google Play (60%), Anzhi (19%), and Appchina (13%). Note that the samples were deduplicated on a per-market basis [1] to avoid over-counting.

6.2 Evaluator and Post-processing

Once the overall JSON report for all APKs in the dataset is acquired according to the pipeline described in Sect. 5, we post-process the results by automatically generating CSV files containing usage statistics and the related plots for all categories (and their sub-categories) described in Sect. 3.1. Apart from that, useful general information about the nature of the dataset is provided in the report. The resulting data serves as input for the pipeline of a cryptographic learning model.

[7] virustotal.com. The number of VirusTotal positive flags is already contained in the Androzoo dataset.

6.3 System Deployment

The parallel processing of all 604 thousand samples took 16 days on 42 cores of Intel Xeon X7560, and each core consumed approximately 1.6 GB of RAM. That is the equivalent of processing 7 thousand APKs per 24 h on a single CPU with 4 cores and 16 GB of RAM, making the system well scalable. The subsequent post-processing of the JSON record to the form of the cryptography usage report takes 5 min on a regular laptop with 4 cores.

6.4 General API Distribution

Application Obfuscation. The first interesting trend of this study is a decreasing ratio of malicious applications for which we detect usage of cryptographic API, as depicted in Fig. 1a. However, such a ratio is not visible for benign applications. We conjecture that this drop does not represent a genuine decrease in usage of cryptographic functionality in time but rather a consequence of an increasing ratio of obfuscated malicious applications. To confirm this hypothesis, we randomly sampled 4444 malicious applications from 2018–2020 that allegedly contained no cryptographic API or third-party libraries. We dissected them using commercial dynamic analysis tool `apklab`[8] and searched for clues of obfuscation. We identified that 98% applications use some form of Android packer, with `jiagu` being the most popular. Each packed application also uses reflection API and dynamic library loading, which prevent static analysis from registering cryptographic API call sites. We also report that 83% of applications use some form of encryption API (AES being the most prevalent, followed by RSA), often to decrypt application resources. Such reduced prevalence of crypto API constitutes a limitation of our study, further discussed in Sect. 8.

Third-Party Packages and Crypto Libraries. Another closely related trend is the dropping ratio of third-party packages captured by `LiteRadar` in malicious applications. Before 2018, we documented a high ratio of malware employing third-party packages (86%). Starting with 2018, this ratio quickly drops as depicted in Fig. 1b. Similar to obfuscation, this drop is not evident in benign applications. Overall, `LiteRadar` was able to identify at least one third-party package in 94.6% of analyzed goodware with little variance between years (see Fig. 1b). On average, 8 packages were identified in benign APKs. This underpins the importance of robust third-party package detection. In contrast to prior work that did not consider third-party package filtering, we discarded over 4 million third-party packages with at least 44 thousand unique package names from the analysis.

Apart from Android API, cryptographic functions can also be delivered by third-party libraries, typically adopted to integrate functionality missing in system-based libraries. To our best knowledge, no curated list of third-party

[8] Kindly provided by Avast, available at http://apklab.io.

Table 1. List of 23 third-party cryptographic libraries that were searched in each of the studied samples. The Java libraries were identified using the `LiteRadar` tool, whereas the native libraries were matched as case-insensitive regular expressions inside the import statements `ReLinker.loadLibrary`, `System.loadLibrary`, `Native.loadLibrary` from the decompiled source code.

3rd-party cryptographic libraries
Java
`whispersystems/curve25519`
`guardianproject/netcipher`
`springframework/security/crypto`
`gnu/crypto`
`apache/shiro/crypto`
`rsa/crypto`
`keyczar`
`jasypt`
`googlecode/gwt/crypto`
`sqlcipher`
`spongycastle`
`bouncycastle`
`facebook/crypt`
native
`crypto-algorithms`
`libgcrypt`
`monocypher`
`PolarSSL`
`tint-AES-C`
`xxHash`
`libsodium`
`openssl`
`libressl`
`wolfssl`

cryptographic libraries for Android exists. We manually selected 13 Java and 10 native candidate libraries to be searched for. These candidates were found through the Google search engine and in popular databases [5], and their fit was confirmed by manual inspection. Although this process is inherently incomplete, and some libraries could have been missed out, we argue that this is not a practical limitation since the most prevalent libraries were unlikely to be missed, and even these are rarely used. The full list of third-party cryptographic libraries searched in the samples can be found in Table 1.

We identified only 796 benign and 198 malicious applications that import third-party cryptographic libraries. Of the studied libraries, `sqlcipher` was most popular in goodware (found in 622 samples), and `keyczar` was most popular in malware (found in 124 samples). The ratio of these applications has been stable throughout the studied timeline. As for the native libraries, not a single call to a native cryptographic library was detected in the malicious dataset, and merely 91 imports of `OpenSSL` occurred in the benign dataset.

From these results, it is possible to observe that third-party cryptographic libraries are not widely used in Android applications. This aspect demonstrates that attackers often resort to standard crypto functionalities provided by system libraries (that can use various backends, e.g., BouncyCastle).

Crypto API in Goodware and Malware. We now describe the general prevalence of cryptographic API in the dataset presented in Sect. 6.1 by showing the differences between malicious and benign applications and comparing our results with two studies conducted on benign datasets. For this comparison, we employed: *(i)* A dataset collected in 2012 as a part of the study CryptoLint [11] that we refer to as CryptoLint-B12; *(ii)* A dataset collected in 2016 as a part of Binsight study [31] that we refer to as Binsight-B16. To avoid temporal data drift, we cast four subsets of our dataset: Androzoo-B12, Androzoo-M12, Androzoo-B16, and Androzoo-M16, limited to malicious (M), and benign (B) samples from years 2012 (12), and 2016 (16). As explained in Sect. 3, our goal is to analyze only cryptographic APIs contained in user-defined code. From this respect, both [11,31] employ weaker methodologies to filter third-party libraries, relying on whitelisting and package names. Conversely, our approach of `LiteRadar` filtering captures the code written by the application authors more reliably. The numbers drawn from the Androzoo datasets serve as conservative estimates, with the real number of cryptographic API call sites even higher. The overall comparison with benign datasets is depicted in Table 2 (also reported in [18]). It can be seen that the malicious datasets have a dramatically higher density of cryptographic API call sites than their benign counterparts.

CryptoLint-Androzoo Comparison. The CryptoLint-B12 dataset resulted from scanning 145 095 samples for the presence of cryptographic API (and its misuse). The study concluded that 15 134 (10.4%) of APKs contain some cryptographic call sites. However, the subsequent BinSight study attributed 79.5% of these call sites to the ignored third-party packages, showing that the original CryptoLint study suffered from overcounting.

In contrast, we report that 27.4% of Androzoo-B12 contains cryptographic API call sites and nearly twice as much malware from Androzoo-M12 (53.1%). This highlights the extensive use of cryptographic API in malicious applications compared to the benign landscape. A closer examination of symmetric ciphers in Table 3 (also reported in [18])reveals considerable differences between malicious and benign datasets. AES dominates benign datasets with 58.9% in CryptoLint-B12 and 52.4% in Andozoo-B12. The situation is strikingly different in the malicious dataset. In Androzoo-M12, the most popular primitive is DES

Table 2. Comparison of cryptographic API spread in benign vs. malicious datasets. The last column normalizes by the size of the datasets, allowing for direct comparison [18].

Dataset	#APKs	#User-def. call sites	#User-def. call sites/10k samples
CryptoLint-B12	145 095	20 967	1445
BinSight-B16	115 683	78 163	7006
Androzoo-B12	39 838	81 698	20 507
Androzoo-B16	37 493	124 705	33 260
Androzoo-M12	39 767	125 225	31 489
Androzoo-M16	39 325	208 625	53 051

Table 3. Distribution of symmetric ciphers in benign and malicious datasets with AES dominating all but Androzoo-M12 [18].

Dataset	AES	DES	3DES	RC4	Blowfish	Unknown
CryptoLint-B12	**58.9%**	19.0%	8.8%	0.4%	1.9%	10.9%
BinSight-B16	**64.4%**	14.3%	1.1%	2.1%	0.9%	17.2%
Androzoo-B12	**52.4%**	16.9%	3.8%	0%	0.0%	26.8%
Androzoo-B16	**59.0%**	12.2%	2.0%	0.1%	0.0%	26.8%
Androzoo-M12	12.1%	**56.0%**	0.9%	0.0%	0.0%	31.0%
Androzoo-M16	**45.1%**	22.8%	2.1%	0.0%	0.0%	30.0%

with 56% of call sites, followed by AES (12.1%) and 3DES (0.9%). We provide a more in-depth comparison of individual ciphers and their modes of operation in Appendix A.

BinSight-Androzoo Comparison. The BinSight paper aimed to answer what proportion of cryptographic API misuse can be attributed to third-party packages. The authors identified 638 distinct third-party packages in 115 683 unique samples in BinSight-B16, relying on the package name as an identifier. The authors attributed at least 90.7% of the call sites to third-party packages, underlying the need for their robust detection. Even after we discarded 9 870 third-party packages from Androzoo-M16, the malicious dataset still contains much more cryptographic API in the user-authored codebase. Again, the relations between Androzoo-M16 and BinSight-B16 are depicted in Table 2. Interestingly, in 2016, AES was dominant in Androzoo-M16 as well with 45.1% of call sites, followed by DES (22.8%). We depict the time evolution of AES vs. DES in Androzoo dataset in Fig. 1 (also reported in [18]), showing that it was only in 2015 when AES outran DES in malicious applications.

6.5 Crypto API Categories in Malware

Apart from the comparison to benign applications, we also report a broad view of the distribution of cryptographic API in *malicious* applications, concentrating on the years 2012–2018, for which we can rely on a set of representative samples not clouded with high ratios of obfuscated applications.

Table 4 (also reported in [18]) illustrates that the majority of call sites from this period can be attributed to hash functions (66%) and symmetric encryption (26%), which leaves the rest of the categories rarely used. Nevertheless, we comment on our findings in all categories, observing the time evolution trends and showing the most prevailing primitives. We could not attribute 21% of the identified constructors to the exact cryptographic primitive (partial obfuscation) during our experiments. We still manage to pinpoint their presence and category, as the system-based API calls are challenging to obfuscate entirely.

Hash Functions. The hash functions are by far the most popular category of cryptographic API in malicious applications, as they are present in 40% of all studied APKs and responsible for 424 858 call sites in our dataset. Interestingly, the majority of the call sites resort to primitives MD5 or SHA-1 that were already shown to be broken [41,43]. Specifically, MD5 can be attributed to more than 80% of these call sites and does not lose any popularity in time. This may suggest that MD5 is either not meant to provide secure integrity protection for the authors or that the developers are unaware of its weakness. The time evolution of SHA-1 and SHA-256 points to the former case. Indeed, the overall dominant SHA-1 (almost 16% of call sites) is gradually decreasing over time in favor of the more secure SHA-256 (3% overall). In 2018, SHA-256 was present in more APKs (708) than SHA-1 (528). This phenomenon can mean that, when secure integrity protection is needed, more secure SHA-256 is nowadays being selected instead of SHA-1. Still, MD5 is preferred by malware creators for other use cases. Apart from the hash functions mentioned above, only SHA-512 and SHA-384 are represented in the dataset, but these are responsible for less than 1000 call sites in total.

Symmetric Encryption. A large portion of the symmetric encryption API landscape was already described in Sect. 6.4, but some important aspects were yet omitted. Overall, our dataset contains 165 994 symmetric encryption call sites distributed in approximately 20% of APKs. A large portion of the call sites (26%) is obfuscated. Besides AES and DES, only 3DES is used in more than 1000 APKs. We also report that the concept of password-based encryption is applied merely in 837 APKs. A closer look at the encryption modes offers an interesting perspective. Our observations confirm that the authors favor the default constructors (`"AES"` and `"DES"`) compared to constructors that specify encryption mode and padding (e.g., `"AES/CBC/PKCS5PADDING"`). The default constructors fall back into the ECB mode with PKCS#7 padding, which is (under most circumstances) considered insecure [30].

Public-key Encryption. The only asymmetric encryption scheme appearing in the Android API is RSA. The RSA encryption occurs in approximately 1.55%

of all APKs in our dataset. Until 2013, RSA appeared very rarely, but then it peaked within two years at almost 1 800 APKs in 2015.

Table 4. Popularity distribution of cryptographic API categories. The ratio of APKs for symmetric encryption and RSA is approximate since one cannot differentiate the obfuscated constructors of these two categories. Note that approximately 1% of APKs contain cryptographic API outside of these categories [18].

Category	#call sites	%obfusc.	%APK
Hash functions	424 858	16.8%	39.7%
Symmetric enc	165 994	25.9%	19.4%
Public-key enc	13 262	25.9%	1.5%
Digital sig. alg	17 505	81.4%	4.5%
MAC	11 661	46.4%	3.0%
PRNGs	10 381	6.6%	2.9%
Key agreement	87	29.9%	0%
Sum	646 018	21.5%	44.6%

Digital Signature Algorithms. Surprisingly, digital signature algorithms occupy 4.5% of the malicious APKs and are present in 17 505 call sites. Considering possible applications of digital signature primitives in malware, this constitutes a rather large number. Despite the highest obfuscation rate among categories (81.43%), the `SHA1withRSA` primitive is responsible for almost 80% of the unobfuscated call sites. As in the case of the hash functions, `SHA256withRSA` is on the rise in time, first appearing in 2015 and steadily increasing the fraction of APKs it appears in ever since. Still, in 2018 it is less than four times probable to appear compared to `SHA1withRSA`.

While multiple schemes supporting elliptic curves over RSA or DSA are offered in the API, these are explicitly specified only in 19 APKs in total, with the first use appearing in 2014.

MAC Algorithms. The situation with MAC algorithms is similar to that of digital signature algorithms. The MAC systems are responsible for 11 661 call sites and are present in 3% of APKs. Still, a large portion (46.4%) of the call sites are obfuscated. Nevertheless, only two functions are called in more than 1% of the call sites – `HMACSHA1` and `HMACSHA256`. The former is heavily dominant throughout the studied timeline, being responsible for 70% of the MAC call sites.

PRNGs. The functionality of PRNGs is utilized in nearly 3% of the APKs, being responsible for 10 381 call sites. A relatively small fraction of the call sites (6.6%) are obfuscated, and virtually all unobfuscated call sites (over 90%) can be attributed to `SHA1PRNG`.

Key Agreement Protocols. The key agreement API's functionality consists purely of the Diffie-Hellman protocol (DH) for key exchange. Concerning the

DH protocol parameters, we can only differentiate between the use of DH over finite fields or elliptic curves. The key agreement API appears only in 53 APKs over the nine years, occupying 87 call sites in total. 36 of the APKs use elliptic curves, whereas 20 APKs use obfuscated calls. Interestingly, only a single APK was detected to be explicitly using DH over finite fields. The dominant use of elliptic curves over finite fields is in contrast with the situation in digital signature algorithms.

Worth noting, we did not thoroughly explore how cryptographic primitives were employed in the *context* of the applications (e.g., to send SMS, encrypt data, et cetera). This analysis is extremely complex due to the variety of application contexts, and it is hardly feasible with static analysis. However, to give readers possible directions about the motivations for using cryptography in malware, we manually inspected a small subset of samples during our study. For the categories defined in Sect. 3.1 we documented the following use-cases: *(i) Hash functions* are generally used to fingerprint the attributes of a device (IMEI, Android version, etc.), to hash whole file or string, or to construct home-brew MACs or signature primitives; *(ii) Public-key encryption* was witnessed to provide hybrid encryption or to construct digital signature algorithms from its basic blocks; *(iii) Symmetric encryption* is used to encrypt files, as well as strings, and to obfuscate expressions directly in the source code. We also witnessed the use of *PRNG* to generate random keys (often with static seeds) or to provide nonces for more complex scenarios; *(iv)* Both *key agreement protocols* and *digital signature algorithms* were found to empower more complex network protocols, e.g., SASL (Simple Authentication and Security Layer [17]); *(v)* We report no surprising use-cases for *MAC* primitives that serve their original purpose of data authentication.

7 Machine Learning and Cryptographic API

In this section, we answer RQ.2: *How features related to cryptography affect the performances of Android malware detectors?* To do so, we analyze the outcome of the experiments outlined in Sect. 4.

Cryptography-Based Learning Model. According to the preliminary results reported in Sect. 4, we trained a random forest model based only on cryptography-related features described in the same Section and compared its performance to `R-PackDroid`. To obtain a valid comparison, we replicated the experimental setup of the original `R-PackDroid` paper [26], considering10 thousand applications divided 50:50 into benign/malicious and split 50:50 into training/test sets. The proposed classifier achieved 62.4% F1 score on the malicious samples set (see also Table 5), showing that cryptographic information is discriminant enough to separate malicious from benign samples. Even though `R-PackDroid` performs significantly better than the proposed system[9], the pro-

[9] Remember that our goal was not to build a better classifier but to show that it is possible to distinguish between malicious and benign Android applications by resorting to their cryptographic API usage only.

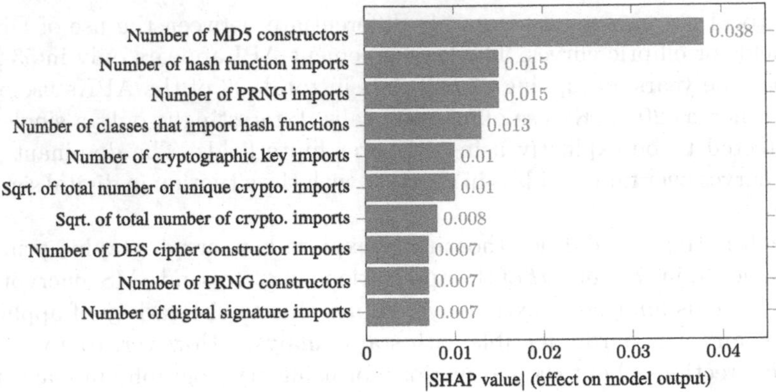

Fig. 2. A representation of 10 most influential features (their |SHAP| values are high, averaged over all samples). These represent the spots in cryptographic API with the largest difference in usage between malicious and benign samples. The x-axis shows the average effect on the model output in either direction. The model outputs values from 0 (benign) to 1 (malicious) [18].

posed classifier was able to correctly identify 88/180 malicious samples that were misclassified as benign by `R-PackDroid` (with all 211 features). This shows that cryptographic API can assist the classification of samples that would otherwise fly under the radar of existing classifiers that does not include specific features related to cryptographic usage.

Explanations of Decisions. Fig. 2 (also reported in [18]) shows the 10 most influential features of the cryptographic-API classifier, based on the SHAP values calculated for the whole dataset (i.e., global explanations) according to the methodology described in Sect. 4. Model outputs are mapped as follows: values range from 0 (benign) to 1 (malicious), and the expected value of the model on a balanced dataset is hence 0.5. The SHAP value of a feature thus represents a deviation from this expected value after inspecting a particular feature.

It is rather interesting to see that the usage of certain hashing functions is discriminative w.r.t. maliciousness of the samples. More specifically, weak hash functions (MD5) are especially used in malicious samples (as also reported by the analysis in Sect. 6.4), and they constitute an important indicator of maliciousness. Additionally, the classifier is also sensitive to the general number of imported cryptographic functions. An increasing number of imported functions lead to an increasing suspicion of maliciousness. We can thus conclude that the statistical analysis reported in the previous Section is confirmed by the analysis of explanations provided by Android malware classifiers.

Concerning the local explanation, we present an example related to the malware samples with MD5 hash `e1001da40929df64443f6d4037aa3a9f`. VirusTotal classifies this sample as a riskware of type SMSpay. By extracting the local SHAP values (Fig. 3, also reported in [18]), it is possible to see the significant importance of a DES encryption that steers the classifiers' decision towards maliciousness. Driven by this explanation, we manually disassembled the sample and looked for the usage of DES-related cryptographic API. We found that, in this case, DES is used to encrypt sensitive information, such as the phone device id, which is then subsequently exfiltrated to a remote server. This detail is especially useful to attract the attention of the analyst toward malicious operations carried out by the sample. Also, note that this sample employs name obfuscation, and the required effort to carry out a similar analysis without such guidance would be higher. Explanations can thus provide further insights into the malicious behavior of malware samples, confirming once again that effective threat analysis requires the usage of multiple different tools.

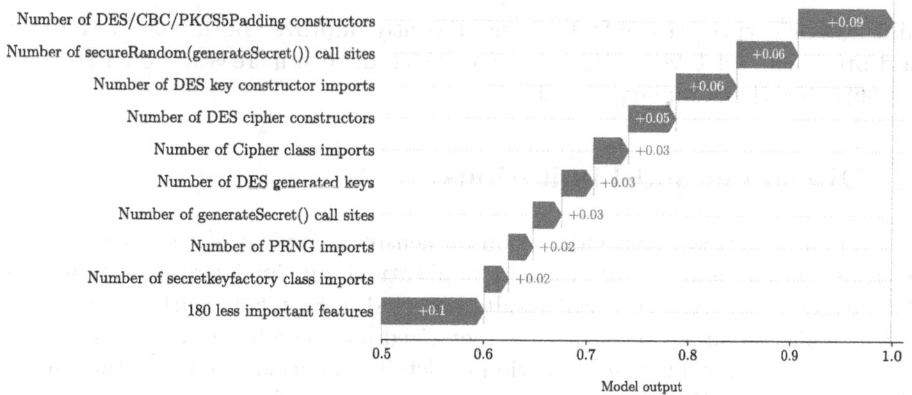

Fig. 3. Local impact of the 10 most influential features w.r.t the models' prediction *on a particular sample.* The shown APK is a malware sample of the SMSpay type. It exfiltrated DES-encrypted data through SMS. Apart from the features, the figure also depicts how the value of each feature shifts the models' output from a neutral score of 0.5 to the final output of 1 which labels the APK as malware [18].

Enhancing Existing Classifier with Cryptographic API Features. In the original work, `R-PackDroid` achieved a 97% F1 score distinguishing between three classes (ransomware in addition to malware/benign). Leveraging on the source code provided by the authors, we achieved a 92.71% F1 score with `R-PackDroid` on the Androzoo dataset. Thus, enhancing this classifier would be a hard task, as it would result in a not significant performance gain. Hence, we decided to rely on a *light* version of `R-PackDroid` that employs a reduced feature set made up of 10 features, reducing the F1 score to 74.47% when averaged over different 10-tuples of features. We then added the cryptographic features following the methodology reported in Sect. 4.

This experimental setup allowed us to better appreciate the influence of crypto features in increasing the classifiers' performance. Reported results show

Table 5. Comparison of the performance of malware classifiers without and with cryptographic API features. The performance metrics measure the result of the malicious samples. Enhancing the limited RPackDroid with cryptographic features causes a 4.18% increase in precision and 5.61% increase of recall on the Androzoo dataset, projecting into a 4.86% F1 score increase [18].

Classifier	# features	F1 score
Cryptographic API	189	62.40%
RPackDroid (full)	211	92.71%
RPackDroid (limited)	10	76.47%
RPackDroid + cryptoAPI	10 + 189	81.33%

that adding cryptographic features significantly improved both recall (+5.61%), and precision (+4.18%) of the classifier, which in turn increases the F1 score by +4.86%. See the summary in Table 5.

8 Discussion and Limitations

Our main goal was to provide a comprehensive overview of the role of cryptography in the analysis of Android applications and malware detection. The description of the experimental results reported in Sect. 6.4 clearly showed that recent malicious applications are characterized by a significant amount of obfuscation, thus preventing the extraction of detailed information about their usage of cryptography. We recognize that this is an inherent limitation of static analysis. While other static techniques such as program slicing may provide additional insights, we consider dynamic analysis as the only reliable way to cope with dynamic code loading and other types of packing. On the other hand, it is infeasible to analyze more than half a million of APKs with dynamic analysis only. Hence, we support our proposed approach as providing an effective balance between effectiveness, precision, and analysis time.

The results reported in this paper can be affected by possible biases that can be present in the data we analyzed. In particular, we did not have control over the contents of the Androzoo dataset. According to the indications provided by the Androzoo authors [1], we can safely rule out the presence of possible duplicates for applications coming from the same sources (e.g., the same stores). We point out that the risk of finding duplicates across stores is significantly lower for malicious applications than benign ones. Nevertheless, even if such duplicates were found, their number should not influence a large-scale analysis.

9 Related Work

Most of the research on cryptographic API in Android is mainly focused on benign applications where the ultimate goal is to mitigate its misuse. Several steps are needed to achieve this, and the respective works usually treat one or two steps at a time. We can summarize these steps as follows: *(i)* Inferring the rules of cryptographic API misuse; *(ii)* Evaluation of cryptographic API misuse; *(ii)* Attribution of cryptographic API misuse; *(iv)* Automatic cryptographic API repairs. The following paragraphs discuss the related research for all these steps mentioned above.

Inferring Rules of Cryptographic API Misuse. In the area of inferring the rules of cryptographic API misuse, the goal is to create a list of specifications for developers and researchers that imply the insecure use of cryptography. Such rules can be crafted manually as done in [8,11,39]. However, this approach does not scale well, leading to the works [13,33] that attempt to infer these rules from git commits, conjecturing that newly introduced commits typically eliminate security vulnerabilities from the code. Surprisingly, Paletov et al. [33] reported success with this approach, whereas chronologically later work [13] commends against the initial assumption.

Evaluation of Cryptographic API Misuse. After having a set of rules that suggest security violations at hand, it is vital to explore these violations in the Android applications market. While more powerful dynamic analysis is employed in [8,39] to show that more than half of the examined applications violate the static set of rules, the application dataset is relatively small (size < 100). On the contrary, the static analysis approach used by Egele et al. in [11] allowed examining a large dataset of 145 thousand benign applications to reveal that 10.4% of them uses some form of cryptography. 88% of such applications were found to violate some rules of secure cryptography usage. These results were confirmed by a later study [31] that gathered a new dataset of 109 thousand APKs that contain at least one cryptographic API call and showed the analogical proportion of insecure applications. Static rules were substituted by a more sophisticated definition language in [19] where 10 000 Android applications were analyzed and misuses detected in over 95% of cases.

Some of the solutions above are impractical to run against large projects due to many false positives. This is treated by `CryptoGuard` [36] that prunes the alerts to achieve 98% precision and is successfully run against real-world projects. As of early 2022, an open-source project named `CRYLOGGER` [34] can well complement `CryptoGuard`, as it is based on dynamic analysis and was tested on a sufficiently large dataset (approx. 1800 applications). In 2021, the first systematic evaluation study [2] was published that allows measuring the quality of such detectors and reveals many flaws in their design or implementation.

Concentrating on the TLS protocol, this work from 2012 [12] analyzed 13 thousand Android applications to reveal inadequate TLS usage in 8% of cases. The authors also managed to launch 41 MiTM attacks against selected applications. Iterating on this effort, another paper [32] studied Network Security Configuration files[10] in Android. The authors revealed that 88% of applications employing custom settings downgrade the security compared to the default con-

[10] developer.android.com/training/articles/security-config.

figuration. Also, the authors penetrated Google Play safeguards that are supposed to protect from publishing applications vulnerable to MiTM.

Attribution of Cryptographic API Misuse. Reliable third-party package detection is central for attribution of misuse. This problem has been addressed, e.g., in [4,24,42] where matching algorithms were proposed to reliably detect third-party libraries. As already discussed, a systematic review [44] then compared these detectors from various perspectives confirming that `LibRadar` is superior to others when used for large-scale analysis due to result quality comparable with the most precise tools, yet running much faster.

Automatic Cryptographic API Repairs. More distant to our research are papers that concentrated on automatic cryptographic API misuse repairs. From this area of research, we refer the reader to [23,45].

Study of Cryptography in Android Malware. We point out that all the aforementioned research results on the Android platform did not focus on the usage of cryptographic API in malicious applications or in its comparison to the benign landscape. The work presented in this paper aims to fill this knowledge gap.

10 Conclusions and Future Work

The main motivation behind this research work is the qualitative observation of the increased use of cryptographic APIs in Android malware. Cryptography is used in various malware modules such as external communication, file encryption, etc. Moreover, cryptography is also employed to obfuscate the malware content and behavior.

We thus performed a quantitative evaluation based on collecting a large number of malware samples covering the past decade. We designed a system based on the static analysis of Android applications to assess the use of cryptographic APIs and computing the related statistical measures. The results of this first phase provided a clear picture of the evolution in the use of cryptographic APIs in Android malware and the difference between goodware and malware in the use of cryptographic APIs.

To get more quantitative information, we trained machine learning classifiers to discriminate between goodware and malware according to the statistical measures on cryptographic APIs computed in the first phase. Thus, we could assess the extent to which features related to the use of cryptographic APIs contribute to the discrimination between goodware and malware. Then, we also ranked the features according to the *explanation* of their influence in the final decision of the classifier.

The result of this analysis is twofold: on the one hand, the developed tool allows a deeper understanding of the internals of a malware sample. On the other hand, we showed that the highest-ranked features could be used to improve the classification performance of malware detectors. This is a clear advance with respect to the state of the art, as cryptographic features until now have been neglected in the design of Android malware detectors.

Reported results have been obtained through the analysis of 603 937 applications and the extraction of over 1 million call sites. The most prominent facts can be summarised as follows:

1. *Use of weak hash functions.* Most malicious applications featuring cryptographic routines resorted to weak MD5 hash functions.
2. *Late transition from DES to AES.* In the symmetric cipher category, malware authors switched from weak DES to modern AES only in 2015, while AES was the most popular cipher in benign samples already in 2012.
3. *Very limited use of third-party cryptographic libraries.* Android application authors favor using system-based libraries to deliver cryptographic functionality.
4. *Contrast between malicious and benign usage of cryptography.* Our study shows that cryptographic API is generally more frequent in malware than in benign samples (in relative measures).

The results in this paper open the door to several follow-up research projects. On the one hand, malware samples could be clustered into families according to their usage of cryptography. On the other hand, it would also be of interest to understand for which *main purpose* specific crypto-routines have been included, to better understand and profile the characteristics of malware authors.

Finally, as the results of this work are entirely based on static analysis, it could be complemented by dynamic analysis to check if our findings also hold for packed and obfuscated applications.

Acknowledgements.. Davide Maiorca was supported by the project PON AIM Research and Innovation 2014–2020 - Attraction and International Mobility, funded by the Italian Ministry of Education, University and Research; and by the European cybersecurity pilot CyberSec4Europe. Giorgio Giacinto was supported by Fondazione di Sardegna under the project "TrustML: Towards Machine Learning that Humans Can Trust", CUP: F73C22001320007. Vashek Matyas was supported by Czech Science Foundation project GA20-03426S. Adam Janovsky was supported by Invasys company. We are grateful to Jonas Konecny who ran the initial machine-learning experiments. We also thank Avast for providing the dynamic-analysis tool apklab.io.

A Detailed Comparison of Symmetric Ciphers Between Androzoo-M12 and CryptoLint-B12

Table 6 displays an in-depth comparison between symmetric encryption schemes in the datasets CryptoLint-B12 and Androzoo-M12. It should be stressed that even though the absolute number of call sites in CryptoLint-B12 is higher (15 598) than in Androzoo-M12 (9729), this comparison is severely skewed by the overall distribution characteristics of CryptoLint-B12 vs. Androzoo-M12. In other words, it takes 145 thousand of benign applications (where only each fifth

Table 6. Comparison of distribution of symmetric encryption schemes in malicious vs. benign applications (Androzoo-M12 and CryptoLint-B12). The frequency of malicious encryption schemes was normalized to fit the size of the benign dataset. In the benign set, only the schemes with frequency > 100 were taken. There is no prevalent malicious scheme (freq. > 100) that would not appear in the benign dataset. The default schemes marked with * symbol fall back into the ECB mode with PKCS7 padding.

Symmetric encryption scheme	Androzoo-M12	CryptoLint-B12
DES*	6356	741
DES/CBC/PKCS5Padding	1203	205
AES*	924	4803
AES/CBC/PKCS5Padding	786	5878
DESede/ECB/PKCS5Padding	231	473
AES/ECB/PKCS5Padding	122	443
DESede*	107	501
DES/ECB/PKCS5Padding	93	221
DES/ECB/NoPadding	68	1151
AES/CBC/NoPadding	43	468
AES/ECB/NoPadding	41	220
AES/CBC/PKCS7Padding	37	235
AES/CFB8/NoPadding	24	104
AES/ECB/PKCS7Padding	1	155
Sum AES where freq. > 100	1832	12306
Sum DES where freq. > 100	7559	2318
Sum DESede where freq. > 100	338	974
Sum where freq. > 100	9729	15598

call originates from user-defined codebase) to get 15 thousand calls, whereas 34 thousand of malicious applications would provide a similar number of symmetric encryption API call sites.

References

1. Allix, K., Bissyandé, T.F., Klein, J., Le Traon, Y.: AndroZoo: collecting millions of Android apps for the research community. In: Proceedings of MSR '16, pp. 468–471. ACM (2016)
2. Ami, A.S., Cooper, N., Kafle, K., Moran, K., Poshyvanyk, D., Nadkarni, A.: Why Crypto-detectors Fail: A Systematic Evaluation of Cryptographic Misuse Detection Techniques. arXiv:2107.07065 [cs], August 2021
3. Anthony, D., Geoffroy, G.: Androguard (2012). https://github.com/androguard/androguard. Accessed 4 Aug 2019
4. Backes, M., Bugiel, S., Derr, E.: Reliable third-party library detection in android and its security applications. In: Proceedings of CCS '16, pp. 356–367. ACM (2016)

5. Bauer, V.: Android Arsenal (2014). https://android-arsenal.com, 5 June 2020
6. Biham, E., Shamir, A.: Differential cryptanalysis of DES-like cryptosystems. J. Cryptol. **4**(1), 3–72 (1991)
7. BusinessOfApps: Android statistics (2022). http://businessofapps.com/data/android-statistics
8. Chatzikonstantinou, A., Ntantogian, C., Karopoulos, G., Xenakis, C.: Evaluation of Cryptography Usage in Android Applications. In: Proceedings of EAI BCT '16, pp. 83–90. ACM (2016)
9. Chen, S., Xue, M., Tang, Z., Xu, L., Zhu, H.: Stormdroid: a streaminglized machine learning-based system for detecting android malware. In: Proceedings of the 11th ACM on Asia Conference on Computer and Communications Security, ASIA CCS 2016, pp. 377–388. ACM, New York (2016)
10. Daniel, A., Michael, S., Malte, H., Hugo, G., Rieck, K.: Drebin: efficient and explainable detection of android malware in your pocket. In: Proceedings 2014 Network and Distributed System Security Symposium, pp. 23–26. The Internet Society, San Diego (2014)
11. Egele, M., Brumley, D., Fratantonio, Y., Kruegel, C.: An empirical study of cryptographic misuse in android applications. In: Proceedings of CCS'13, pp. 73–84. ACM (2013)
12. Fahl, S., Harbach, M., Muders, T., Smith, M., Baumgärtner, L., Freisleben, B.: Why eve and mallory love android: An analysis of android SSL (in)security. In: Proceedings of CCS '12, pp. 50–61. ACM (2012)
13. Gao, J., Kong, P., Li, L., Bissyande, T.F., Klein, J.: Negative results on mining crypto-API usage rules in android apps. In: Proceedings of MSR '19, pp. 388–398. IEEE (2019)
14. Google: Android Cryptography API Guide (2020). https://developer.android.com/guide/topics/security/cryptography. Accessed 4 Mar 2020
15. Google, i.: Conscrypt - a java security provider (2013). https://github.com/google/conscrypt. Accessed 5 June 2020
16. Hoffmann, J., Rytilahti, T., Maiorca, D., Winandy, M., Giacinto, G., Holz, T.: Evaluating analysis tools for android apps: status quo and robustness against obfuscation. In: Proceedings of the Sixth ACM Conference on Data and Application Security and Privacy, pp. 139–141. Association for Computing Machinery, New York (2016)
17. Isode Limited, OpenLDAP Foundation: RFC 4422 - simple authentication and security layer (sasl) (2006). http://tools.ietf.org/html/rfc4422, March 2, 2022
18. Janovsky., A., Maiorca., D., Macko., D., Matyas., V., Giacinto., G.: A longitudinal study of cryptographic api: a decade of android malware. In: Proceedings of the 19th International Conference on Security and Cryptography - SECRYPT, pp. 121–133. INSTICC, SciTePress (2022). https://doi.org/10.5220/0011265300003283
19. Krüger, S., Späth, J., Ali, K., Bodden, E., Mezini, M.: CrySL: An Extensible Approach to Validating the Correct Usage of Cryptographic APIs. In: Proceedings of ECOOP 2018, pp. 10:1–10:27. LIPIcs, vol. 109, LZI (2018)
20. Kursa, M.B., Rudnicki, W.R., et al.: Feature selection with the boruta package. J. Stat. Softw. **36**(11), 1–13 (2010)
21. Legion of the Bouncy Castle Inc.: The Legion of the Bouncy Castle (2020). https://www.bouncycastle.org/java.html. Accessed 6 Apr 2020
22. Lundberg, S.M., Lee, S.I.: A unified approach to interpreting model predictions. In: Proceedings of NIPS 2017, pp. 4765–4774. Curran Associates, Inc. (2017). http://papers.nips.cc/paper/7062-a-unified-approach-to-interpreting-model-predictions.pdf

23. Ma, S., Lo, D., Li, T., Deng, R.H.: CDRep: automatic repair of cryptographic misuses in android applications. In: Proceedings of ASIACCS 2016, pp. 711–722. ACM, Xi'an, China (2016)
24. Ma, Z., Wang, H., Guo, Y., Chen, X.: LibRadar: fast and accurate detection of third-party libraries in Android apps. In: Proceedings of ICSE 2016, pp. 653–656. ACM, Austin, Texas (2016)
25. Maiorca, D., Ariu, D., Corona, I., Aresu, M., Giacinto, G.: Stealth attacks: an extended insight into the obfuscation effects on android malware. Comput. Secur. **51**(C), 16–31 (2015)
26. Maiorca, D., Mercaldo, F., Giacinto, G., Visaggio, C.A., Martinelli, F.: R-PackDroid: API package-based characterization and detection of mobile ransomware. In: Proceedings of SAC 2017, pp. 1718–1723. ACM (2017)
27. McAfee Labs: McAfee labs threats report, august 2019 (2019). http://mcafee.com/enterprise/en-us/threat-center/mcafee-labs/reports.html. 7 March 2022
28. Melis, M., Maiorca, D., Biggio, B., Giacinto, G., Roli, F.: Explaining black-box android malware detection. In: 26th European Signal Processing Conference. EUSIPCO 2018, pp. 524–528. IEEE, Rome, Italy (2018)
29. Melis, M., Scalas, M., Demontis, A., Maiorca, D., Biggio, B., Giacinto, G., Roli, F.: Do gradient-based explanations tell anything about adversarial robustness to android malware? Int. J. Mach. Learn. Cybern. **13**(1), 217–232 (2022). https://doi.org/10.1007/s13042-021-01393-7
30. Menezes, A.J., Katz, J., Van Oorschot, P.C., Vanstone, S.A.: Handbook of Applied cryptography. CRC Press (1996)
31. Muslukhov, I., Boshmaf, Y., Beznosov, K.: Source attribution of cryptographic API misuse in android applications. In: Proceedings of ASIACCS 2018, pp. 133–146. ACM (2018)
32. Oltrogge, M., Huaman, N., Amft, S., Acar, Y., Backes, M., Fahl, S.: Why eve and mallory still love android: Revisiting TLS (In)Security in android applications. In: Proceedings of USENIX '21, pp. 4347–4364. USENIX (2021)
33. Paletov, R., Tsankov, P., Raychev, V., Vechev, M.: Inferring crypto API rules from code changes. In: Proceedings of PLDI 2018, pp. 450–464. ACM (2018)
34. Piccolboni, L., Guglielmo, G.D., Carloni, L.P., Sethumadhavan, S.: CRYLOGGER: detecting crypto misuses dynamically. In: Proceedings of IEEE SP 2021, pp. 1972–1989. IEEE (2021)
35. Platform, J.: Java Cryptography Architecture (JCA) Reference Guide (2017). https://docs.oracle.com/javase/7/docs/technotes/guides/security/crypto/CryptoSpec.html. Accessed 4 Mar 2020
36. Rahaman, S., et al.: CryptoGuard: high precision detection of cryptographic vulnerabilities in massive-sized java projects. In: Proceedings of CCS 2019, pp. 2455–2472. ACM (2019)
37. Salem, A.: Towards accurate labeling of Android apps for reliable malware detection. arXiv preprint arXiv:2007.00464 (2020)
38. Shapley, L.: A value for n-person games. contributions to the theory of games. Annals of mathematics studies (2) (1953)
39. Shuai, S., Guowei, D., Tao, G., Tianchang, Y., Chenjie, S.: Modelling analysis and auto-detection of cryptographic misuse in android applications. In: Proceedings of DASC 2014, pp. 75–80. IEEE (2014)
40. skylot: Jadx decompiler (2020). https://github.com/skylot/jadx, 15 December 2019

41. Stevens, M., Bursztein, E., Karpman, P., Albertini, A., Markov, Y.: The first collision for full SHA-1. In: Katz, J., Shacham, H. (eds.) CRYPTO 2017. LNCS, vol. 10401, pp. 570–596. Springer, Cham (2017). https://doi.org/10.1007/978-3-319-63688-7_19
42. Wang, H., Guo, Y., Ma, Z., Chen, X.: WuKong: a scalable and accurate two-phase approach to Android app clone detection. In: Proceedings of ISSTA 2015, pp. 71–82. ACM (2015)
43. Wang, X., Yu, H.: How to Break MD5 and other hash functions. In: Cramer, R. (ed.) EUROCRYPT 2005. LNCS, vol. 3494, pp. 19–35. Springer, Heidelberg (2005). https://doi.org/10.1007/11426639_2
44. Zhan, X., et al.: Automated third-party library detection for Android applications: are we there yet? In: Proceedings of ASE 2020, pp. 919–930. ACM, December 2020
45. Zhang, X., Zhang, Y., Li, J., Hu, Y., Li, H., Gu, D.: Embroidery: patching vulnerable binary code of fragmentized android devices. In: Proceedings of ICSME 2017, pp. 47–57. IEEE (2017)

Towards a Realistic Decentralized Naive Bayes with Differential Privacy

Lodovico Giaretta[1], Thomas Marchioro[2(✉)], Evangelos Markatos[2], and Sarunas Girdzijauskas[1]

[1] KTH Royal Institute of Technology, Isafjordsgatan 22, 16440 Kista, Sweden
{lodovico,sarunasg}@kth.se

[2] Foundation for Research and Technology Hellas, Nikolaou Plastira 100, 70013 Heraklion, Greece
{marchiorot,markatos}@ics.forth.gr

Abstract. This is an extended version of our work in [16]. In this paper, we introduce two novel algorithms to collaboratively train Naive Bayes models across multiple private data sources: Federated Naive Bayes and Gossip Naive Bayes. Instead of directly providing access to their data, the data owners compute local updates that are then aggregated to build a global model. In order to also prevent indirect privacy leaks from the updates or from the final model, our algorithms protect the exchanged information with differential privacy. We experimentally evaluate our proposed approaches, examining different scenarios and focusing on potential real-world issues, such as different data owner offering different amounts of data or requesting different levels of privacy. Our results show that both Federated and Gossip Naive Bayes achieve similar accuracy to a "vanilla" Naive Bayes while maintaining reasonable privacy guarantees, while being extremely robust to heterogeneous data owners.

Keywords: Federated learning · Gossip learning · Differential privacy · Naive Bayes

1 Introduction

Machine learning has reached unprecedented popularity in recent years, its successes enabling previously unthinkable digital services. However, training

---

This project has received funding from the European Union's Horizon 2020 research and innovation programme under the Marie Skłodowska-Curie grant agreement No 813162: RAIS - Real-time Analytics for the Internet of Sports. The content of this paper reflects the views only of their author(s). The European Commission/Research Executive Agency are not responsible for any use that may be made of the information it contains.

M. Van Sinderen et al. (Eds.): ICSBT/SECRYPT 2022, CCIS 1849, pp. 98–121, 2023.
https://doi.org/10.1007/978-3-031-45137-9_5

machine learning models typically requires the collection, storage and processing of large amounts of personal and potentially sensitive data, causing privacy and scalability issues.

Thence, a variety of approaches have been developed to train machine learning models on decentralized, private data. Among these, the most popular is federated learning [17], which allows multiple data owners to cooperatively train a model without having to transfer or disclose their data. The training procedure under federated learning requires the data owners to iteratively compute local model updates and share them with a central aggregator. The aggregator, in turn, combines such updates to produce a global model, containing information from all data sources.

One limitation of federated learning is its requirement for a central, trusted entity to perform the aggregation step. Different approaches have been proposed to overcome this issue, the most notable being gossip learning [19], which instead employs peer-to-peer communication protocols to perform the aggregation.

However, federated and gossip learning alone cannot shield from all possible privacy leaks [21,27]. Thus, they are often combined with differential privacy [7,11,24], a family of techniques to inject properly calibrated noise into the outputs shared by the data owners. When properly implemented, differential privacy provides strong mathematical guarantees that no private information can be inferred from the values that are shared.

While substantial efforts have been devolved to study differentially-private federated learning on deep models, in [16] we argued that, in many practical applications, simpler yet robust models like Naive Bayes classifiers are preferable. Therefore, we proceeded to provide the first (to our knowledge) implementation and evaluation of Federated Naive Bayes with differential privacy, showing that in most cases it can achieve nearly the same performance as a traditional, non-data-private counterpart.

In this extended version of [16], we provide additional algorithms and experimental results, with the focus on enabling certain realistic scenarios that were not discussed in the original work.

First, we experimentally evaluate cases where different data owners own substantially different amounts of data points or require different degrees of privacy. We provide insights into how these metrics affect the amount of noise injected by the data owners, and we show that Federated Naive Bayes is extremely robust to variable size of the data partitions and privacy budget distribution.

Additionally, we propose and evaluate Gossip Naive Bayes, a counterpart to Federated Naive Bayes that uses iterative gossip-based communications, replacing the central aggregator of the latter. Our results show that Gossip Naive Bayes converges to the same accuracy as Federated Naive Bayes in just a few iterations of the protocol, providing a high degree of scalability and privacy in fully-decentralized scenarios.

2 Background, Notation, and Terminology

2.1 Naive Bayes

Naive Bayes is well established as a simple-yet-effective machine learning algorithm for classification. Naive Bayes classifies data points according to bayesian inference, following the maximum a posteriori probability (MAP) criterion (Table 1):

$$\begin{aligned}\hat{y}(x) &= \arg\max_{y\in\mathcal{Y}} \Pr[\mathbf{y} = y|\mathbf{x} = x] \\ &= \arg\max_{y\in\mathcal{Y}} \Pr[\mathbf{y} = y] \Pr[\mathbf{x} = x|\mathbf{y} = y].\end{aligned} \quad (1)$$

Table 1. Notation used in the paper.

Symbol	Description
$\mathbf{x}$	Random variable
x	Observation of $\mathbf{x}$
$x^{(i)}$	Samples owned by i-th node
x_j	j-th sample
x_ϕ	Feature ϕ of x
$y^{(i)}$	Labels owned by i-th node
n_y	Count of data points in class y
$m_{x_\phi y}$	Count of data points with categorical feature ϕ equal to x_ϕ
$\mu_{\phi y}$	Average of numerical feature ϕ for class y
$\mu_{\phi y}$	Standard deviation of numerical feature ϕ for class y
$\mathcal{X}$	Set of possible values of x
$\mathcal{F}$	Set of features
$\mathcal{F}_{\text{cat}}$	Set of categorical features
$\mathcal{F}_{\text{num}}$	Set of numerical features
N_{nodes}	Number of nodes
$N^{(i)}_{\text{samples}}$	Number of data points owned by the i-th node

An underlying assumption of this algorithm is that the features $\mathbf{x}_1, \ldots, \mathbf{x}_\Phi$ are independent when conditioned with respect to the class variable Y. The MAP criterion under such assumption becomes:

$$\hat{y}(x) = \arg\max_{y\in\mathcal{Y}} \Pr[\mathbf{y} = y] \prod_{\phi\in\mathcal{F}} \Pr[\mathbf{x}_\phi = x_\phi|\mathbf{y} = y]. \quad (2)$$

Equation 2 is the criterion adopted by Naive Bayes to predict the most likely class $\hat{y} \in \mathcal{Y}$ to which a sample $x \in \mathcal{X}$ belongs. However, the a priori probability distribution of the classes $\Pr[\mathbf{y} = y]$ and the conditional likelihood of each feature $\Pr[\mathbf{x}_\phi = x_\phi | \mathbf{y} = y]$ are unknown. "Training" a Naive Bayes classifier consists of estimating such probabilities from the training dataset $\mathcal{D}_{\text{train}}$, which is a collection of example/class pairs $(x_j, y_j) \in \mathcal{X} \times \mathcal{Y}$. The prior probabilities of the classes are estimated as the normalized frequency for each class, i.e.,

$$p_y = \frac{n_y}{\sum_{y' \in \mathcal{Y}} n_{y'}}, \text{ with } n_y = \sum_{j=1}^{|\mathcal{D}_{\text{train}}|} \chi\{y_j = y\}, \tag{3}$$

where χ denotes the indicator function. Simply put, n_y is the number of training examples that belong to class y. The way conditional likelihoods are estimated depends on the nature of the features.

- **Categorical Features:** For categorical features, the most common approach is again to compute the normalized frequency, this time normalized with respect to the categories:

$$p_{x_\phi | y} = \frac{m_{x_\phi y}}{\sum_{x'_\phi \in \mathcal{X}_\phi} m_{x'_\phi y}}, \text{ with } m_{x_\phi y} = \sum_{j=1}^{|\mathcal{D}_{\text{train}}|} \chi\{x_{j\phi} = x_\phi \wedge y_j = y\}. \tag{4}$$

- **Numerical Features:** For numerical features, the conditional likelihood $\Pr[\mathbf{x}_\phi = x_\phi | \mathbf{y} = y]$ is proportional to a probability density function (PDF) $\rho_{\mathbf{x}_\phi | \mathbf{y}}$ in Eq. 2. A PDF cannot be estimated by counting occurrences, since the number of possible values is infinite. Instead, the most common approach is to assume that the underlying PDF follows a certain parametric distribution. The usual choice is a normal distribution, in which case the algorithm takes the name of *Gaussian Naive Bayes.* A normal distribution is characterized by its mean $\mu_{\phi y}$ and variance $\sigma^2_{\phi y}$, which are estimated as follows:

$$\mu_{\phi y} = \frac{1}{n_y} \sum_{j: y_j = y} x_{j\phi}, \; \sigma^2_{\phi y} = \frac{1}{n_y - 1} \sum_{j: y_j = y} (x_{j\phi} - \mu_{\phi y})^2 . \tag{5}$$

The estimate of the probability density for x_ϕ, conditioned w.r.t. class y, is computed as

$$\rho_{\mathbf{x}_\phi | \mathbf{y}}(x_\phi | y) = \frac{1}{\sqrt{2\pi\sigma^2_{\phi y}}} \exp\left(-\frac{(x_\phi - \mu_{\phi y})^2}{2\sigma^2_{\phi y}} \right). \tag{6}$$

Practical Computation and Numerical Stability. Computing the posterior probabilities according to Eq. 2 is problematic in terms of numerical stability, as the products tends to quickly vanish for a large number of features. For this reason, we calculate the posterior log-probabilities, which preserve the arg max value. Log-probabilities allow to rewrite products as sums:

$$\hat{y}(x) = \arg\max_{y \in \mathcal{Y}} \log \left(p_y \prod_{\phi \in \mathcal{F}} p_{x_\phi | y} \right) \tag{7}$$

$$= \arg\max_{y \in \mathcal{Y}} \log p_y + \sum_{\phi \in \mathcal{F}} \log p_{x_\phi | y} \tag{8}$$

The prior log-probabilities can be simplified as

$$\log p_y = \log \left(\frac{n_y}{\sum_{y' \in \mathcal{Y}} n_{y'}} \right) = \log n_y - \log \left(\sum_{y' \in \mathcal{Y}} n_{y'} \right). \tag{9}$$

The normalization term $\log \left(\sum_{y' \in \mathcal{Y}} n_{y'} \right)$ in Eq. 9 is common to all the classes, and can thus be neglected. Likewise, for categorical features, the conditional log-likelihoods become

$$\log p_{x_\phi | y} = \log \left(\frac{m_{x_\phi y}}{\sum_{x'_\phi \in \mathcal{X}_\phi} m_{x'_\phi y}} \right) = \log m_{x_\phi y} - \log n_y. \tag{10}$$

For numerical features, the conditional log-likelihoods are proportional to

$$\log p_{x_\phi | y} \propto -\log \sigma_{\phi y} - \frac{(x_\phi - \mu_{\phi y})^2}{2\sigma_{\phi y}^2}. \tag{11}$$

The normalization terms can be neglected when computing the arg max, since they are common to all classes.

Algorithm 1. Naive Bayes prediction.

Require: Sample x', prior counts n, conditional counts m, means μ and standard deviations σ
  for all classes $y = 1, \ldots, |\mathcal{Y}|$ **do**
    $\text{score}_y(x') \leftarrow \log(n_y)$ ▷ Initialize the scores with the log of the prior counts
    for all categorical features $\phi \in \mathcal{F}_{\text{cat}}$ **do**
      $\text{score}_y(x') \leftarrow \text{score}_y(x') + \log(m_{x'_\phi y})$
    end for
    for all numerical features $\phi \in \mathcal{F}_{\text{num}}$ **do**
      $\text{score}_y(x') \leftarrow \text{score}_y(x') - \log(\sigma_{\phi y}) + \dfrac{(x'_\phi - \mu_{\phi y})^2}{2\sigma_{\phi y}^2}$
    end for
  end for
  $\bar{y}' \leftarrow \text{ArgMax}_y \text{score}(x')$
  return predicted class $\bar{y}'$

2.2 Differential Privacy

Introduced by Dwork et al. [6], differential privacy is an umbrella term covering different techniques to protect the output of an aggregation algorithm (henceforth, aggregated query) against membership inference. Differentially private mechanisms perturb the aggregated queries with noise, in a way that makes it hard to deduce whether a certain data point was included in the aggregation. The level of protection provided by differential privacy is determined by a parameter ε, called *privacy budget*. A lower privacy budget implies a higher level of privacy, but also requires a higher amount of noise. Formally, a randomized query $\tilde{\mathbf{q}}$ satisfies ε-differential privacy if for all adjacent[1] datasets $\mathcal{D}, \mathcal{D}'$, it holds

$$\Pr[\tilde{\mathbf{q}}(\mathcal{D}) \in \mathcal{O}] \leq \varepsilon \Pr[\tilde{\mathbf{q}}(\mathcal{D}') \in \mathcal{O}], \; \forall \mathcal{O} \subseteq \mathcal{Q}. \tag{12}$$

Equation 12 means that the probability for the query output falling in any subset $\mathcal{O}$ of the output space $\mathcal{Q}$ should not change "too much" if one data point is replaced.

Laplace Mechanism. In our algorithm, we use the Laplace mechanism to enforce differential privacy on aggregated queries. This mechanism perturbs the query with additive noise that follows a Laplace distribution:

$$L_{\varepsilon}(q(\mathcal{D})) = q(\mathcal{D}) + \Xi, \; \Xi \sim \text{Lap}\left(0, \frac{\Delta_q}{\varepsilon}\right). \tag{13}$$

As apparent from Eq. 13, the scale of the noise is proportional to Δ_r and inversely proportional to the privacy budget ε. The value Δ_q is called *sensitivity* of the query, and can be defined in two ways:

- global sensitivity: $\Delta_q = \max_{\mathcal{D},\mathcal{D}'} |q(\mathcal{D}) - q(\mathcal{D}')|$;
- local sensitivity: $\Delta_q(\mathcal{D}) = \max_{\mathcal{D}':\mathcal{D}'=\mathcal{D}\setminus\{x_j\},x_j\in\mathcal{D}} |q(\mathcal{D}) - q(\mathcal{D}')|$.

Both notions of sensitivity guarantee that differential privacy is satisfied. However, when local sensitivity is used, the level of noise to be applied depends on the dataset $\mathcal{D}$. With global sensitivity, the noise is determined just by the query and the privacy budget.

Within the scope of our work, the Laplace mechanism is applied to two queries: SUM queries, and COUNT queries. A COUNT query simply counts how many elements satisfy a certain condition. When replacing an element in the dataset, the count can change by at most 1, meaning that the global sensitivity is $\Delta_q = 1$ for COUNT queries. SUM queries, instead, require to add all elements satisfying the condition. Unless the values are in a limited range, the maximum change in a SUM query cannot be determined in advance. Therefore, this must be estimated as a local sensitivity.

[1] Two datasets are adjacent if they differ by exactly one data point.

Properties. In the design of Federated and Gossip Naive Bayes, we make use of two well-known properties of differential privacy:

- *Sequential Composition:* If ℓ independent random queries $\tilde{\mathbf{q}}_1(\mathcal{D}), \ldots, \tilde{\mathbf{q}}_\ell(\mathcal{D})$ are computed on the same data $\mathcal{D}$ under $\frac{\varepsilon}{\ell}$-differential privacy, then any function of them $g(\tilde{\mathbf{q}}_1(\mathcal{D}), \ldots, \tilde{\mathbf{q}}_\ell(\mathcal{D}))$ satisfies ε-differential privacy.
- *Parallel Composition:* If ℓ independent random queries $\tilde{\mathbf{q}}_1(\mathcal{D}^{(1)}), \ldots, \tilde{\mathbf{q}}_\ell(\mathcal{D}^{(\ell)})$ are computed on disjoint subsets of $\mathcal{D}$ under ε-differential privacy, then any function of them $g(\tilde{\mathbf{q}}_1(\mathcal{D}^{(1)}), \ldots, \tilde{\mathbf{q}}_\ell(\mathcal{D}^{(\ell)}))$ satisfies ε-differential privacy.

2.3 Federated and Gossip Learning

Several techniques have been proposed to perform distributed machine learning on private, horizontally-partitioned data sources. The most common and well-studied approach is federated learning [17]. Being typically deployed with deep learning models, federated learning consists of an iterative approach. In each iteration, the devices holding the private data compute a gradient based on a batch of local data. These local gradients are then sent to a central entity, which aggregates them into a global gradient, modifies the model weights accordingly, and distributes the updated model to all participants for the next iteration.

The need for a central aggregator may limit the scalability of federated learning and introduce robustness and trust issues [1]. Gossip learning [8,19] is a less-studied approach that overcomes these issues through decentralization and gossip communication protocols [13]. Data-owning devices directly share their locally-updated models with each other in a peer-to-peer fashion. More specifically, at regular intervals, each device will produce a new model by merging the two most recent models received from peers and then performing a local training step. This new model is then forwarded to a randomly-chosen peer.

Both federated and gossip learning can collaboratively train a model without explicit data sharing among participants. However, neither of them is designed to prevent implicit data leaks. These may occur during training, through the models or gradients shared in each iteration [27] or afterwards, through the final model produced by the process [21]. Therefore, previous works have integrated differential privacy with federated learning to protect from these leaks. Differential privacy can be applied on each local gradient before sharing [24], to ensure the privacy of individual data points, or within the central aggregator [7], thus hiding the identity of whole data owners participating in the protocol.

Both federated and gossip learning have been studied mostly in the context of deep learning models, where the iterative gradient-based approaches described above are necessary. Naive Bayes classifiers, on the other hand, are built based on simple statistics that can be computed by a single pass over the dataset. Furthermore, the focus of both approaches is typically on *massively-distributed* scenarios, with large number of devices each holding few data points. Fewer works [3,7] have considered situations where a relatively small number of data brokers each contribute many data points from different individuals.

3 Algorithms

In this section, we describe our design for Federated and Gossip Naive Bayes. The setting is similar for both algorithms, and can be summarized as follows. Each data owner (henceforth, node) $i \in \{1, \ldots, N_{\text{nodes}}\}$ has a local dataset $\mathcal{D}^{(i)} = (x^{(i)}, y^{(i)})$ of multiple labeled data points. Nodes are unwilling to share their data in plain text, but are willing to participate in the training process of a Naive Bayes model by sharing the required dataset statistics, as long as the information they disclose does not leak information about individual data points. In other words, the information disclosed by each node should satisfy the following property:

> For all labeled data points $(x_j^{(i)}, y_j^{(i)})$ in a data partition $\mathcal{D}^{(i)}$, it should not be possible to infer whether $(x_j^{(i)}, y_j^{(i)})$ is present in $\mathcal{D}^{(i)}$ from the disclosed information.

This guarantees resilience against membership inference and can be achieved by protecting disclosed information with differential privacy.

In both Federated and Gossip Naive Bayes, the training process starts with all nodes independently computing their differentially-private model statistics, which we refer to as local updates. Then, these updates are aggregated to estimate the complete dataset statistics required to construct a Naive Bayes classifier, as introduced in Sect. 2.1. However, the way this aggregation is performed differs in the two approaches. Federated Naive Bayes relies on a central aggregator, which handles the collection and merging of the updates. In Gossip Naive Bayes, instead, the updates are exchanges between nodes in a peer-to-peer fashion.

3.1 Local Update Computation

The local updates are essentially a collection of aggregated parameters that should allow to compute the final model, protected under differential privacy. More specifically, each update is a noisy version of the tuple ($n^{(i)}$, $m^{(i)}$, $S^{(i)}$, $Q^{(i)}$), where these parameters are defined as follows (Fig. 1):

- $n^{(i)}$ is a vector of prior counts $n_y^{(i)}$ for each class $y = 1, \ldots, |\mathcal{Y}|$, computed according to Eq. 3;
- $m^{(i)}$ contains the counts $m_{x_\phi y}^{(i)}$ of each category x_ϕ for each categorical feature $\phi \in \mathcal{F}_{\text{cat}}$ for each class, computed according to Eq. 4;
- $S^{(i)}$ is a matrix of sums

$$S_{\phi y}^{(i)} = \sum_{j:y_j^{(i)}=y} x_{j\phi}^{(i)} \tag{14}$$

  computed for each numerical feature $\phi \in \mathcal{F}_{\text{num}}$ and for each class y;

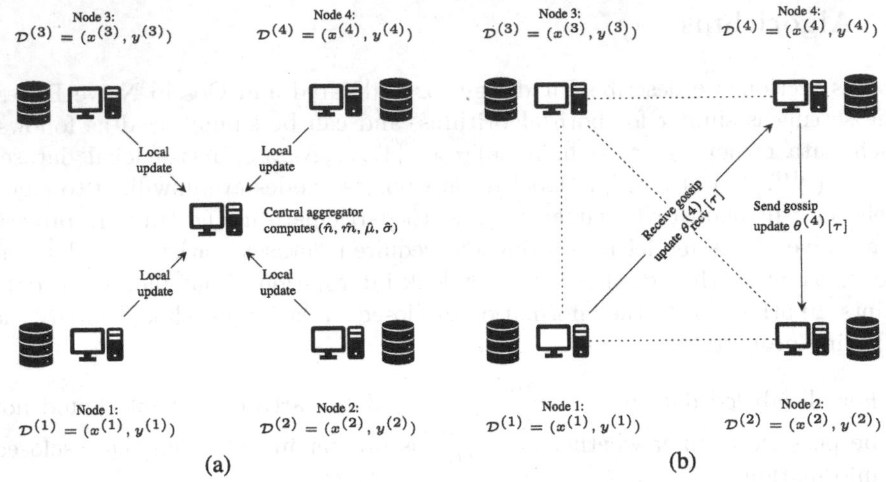

Fig. 1. Settings for Federated Naive Bayes (a) and Gossip Naive Bayes (b).

- $Q^{(i)}$ is a matrix of sums of squares

$$Q^{(i)}_{\phi y} = \sum_{j:y_j^{(i)}=y} \left(x^{(i)}_{j\phi}\right)^2 \tag{15}$$

computed for each numerical feature $\phi \in \mathcal{F}_{\text{num}}$ and for each class y.

All the parameters are perturbed with noise in order to achieve differential privacy. The privacy budget must be distributed equally between the different queries, following the sequential and parallel composition properties of differential privacy (as described in Sect. 2.2). According to parallel composition, the same query executed on different classes counts as a single query from the standpoint of privacy budget distribution. This is due to the fact that such queries are executed on disjoint subsets of the local dataset $\mathcal{D}^{(i)}$. On the other hand, privacy budget must be equally distributed between multiple queries that affect the same class. There is 1 such query to compute $n^{(i)}$, $|\mathcal{F}_{\text{cat}}|$ queries to compute $m^{(i)}$ for all categorical features, and $2|\mathcal{F}_{\text{num}}|$ queries to compute $S^{(i)}$ and $Q^{(i)}$. Hence, each parameter ($n^{(i)}$, $m^{(i)}$, $S^{(i)}$, $Q^{(i)}$) is perturbed with the Laplace mechanism with privacy budget

$$\varepsilon' = \frac{\varepsilon}{1 + |\mathcal{F}_{\text{cat}}| + 2|\mathcal{F}_{\text{num}}|}, \tag{16}$$

yielding ($\tilde{n}^{(i)}$, $\tilde{m}^{(i)}$, $\tilde{S}^{(i)}$, $\tilde{Q}^{(i)}$). The values $\tilde{n}^{(i)}_y$ and $\tilde{m}^{(i)}_{x_\phi y}$ are computed via COUNT queries, thus the sensitivity is $\Delta_q = 1$. The values $S^{(i)}_{\phi y}$ and $Q^{(i)}_{\phi y}$, instead, are computed via SUM queries, meaning that their sensitivity is estimated from the local data, and varies between different features and classes: it is $\Delta_q = \max|x^{(i)}_{j\phi}|$ for $S^{(i)}_{\phi y}$, and $\Delta_q = \max|x^{(i)}_{j\phi}|^2$ for $Q^{(i)}_{\phi y}$. The randomization of each query via the Laplace mechanism is done by sampling independent values from a Laplace distribution with mean 0 and scale Δ_q/ε, and adding such values to each original parameter. The overall procedure is described in Algorithm alg:local.

Algorithm 2. Local update computed by the i-th node.

Require: Local data $\mathcal{D}^{(i)} = (x^{(i)}, y^{(i)})$, privacy budget ε

$\varepsilon' \leftarrow \dfrac{\varepsilon}{1 + |\mathcal{F}_{\text{cat}}| + 2|\mathcal{F}_{\text{num}}|}$ ▷ Allocate the privacy budget among the queries

for all classes $y = 1, \dots, |\mathcal{Y}|$ **do**

  $n_y^{(i)} \leftarrow \text{COUNT}_j(\{j : y_j^{(i)} = y\})$ ▷ Count samples from class y

  for all categorical features $\phi \in \mathcal{F}_{\text{cat}}$ **do**

    for all categories $x_\phi = 1, \dots, |\mathcal{X}_\phi|$ **do**

      $m_{x_\phi y}^{(i)} \leftarrow \text{COUNT}_j(\{j : x_{j\phi}^{(i)} = x_\phi \wedge y_j^{(i)} = y\})$ ▷ Count samples from class y with feature ϕ equal to x_ϕ

      $\xi \leftarrow \text{RANDOMSAMPLE}(\text{Lap}\left(0, \frac{1}{\varepsilon'}\right))$ ▷ Sample Laplace noise

      $\tilde{m}_{x_\phi y}^{(i)} \leftarrow m_{x_\phi y}^{(i)} + \xi$ ▷ Add the noise to the query

    end for

  end for

  for all numerical features $\phi \in \mathcal{F}_{\text{num}}$ **do**

    $S_{\phi y}^{(i)} \leftarrow \text{SUM}_j(\{x_{j\phi}^{(i)} : y_j^{(i)} = y\})$

    $\xi \leftarrow \text{RANDOMSAMPLE}(\text{Lap}\left(0, \frac{\max|x_{j\phi}|}{\varepsilon'}\right))$

    $\tilde{S}_{\phi y}^{(i)} \leftarrow S_{\phi y}^{(i)} + \xi$

    $Q_{\phi y}^{(i)} \leftarrow \text{SUM}_j(\{(x_{j\phi}^{(i)})^2 : y_j^{(i)} = y\})$

    $\xi \leftarrow \text{RANDOMSAMPLE}(\text{Lap}\left(0, \frac{\max(x_{j\phi}^{(i)})^2}{\varepsilon'}\right))$

    $\tilde{Q}_{\phi y}^{(i)} \leftarrow Q_{\phi y}^{(i)} + \xi$

  end for

end for

return $(\tilde{n}^{(i)}, \tilde{m}^{(i)}, \tilde{S}^{(i)}, \tilde{Q}^{(i)})$

3.2 Federated Aggregation

In the case of Federated Naive Bayes, once the local updates ($\tilde{n}^{(i)}$, $\tilde{m}^{(i)}$, $\tilde{S}^{(i)}$, $\tilde{Q}^{(i)}$) are computed by all nodes $i = 1, \dots, N_{\text{nodes}}$, these are collected by the central aggregator and merged into the final model.

A Naive Bayes model requires the overall prior counts n, the category counts m, and the parameters μ and σ to define a normal distribution for numerical features. Prior and category counts are trivially estimated as

$$\hat{n} = \sum_{i=1}^{N_{\text{nodes}}} \tilde{n}^{(i)}, \quad \hat{m} = \sum_{i=1}^{N_{\text{nodes}}} \tilde{m}^{(i)}. \tag{17}$$

Since $\hat{n}$ and $\hat{m}$ are collections of scalars, when we say that we "sum" them we imply that we perform an element-wise sum across the nodes dimension. For instance, this means that the collection $\hat{m}$ contains the counts for all categories of all features for every class, which are obtained by summing those of each node. Regarding the numerical features, the central aggregator first estimates the overall sums and sums of squares:

$$\hat{S} = \sum_{i=1}^{N_{\text{nodes}}} \tilde{S}^{(i)}, \; \hat{Q} = \sum_{i=1}^{N_{\text{nodes}}} \tilde{Q}^{(i)}. \tag{18}$$

These are leveraged to estimate the means and standard deviations of the features. For each feature and class, the mean value of the feature within the class can be estimated simply dividing the sum by the count, using the definition of sample average

$$\hat{\mu}_{\phi y} = \frac{\hat{S}_{\phi y}}{\hat{n}_y}. \tag{19}$$

Typically standard deviation is estimated by computing the root mean square difference between samples $x_{j\phi}$ from class y and $\mu_{\phi y}$, as in Eq. 5. However, this would require an additional exchange with the nodes, as they would need to first receive the aggregated $\hat{\mu}_{\phi y}$ to be able to compute the sum of $(x_{j\phi} - \hat{\mu}_{\phi y})^2$ terms. Instead of doing so, we observe that the variance of a random variable $\mathbf{z}$ can be expressed as the difference between the second moment and the squared mean, i.e. $\text{Var}(\mathbf{z}) = \mathbb{E}[\mathbf{z}^2] - (\mathbb{E}[\mathbf{z}])^2$. The second moment of each feature can be estimated as

$$\hat{\varsigma}_{\phi y} = \frac{\hat{Q}_{\phi y}}{\hat{n}_y}, \tag{20}$$

and thus the variance is approximated as

$$\hat{\sigma}^2_{\phi y} = \hat{\varsigma}_{\phi y} - \hat{\mu}^2_{\phi y} = \frac{\hat{Q}_{\phi y}}{\hat{n}_y} - \hat{\mu}^2_{\phi y}. \tag{21}$$

Indeed, this is not the most accurate approximation, and contrarily to Eq. 5, it can yield negative values. When that happens, we replace negative values with a small positive value, namely 10^{-6}, before taking the square root to obtain the estimated standard deviation. We do the same with prior and categorical counts, as in some instances the noise can turn small positive counts into negative values, especially for categorical ones. The central aggregation is summarized by Algorithm alg:centralaggr.

Online Updates. In many practical cases, the exchanges between different nodes and the central aggregator will happen asynchronously. Furthermore, new nodes may join the collaborative training after the model has already been computed. In such cases, the simplest solution is to keep the collection of submitted updates $(\tilde{n}^{(i)}, \tilde{m}^{(i)}, \tilde{S}^{(i)}, \tilde{Q}^{(i)})$ by each users $i = 1, \ldots, N_{\text{nodes}}$, and just recompute the parameters adding the new updates. However, in the event that the complete collection of updates is not available,

Algorithm 3. Central aggregation.

Require: Collection of local updates $\{(\tilde{n}^{(i)}, \tilde{m}^{(i)}, \tilde{S}^{(i)}, \tilde{Q}^{(i)}), i = 1, \ldots, N_{\text{nodes}}\}$
  $\hat{n} \leftarrow \text{SUM}_i(\{\tilde{n}^{(i)}, i = 1, \ldots, N_{\text{nodes}}\})$
  $\hat{m} \leftarrow \text{SUM}_i(\{\tilde{m}^{(i)}, i = 1, \ldots, N_{\text{nodes}}\})$
  $\hat{S} \leftarrow \text{SUM}_i(\{\tilde{S}^{(i)}, i = 1, \ldots, N_{\text{nodes}}\})$
  $\hat{Q} \leftarrow \text{SUM}_i(\{\tilde{Q}^{(i)}, i = 1, \ldots, N_{\text{nodes}}\})$
  for all classes $y = 1, \ldots, |\mathcal{Y}|$ **do**
    for all numerical features $\phi \in \mathcal{F}_{\text{num}}$ **do**

$$\hat{\mu}_{\phi y} \leftarrow \frac{\hat{S}_{\phi y}}{\hat{n}_y}$$

$$\hat{\sigma}_{\phi y} \leftarrow \sqrt{\frac{\hat{Q}_{\phi y}}{\hat{n}_y} - \hat{\mu}_{\phi y}^2}$$

    end for

  end for
  return $(\hat{n}, \hat{m}, \hat{\mu}, \hat{\sigma})$

it is still possible to update the model with a new update $(\tilde{n}^{(N_{\text{nodes}}+1)}, \tilde{m}^{(N_{\text{nodes}}+1)}, \tilde{S}^{(N_{\text{nodes}}+1)}, \tilde{Q}^{(N_{\text{nodes}}+1)})$. The parameters $\hat{n}$ and $\hat{m}$ can be updated as

$$\hat{n}[\tau+1] = \hat{n}[\tau] + \tilde{n}^{(N_{\text{nodes}}+1)}, \hat{m}[\tau+1] = \hat{m}[\tau] + \tilde{m}^{(N_{\text{nodes}}+1)} \tag{22}$$

where the τ temporal index is simply used to distinguish between the new and old parameters. The new mean values $\hat{\mu}_{\phi y}[\tau+1]$ are a weighted average computed between the old means $\hat{\mu}_{\phi y}[\tau]$ and the received sums $\tilde{S}_{\phi y}^{(N_{\text{nodes}}+1)}$

$$\hat{\mu}_{\phi y}[\tau+1] = \frac{\hat{n}[\tau]}{\hat{n}[\tau+1]}\hat{\mu}_{\phi y}[\tau] + \frac{1}{\hat{n}[\tau+1]}\tilde{S}_{\phi y}^{(N_{\text{nodes}}+1)}. \tag{23}$$

The same holds for the second moments and the newly received sums of squares, for which it holds

$$\hat{\varsigma}_{\phi y}[\tau+1] = \frac{\hat{n}[\tau]}{\hat{n}[\tau+1]}\hat{\varsigma}_{\phi y}[\tau] + \frac{1}{\hat{n}[\tau+1]}\tilde{Q}_{\phi y}^{(N_{\text{nodes}}+1)}. \tag{24}$$

If also the previous value of $\hat{\varsigma}_{\phi y}[\tau]$ was not kept, it can be retrieved from the standard deviation as $\hat{\varsigma}_{\phi y}[\tau] = (\hat{\sigma}_{\phi y}[\tau])^2 + (\hat{\mu}_{\phi y}[\tau])^2$.

3.3 Gossip Naive Bayes

While in Federated Naive Bayes the central aggregator can trivially compute the sum ($\hat{n}$, $\hat{m}$, $\hat{S}$, $\hat{Q}$) of the local updates ($\tilde{n}^{(i)}$, $\tilde{m}^{(i)}$, $\tilde{S}^{(i)}$, $\tilde{Q}^{(i)}$), in Gossip Naive Bayes this is not possible. Instead, each node maintains a local estimates ($\hat{n}^{(i)}[\tau]$, $\hat{m}^{(i)}[\tau]$, $\hat{S}^{(i)}[\tau]$, $\hat{Q}^{(i)}[\tau]$) of the global statistics, which is updated and shared with peers in each iteration τ of the gossiping process.

To do this, each node i keeps track of the last and next-to-last estimates received from other peers, notated as ($\hat{n}_{\text{recv}}^{(i)}[\tau]$, $\hat{m}_{\text{recv}}^{(i)}[\tau]$, $\hat{S}_{\text{recv}}^{(i)}[\tau]$, $\hat{Q}_{\text{recv}}^{(i)}[\tau]$) and

$(\hat{n}^{(i)}_{\text{prev}}[\tau],\ \hat{m}^{(i)}_{\text{prev}}[\tau],\ \hat{S}^{(i)}_{\text{prev}}[\tau],\ \hat{Q}^{(i)}_{\text{prev}}[\tau])$ respectively. At regular intervals, every node performs one gossiping iteration by computing each component $\hat{\theta}^{(i)}[\tau]$ in the local estimate $(\hat{n}^{(i)}[\tau],\ \hat{m}^{(i)}[\tau],\ \hat{S}^{(i)}[\tau],\ \hat{Q}^{(i)}[\tau])$, based on the corresponding local update $\tilde{\theta}^{(i)}$ and the corresponding values in the latest two estimates received from peers, as

$$\hat{\theta}^{(i)}[\tau] = \hat{\theta}^{(i)}_{\text{prev}}[\tau] + \hat{\theta}^{(i)}_{\text{recv}}[\tau] + \tilde{\theta}^{(i)} \tag{25}$$

The node then sends its updated estimate to a randomly-chosen peer in the network.

To gain an intuition of this update rule, it is useful to look at the system not from the perspective of the nodes, but rather of the estimates themselves. These can be seen as acting like random walks over the network of nodes. Disregarding the first right-hand side term, Eq. 25 shows that, at each step of its random walk, the estimate adds to its own values the local updates of the currently-visited node. After T steps, the estimate would have visited each node on average T/N_{nodes} times, and thus with a sufficiently large T its values would converge to the correct $(\hat{n},\ \hat{m},\ \hat{S},\ \hat{Q})$, multiplied by a factor of T/N_{nodes}. This factor would then disappear when using the estimate to build a Naive Bayes classifier as explained in Sect. 2.1.

With such behaviour, $O(N_{\text{nodes}})$ gossiping steps would be necessary to ensure that the latest estimate at each node has converged to the correct values, which would not be scalable. Thus, the first term in Eq. 25 is introduced, which brings the requirement down to $O(\log N_{\text{nodes}})$. Intuitively, it allows each estimate to not only visit the current node and learn about its local update, but also "meet" the estimate that last visited the current node and learn of all the local updates that that estimate had previously witnessed. As that previous estimate will have typically visited the node no more than a few iterations priors, this amounts to an almost doubling of the number of local updates contributing to the estimate.

Algorithm 4. Gossip aggregation at the i-th node.

Require: Local update $(\tilde{n}^{(i)}[\tau],\ \tilde{m}^{(i)}[\tau],\ \tilde{S}^{(i)}[\tau],\ \tilde{Q}^{(i)}[\tau])$, last two estimates received from peers $(t^{(i)}_{\text{recv}}[\tau],\ \hat{n}^{(i)}_{\text{recv}}[\tau],\ \hat{m}^{(i)}_{\text{recv}}[\tau],\ \hat{S}^{(i)}_{\text{recv}}[\tau],\ \hat{Q}^{(i)}_{\text{recv}}[\tau])$ and $(t^{(i)}_{\text{prev}}[\tau],\ \hat{n}^{(i)}_{\text{prev}}[\tau],\ \hat{m}^{(i)}_{\text{prev}}[\tau],\ \hat{S}^{(i)}_{\text{prev}}[\tau],\ \hat{Q}^{(i)}_{\text{prev}}[\tau])$

$t^{(i)}[\tau] \leftarrow t^{(i)}_{\text{recv}}[\tau] + 1$

$t^{(i)}_{\text{tot}}[\tau] \leftarrow t^{(i)}_{\text{prev}}[\tau] + t^{(i)}_{\text{recv}}[\tau] + 1$

$\hat{n}^{(i)}[\tau] \leftarrow \frac{t^{(i)}_{\text{prev}}[\tau]}{t^{(i)}_{\text{tot}}[\tau]}\hat{n}^{(i)}_{\text{prev}}[\tau] + \frac{t^{(i)}_{\text{recv}}[\tau]}{t^{(i)}_{\text{tot}}[\tau]}\hat{n}^{(i)}_{\text{recv}}[\tau] + \frac{1}{t^{(i)}_{\text{tot}}[\tau]}\tilde{n}^{(i)}$

$\hat{m}^{(i)}[\tau] \leftarrow \frac{t^{(i)}_{\text{prev}}[\tau]}{t^{(i)}_{\text{tot}}[\tau]}\hat{m}^{(i)}_{\text{prev}}[\tau] + \frac{t^{(i)}_{\text{recv}}[\tau]}{t^{(i)}_{\text{tot}}[\tau]}\hat{m}^{(i)}_{\text{recv}}[\tau] + \frac{1}{t^{(i)}_{\text{tot}}[\tau]}\tilde{m}^{(i)}$

$\hat{S}^{(i)}[\tau] \leftarrow \frac{t^{(i)}_{\text{prev}}[\tau]}{t^{(i)}_{\text{tot}}[\tau]}\hat{S}^{(i)}_{\text{prev}}[\tau] + \frac{t^{(i)}_{\text{recv}}[\tau]}{t^{(i)}_{\text{tot}}[\tau]}\hat{S}^{(i)}_{\text{recv}}[\tau] + \frac{1}{t^{(i)}_{\text{tot}}[\tau]}\tilde{S}^{(i)}$

$\hat{Q}^{(i)}[\tau] \leftarrow \frac{t^{(i)}_{\text{prev}}[\tau]}{t^{(i)}_{\text{tot}}[\tau]}\hat{Q}^{(i)}_{\text{prev}}[\tau] + \frac{t^{(i)}_{\text{recv}}[\tau]}{t^{(i)}_{\text{tot}}[\tau]}\hat{Q}^{(i)}_{\text{recv}}[\tau] + \frac{1}{t^{(i)}_{\text{tot}}[\tau]}\tilde{Q}^{(i)}$

return new local estimate $(t^{(i)}[\tau],\ \hat{n}^{(i)}[\tau],\ \hat{m}^{(i)}[\tau],\ \hat{S}^{(i)}[\tau],\ \hat{Q}^{(i)}[\tau])$

This fast aggregation of many local updates also brings an issue: the magnitude of the components in the estimate can quickly grow, leading to a loss of floating point precision after just a few gossiping steps. Thus, we includc with each estimate a step counter t, which is increased with every node visited by the estimate, and which is used as a normalization factor to maintain all scalars within a constant range. Thus, Eq. 25 becomes

$$\hat{\theta}^{(i)}[\tau] = \frac{t^{(i)}_{\text{prev}}[\tau]}{t^{(i)}_{\text{tot}}[\tau]}\hat{\theta}^{(i)}_{\text{prev}}[\tau] + \frac{t^{(i)}_{\text{recv}}[\tau]}{t^{(i)}_{\text{tot}}[\tau]}\hat{\theta}^{(i)}_{\text{recv}}[\tau] + \frac{1}{t^{(i)}_{\text{tot}}[\tau]}\tilde{\theta}^{(i)} \tag{26}$$

$$\text{where } t^{(i)}_{\text{tot}}[\tau] = t^{(i)}_{\text{prev}}[\tau] + t^{(i)}_{\text{recv}}[\tau] + 1 \tag{27}$$

Equation 4 shows the pseudocode for this aggregation step, while Algorithm 5 presents a high-level view of the full gossiping protocol performed by each node.

Algorithm 5. Overall gossip protocol at the i-th node.

Require: local dataset $\mathcal{D}^{(i)}$, gossiping delay Δ

$\tilde{\theta}^{(i)} \leftarrow$ ComputeLocalUpdate($\mathcal{D}^{(i)}$) $\triangleright$ $(\tilde{n}^{(i)}, \tilde{m}^{(i)}, \tilde{S}^{(i)}, \tilde{Q}^{(i)})$
$\hat{\theta}_{\text{prev}} \leftarrow 0$ $\triangleright$ $(t^{(i)}_{\text{prev}}[\tau], \hat{n}^{(i)}_{\text{prev}}[\tau], \hat{m}^{(i)}_{\text{prev}}[\tau], \hat{S}^{(i)}_{\text{prev}}[\tau], \hat{Q}^{(i)}_{\text{prev}}[\tau])$
$\hat{\theta}_{\text{recv}} \leftarrow 0$ $\triangleright$ $(t^{(i)}_{\text{recv}}[\tau], \hat{n}^{(i)}_{\text{recv}}[\tau], \hat{m}^{(i)}_{\text{recv}}[\tau], \hat{S}^{(i)}_{\text{recv}}[\tau], \hat{Q}^{(i)}_{\text{recv}}[\tau])$
loop
  Wait(Δ)
  $\hat{\theta} \leftarrow$ Aggregate($\hat{\theta}_{\text{prev}}, \hat{\theta}_{\text{recv}}, \tilde{\theta}^{(i)}$) $\triangleright$ Algorithm 4
  $p \leftarrow$ RandomPeer
  Send($p, \hat{\theta}$)
end loop

function OnReceive($\hat{\theta}'$)
  $\hat{\theta}_{\text{prev}} \leftarrow \hat{\theta}_{\text{recv}}$
  $\hat{\theta}_{\text{recv}} \leftarrow \hat{\theta}'$
end function

At any point during the gossip protocol, each node can use its latest local estimate $(\hat{n}^{(i)}[\tau], \hat{m}^{(i)}[\tau], \hat{S}^{(i)}[\tau], \hat{Q}^{(i)}[\tau])$ to build a local Naive Bayes classifier as shown in Sect. 2.1. Once a sufficient number of gossiping steps have been performed, and the estimates have reached convergence, the local classifiers of every node will be almost identical to each other and to the one that would have been built by a federated approach.

4 Experiments

We thoroughly evaluate the performance of Federated and Gossip Nave Bayes on six popular benchmark datasets, all from the UCI repository[2]. The majority

[2] https://archive.ics.uci.edu/ml/datasets.php.

of the datasets comprises either only numerical or only categorical features, with the exception of Adults, which has both types. The details of each dataset are summarized in Table 2. For all datasets that do not provide a default train/test split, we perform a 90/10 split with random seed 42, for reproducibility. All the accuracy results reported in the rest of the section are computed on the test data, which are kept untouched until the evaluation phase.

Table 2. Datasets used in the evaluation. Table from [16].

Dataset	Samples	Labels	F_{num}	F_{cat}	Predefined train/test split
Accelerometer	153,000	3	3	0	no
Adult	48,842	2	6	8	yes (2:1)
Congressional Voting	435	2	0	16	no
Mushroom	8,124	2	0	22	no
Skin Segmentation	245,057	2	3	0	no
SPECT Heart	267	2	0	22	yes (3:7)

4.1 Federated Naive Bayes: Homogeneous Setting

In the first set of experiments we compare the accuracy of Federated Naive Bayes against two baselines: a centralized ε-differentially-private Naive Bayes implementation by Vaidya et al. [23] and a "vanilla" non-private implementation based on Sect. 2.1.

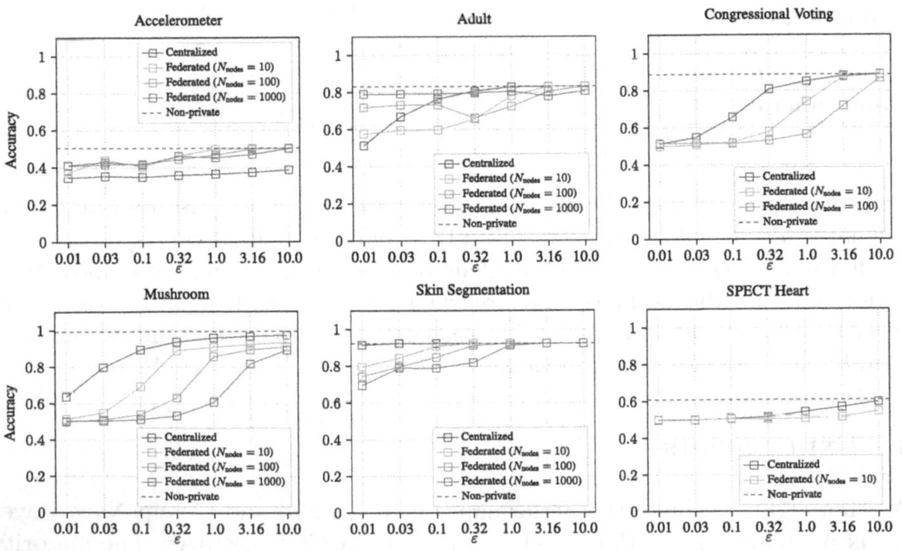

Fig. 2. Accuracy of Federated Naive Bayes for different values of ε and N_{nodes} vs centralized and non-private baselines. Image from [16].

We perform the evaluation on different $(N_{\text{nodes}}, \varepsilon)$ pairs, testing our algorithm for $N_{\text{nodes}} = 1, 10, 100, 1000$ and varying ε from 10^{-2} to 10^{1}. For each pair, we run a Monte Carlo experiment with 1000 trials and average the results. This allows to estimate the accuracy for an average execution of Federate Naive Bayes, accounting for both the variation introduced by differential privacy and by the data distribution. Our results are displayed in Fig. 2.

The plots follow the expected behavior of a differentially-private machine learning algorithm. When ε is low, the noise introduced by the Laplace mechanism completely hinders the prediction. However, for increasing value of ε, Federated Naive Bayes quickly approaches the accuracy value of the original centralized Naive Bayes. The value of ε at which this happens depends on the specific dataset: in Skin Segmentation a value of 1 already yields maximum accuracy in all cases, while SPECT Heart represents the opposite extreme.

It is worth noting that Federated Naive Bayes is not always worse than its centralized counterpart. It provides better accuracy for small values of ε on Adult, and for all values of ε on Accelerometer. The reason behind this counter-intuitive behavior is that Federated Naive Bayes perturbs the numerical parameters $(\tilde{S}^{(i)}, \tilde{Q}^{(i)})$ based on the local sensitivity. When the training data are partitioned across multiple nodes, the local sensitivity at each node may decrease, reducing the scale of Laplace noise. This hypothesis is confirmed by Fig. 3, which shows the local sensitivity of numerical features for $N = 10$ and $N = 100$, normalized with respect to the $N = 1$ case.

Note that the presence of numerical features does not guarantee this behavior. The distribution of the numerical features also matters, as it influences the chance of each node to have lower local sensitivity. This can be seen by looking at the Skin Segmentation dataset in Fig. 2 and 3: despite having only numerical features, its local sensitivity does not decrease significantly as the number of nodes increases, and thus Federated Naive Bayes does not gain an advantage on its centralized counterpart.

For datasets of categorical features, on the other hand, the noise is applied with a global sensitivity of 1. In such cases, perturbing multiple partitions of the data only increases the overall amount of noise. Hence, the accuracy decreases for a larger number of nodes.

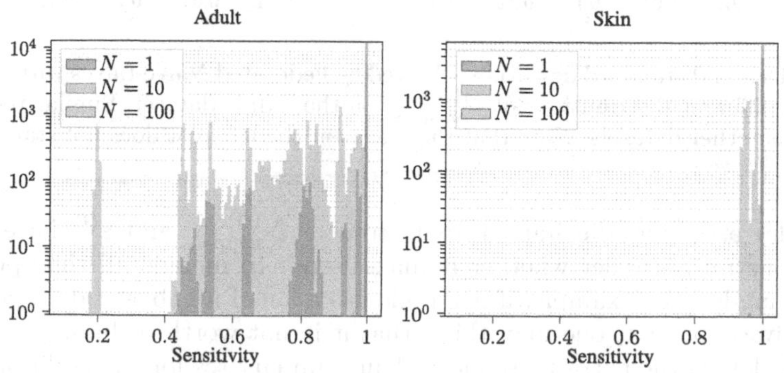

Fig. 3. Sensitivity distribution of $\tilde{S}^{(i)}$ for different numbers of nodes. Image from [16].

Overall, while the performance of Federated Naive Bayes depends on the characteristics of the dataset, in most cases it achieves similar accuracy to its centralized counterparts with the same or only slightly higher privacy budget.

4.2 Federated Naive Bayes: Heterogeneous Setting

In the experiments above, we assume that all nodes possess similar amounts of samples $N^{(i)}_{\text{samples}} \approx N_{\text{train}}/N_{\text{nodes}}$ and adopt the same privacy budget $\varepsilon^{(i)}$ for all nodes $i = 1, \ldots, N_{\text{nodes}}$. However, in realistic scenarios, nodes have a different number of data points and may have different privacy requirements. Therefore, we further evaluate Federated Naive Bayes in a more heterogeneous setting, where we assign $N^{(i)}_{\text{samples}}$ and $\varepsilon^{(i)}$ according to some probability distribution. We start by running the same Monte Carlo experiment as above while distributing the training data according to the two following distributions:

- a uniform distribution $\mathcal{U}([1, 10])$;
- an exponential distribution, Exp(2);

meaning that each node samples a value from such distributions and gets assigned a number of data points proportional to the outcome.

Figure 4 shows the mean and standard deviation of the accuracy achieved on the Adult dataset with different node size distributions. The results suggest that Federated Naive Bayes perform equally well when different nodes have significantly different numbers of local samples.

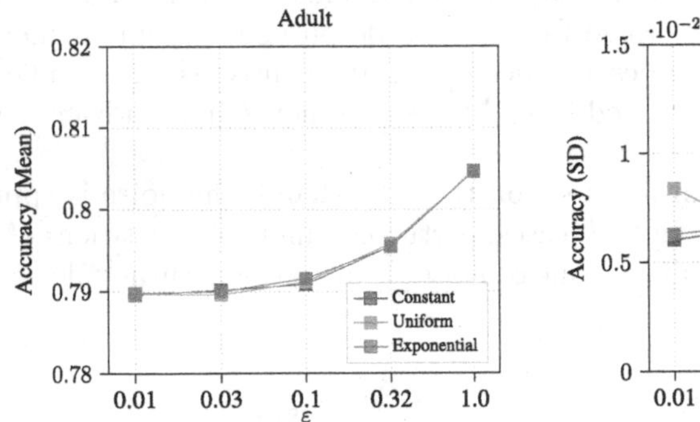

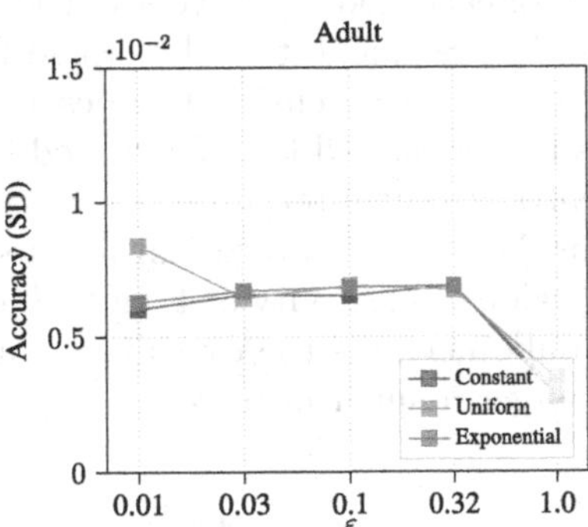

Fig. 4. Mean and standard deviation achieved by Federated Naive Bayes with $N_{\text{nodes}} = 1000$ and different distributions of $N^{(i)}_{\text{samples}}$, on the Adult dataset. Similar results are achieved on other datasets. Note that the y axis on the left plot does not start from 0.

Besides assessing the impact that variable $N^{(i)}_{\text{samples}}$ and $\varepsilon^{(i)}$ have on the results, one may wonder whether it makes sense to include all the updates in the final model. For example, if one node has a small number of data points, or a low privacy budget, one may think that it is not worth including its update in the model, as the extra noise more than compensates for the additional data points.

In order to determine whether this is the case, we run the following experiment. In a Federated Naive Bayes setting, we randomly distribute the entire training set across a number of nodes, such as the number of samples $N^{(i)}_{\text{samples}}$ at each node i follow a log-uniform distribution between 2 and $\log N_{train}/5$. We then assign a privacy budget $\varepsilon^{(i)}$ to each node, again according to a log-uniform distribution between 10^{-2} and 10^{1}. The reason behind this seemingly odd choice is that a log-uniform distribution implies that the node sizes are uniformly distributed in terms of "magnitude". In other words, a node has roughly the same likelihood of being assigned 10, 100, or 1000 data points. Likewise, a log-uniform privacy budget implies that the privacy requirements of the nodes are uniformly distributed, since the definition of differential privacy involves taking the exponential of the privacy budget.

After assigning data points and privacy budgets to all nodes, we compute the local updates normally, and measure the overall relative error as

$$\sum_{y} \frac{|\tilde{n}_y^{(i)} - n_y^{(i)}|}{n_y^{(i)}} + \sum_{y,x_\phi} \frac{|\tilde{m}_{x_\phi y}^{(i)} - m_{x_\phi y}^{(i)}|}{m_{x_\phi y}^{(i)}} + \sum_{y,\phi} \frac{|\tilde{S}_{\phi y}^{(i)} - S_{\phi y}^{(i)}|}{|S_{\phi y}^{(i)}|} + \sum_{y,\phi} \frac{|\tilde{Q}_{\phi y}^{(i)} - Q_{\phi y}^{(i)}|}{Q_{\phi y}^{(i)}} \tag{28}$$

These error values serve to quantify the amount of noise introduced by each node. We use each of them as a threshold, and exclude all the nodes with error above such threshold from the collaborative training.

Our results on two datasets are displayed in Fig. 5, with the other datasets showing similar behaviours. The plot on the left simply show the distribution of $N^{(i)}_{\text{samples}}$ and $\varepsilon^{(i)}$ among the nodes. In addition, the nodes have a different color depending on their error value, with the more noisy nodes being assigned a brighter color. Unsurprisingly, the noise depends mostly on the value of ε, especially when the features are mostly numerical (such as in the Skin Segmentation dataset). However, N_{samples} also has a significant effect on the amount of noise, particularly in the presence of categorical features, as in the Adult dataset, as the sensitivity of COUNT queries is fixed and thus the corresponding relative noise is smaller.

For the central and right plots in Fig. 5, we consider how the accuracy of a Federated Naive Bayes classifier would change if all nodes with noise level above a certain threshold were discarded from the aggregation. Based on the results, this kind of cutoff would not change the *typical* accuracy of the model. However choosing a very high or very low threshold can significantly influence the run-to-run variance. When the threshold is very high (i.e. virtually all contributions are accepted), this confirms the intuition that some nodes may be contributing more noise than information. On the other hand, when the threshold is very low, too much data is lost and high accuracy can only be achieved if the remaining nodes happen to represent very well the overall population. This is made obvious in the right side plots, which highlight how the worst accuracy results are obtained when only a single node is below the threshold.

4.3 Gossip Naive Bayes

As described in Sect. 3.3, nodes in Gossip Naive Bayes compute the same differentially-private local updates as in Federated Naive Bayes, with the only change being the aggregation of these updates happens in a peer-to-peer fashion, rather than via a central aggregator. Thus, in our experiments we investigate whether this gossip-based aggregation can converge to the same results as a federated aggregation, and how many steps this convergence takes.

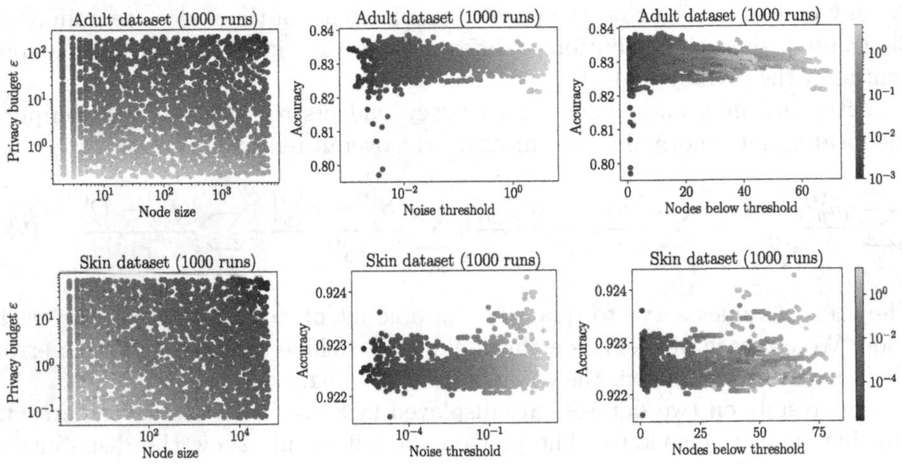

Fig. 5. Impact of noise thresholding on the accuracy of Federated Naive Bayes models.

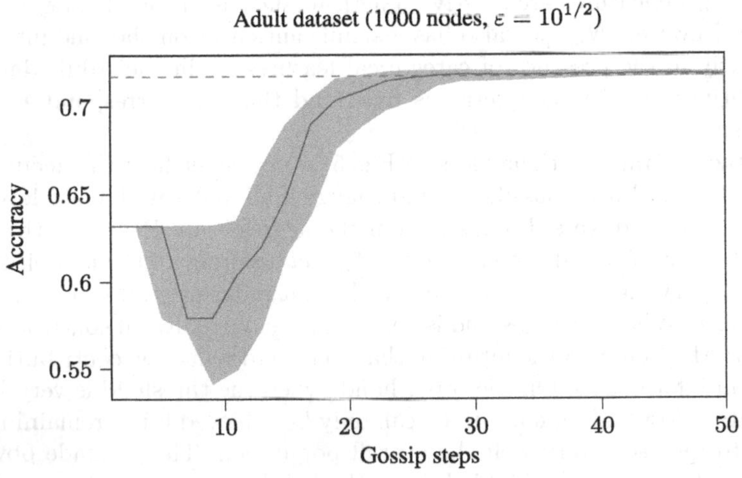

Fig. 6. Accuracy of Gossip Naive Bayes over multiple gossiping steps. The blue line is the median accuracy across 1000 participating nodes, the shaded area represents the inter-quartile range. The dotted line is the accuracy achieved by Federated Naive Bayes on the same set of local updates. (Color figure online)

More specifically, we follow the same setup as in Sect. 4.1 and apply both federated and gossip aggregation on the exact same runs, thus allowing a direct comparison not influenced by randomized dataset partitioning and noise generation.

Figure 6 shows how the accuracy of local Gossip Naive Bayes models evolves as more gossiping iterations are performed, on the Adult dataset with $N_{\text{nodes}} = 1000$ and $\varepsilon = 10^{\frac{1}{2}}$. Similar results were achieved on all datasets. In the first few iterations, as expected, the accuracy is very low, as the local estimates have only "seen" few local updates. Furthermore, the inter-quartile range of the accuracies is relatively wide. However, after just around 30 iterations, a vast majority of the nodes have reached the accuracy of the corresponding Federated Naive Bayes model, and this convergence further improves over additional iterations, with variance across different nodes reducing.

Figure 7 provides a more granular view, enabling a qualitative analysis of how individual Naive Bayes parameters converge over time. Prior probabilities, which on unbalanced datasets are typically the most influential parameters in the

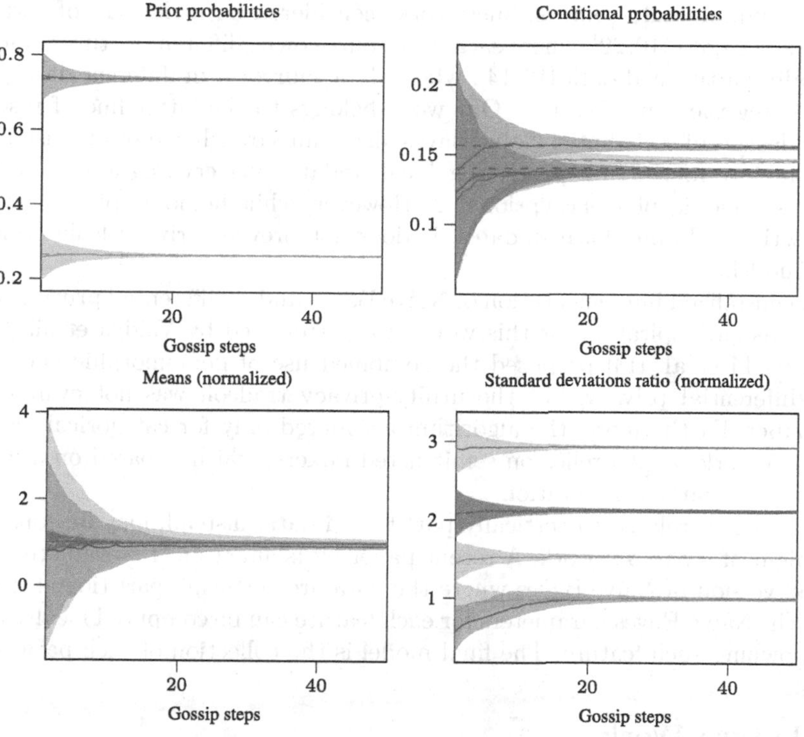

Fig. 7. Distribution of different Naive Bayes parameters across nodes over multiple steps of Gossip Naive Bayes, on the Adult dataset with $N_{\text{nodes}} = 1000$ and $\varepsilon = 10^{\frac{1}{2}}$. Lines and shaded areas of different colors represent median and inter-quartile range of each individual parameter.

prediction, very quickly converge to the correct values. Conditional probabilities of categorical features and means of numerical features converge slightly slower and can show slight deviations from a federated aggregation after convergence. Finally, the standard deviations of numerical features significantly deviates from the expected values after convergence. These different converge speeds and deviations after convergence may be due to error propagation across the different statistics. Prior probabilities are computed directly from $\hat{n}$. Means (resp. conditional probabilities) depend from both $\hat{S}$ (resp. $\hat{m}$) and $\hat{n}$. Standard deviations depend on $\hat{Q}$, $\hat{n}$ and, importantly, the *squares* of the means. Yet, Figure 6 shows that these deviations do not affect the overall accuracy of the model, thus proving the robustness of our differentially-private Naive Bayes scheme.

5 Related Work

Naive Bayes has shown consistent results in multiple applications [20,26], drawing the attention of both researchers and practitioners. Therefore, it is not surprising that prior works explored the possibility of training Naive Bayes models across multiple data sources. Such works considered both the case of vertically partitioned data [10,22], where each data source owns different features, and horizontally partitioned data [12,14], where data sources own different data points comprising the same features. Our work belongs to the latter line of research. Prior designs of distributed Naive Bayes algorithms over horizontally distributed data mainly focused on protecting local updates via cryptographic methods, such as homomorphic encryption [12]. However, while homomorphic encryption is effective in hiding local updates, it does not prevent privacy leaks from the final model.

A centralized implementation of Naive Bayes under differential privacy, which served as an inspiration for this work, was introduced by Vaidya et al. [23]. A work by Li et al. [14] proposed the combined use of homomorphic encryption and differential privacy, but the utility-privacy tradeoff was not evaluated in the paper. Furthermore, the algorithm accounted only for categorical features. Another work by [25] relies on semitrusted mixers, which is based on a form of secure multiparty computation.

The works related to vertically partitioned data, instead, may be considered complementary to our work. A recent paper by Islam et al. [10] evaluated a federated version of Naive Bayes where the data are vertically partitioned. In such case, the Naive Bayes parameters for each feature can be computed locally by the node owning such feature. The final model is the collection of such parameters.

6 Future Work

Non i.i.d. Data Distribution. In this work we evaluated Federated and Gossip Naive Bayes for a varying node size and privacy budget. However, the distribution of the data among the nodes is kept i.i.d. in all our experiments. In order to further generalize our results, future work should explore different data distributions. One case may consist in considering class imbalances between the nodes. Another possibility is to investigate sample biases within the nodes. These may be simulated by clustering data points according to some similarity metric, and assigning each cluster to a node.

Feature Selection. A relevant component of Naive Bayes models is feature selection. Discarding less important features is essential to train a robust model with good generalization capability [5]. This is especially true when differential privacy is applied and needs to be divided between the features, and thus having irrelevant features only contributes to add more noise. A naive idea may be to have each node ranking features locally, and to combine local rankings to select most relevant features. Local ranking can be performed with several well-established feature ranking techniques [18].

Byzantine Resilience. The shift towards decentralized and private data sources leads to the emergence of a new challenge: byzantine data owners. Instead of following the correct protocol, these disseminate maliciously-generated model updates, typically with the goal of preventing model convergence, inserting specific biases in the final model, or causing the training process to leak specific private data. Thus, byzantine-resilient federated learning [2,15] has become an important research area. One of the most common approaches to achieve byzantine resilience is to use median-based aggregation functions [4,9] to filter out contributions that diverge excessively from the majority of the nodes. However, Federated Naive Bayes relies on dataset statistics that are not directly amenable to this approach, as their magnitudes depend on data partition sizes. One option could be for the nodes to compute and share statistics that are independent of partition sizes (e.g. prior probabilities instead of prior counts), but this would significantly increase noise and numerical errors for under-represented classes. Thus, how to effectively achieve byzantine resilience for Federated and Gossip Naive Bayes is an open challenge.

7 Conclusions

This paper introduced two algorithms to collaboratively train a Naive Bayes model across multiple partitions, and under differential privacy guarantees: Federated and Gossip Naive Bayes. Both algorithms have been thoroughly evaluated, exploring the privacy-utility tradeoff for different distribution of node size and of privacy budget. Our results suggest that models trained with Federated or Gossip Naive Bayes offer comparable accuracy to their centralized counterpart, requiring only a slightly higher privacy budget depending on the dataset. Furthermore, both approaches are robust to varying distributions of the nodes' size and privacy budgets, thus making the suitable for real-world scenarios with heterogeneous data owners.

References

1. Alkathiri, A.A., Giaretta, L., Girdzijauskas, S., Sahlgren, M.: Decentralized word2 vec using gossip learning. In: 23rd Nordic Conference on Computational Linguistics (NoDaLiDa 2021) (2021)
2. Awan, S., Luo, B., Li, F.: CONTRA: defending against poisoning attacks in federated learning. In: Bertino, E., Shulman, H., Waidner, M. (eds.) ESORICS 2021. LNCS, vol. 12972, pp. 455–475. Springer, Cham (2021). https://doi.org/10.1007/978-3-030-88418-5_22
3. Bernal, D.G., Giaretta, L., Girdzijauskas, S., Sahlgren, M.: Federated word2vec: leveraging federated learning to encourage collaborative representation learning. arXiv preprint arXiv:2105.00831 (2021)
4. Blanchard, P., El Mhamdi, E.M., Guerraoui, R., Stainer, J.: Machine learning with adversaries: byzantine tolerant gradient descent. Adv. Neural Inf. Process. Syst. **30**, 1–11 (2017)
5. Chen, J., Huang, H., Tian, S., Qu, Y.: Feature selection for text classification with naïve bayes. Expert Syst. Appl. **36**(3), 5432–5435 (2009)
6. Dwork, C., Roth, A., et al.: The algorithmic foundations of differential privacy. Found. Trends Theor. Comput. Sci. **9**(3–4), 211–407 (2014)
7. Geyer, R.C., Klein, T., Nabi, M.: Differentially private federated learning: a client level perspective. arXiv preprint arXiv:1712.07557 (2017)
8. Giaretta, L., Girdzijauskas, v.: Gossip learning: off the beaten path. In: 2019 IEEE International Conference on Big Data (Big Data), pp. 1117–1124 (2019). https://doi.org/10.1109/BigData47090.2019.9006216
9. Guerraoui, R., Rouault, S., et al.: The hidden vulnerability of distributed learning in byzantium. In: International Conference on Machine Learning, pp. 3521–3530. PMLR (2018)
10. Islam, T.U., Ghasemi, R., Mohammed, N.: Privacy-preserving federated learning model for healthcare data. In: 2022 IEEE 12th Annual Computing and Communication Workshop and Conference (CCWC), pp. 0281–0287. IEEE (2022)
11. Ji, Z., Lipton, Z.C., Elkan, C.: Differential privacy and machine learning: a survey and review. arXiv preprint arXiv:1412.7584 (2014)
12. Kantarcıoglu, M., Vaidya, J., Clifton, C.: Privacy preserving naive bayes classifier for horizontally partitioned data. In: IEEE ICDM Workshop on Privacy Preserving Data Mining, pp. 3–9 (2003)
13. Kempe, D., Dobra, A., Gehrke, J.: Gossip-based computation of aggregate information. In: 44th Annual IEEE Symposium on Foundations of Computer Science, 2003, Proceedings, pp. 482–491. IEEE (2003)
14. Li, T., Li, J., Liu, Z., Li, P., Jia, C.: Differentially private naive bayes learning over multiple data sources. Inf. Sci. **444**, 89–104 (2018)
15. Lyu, L., et al.: Privacy and robustness in federated learning: attacks and defenses. arXiv preprint arXiv:2012.06337 (2020)
16. Marchioro, T., Giaretta, L., Markatos, E., Girdzijauskas, Š.: Federated naive bayes under differential privacy. In: 19th International Conference on Security and Cryptography (SECRYPT), Lisbon, Portugal, 11–13 July 2022, pp. 170–180. Scitepress (2022)
17. McMahan, B., Moore, E., Ramage, D., Hampson, S., Arcas, B.A.y.: Communication-efficient learning of deep networks from decentralized data. In: Singh, A., Zhu, J. (eds.) Proceedings of the 20th International Conference on Artificial Intelligence and Statistics. Proceedings of Machine Learning Research, vol. 54, pp. 1273–1282. PMLR (2017). https://proceedings.mlr.press/v54/mcmahan17a.html

18. Novakovic, J.: The impact of feature selection on the accuracy of naïve bayes classifier. In: 18th Telecommunications forum TELFOR, vol. 2, pp. 1113–1116 (2010)
19. Ormándi, R., Hegedűs, I., Jelasity, M.: Gossip learning with linear models on fully distributed data. Concurr. Comput. Pract. Exp. **25**(4), 556–571 (2013)
20. Rish, I., et al.: An empirical study of the naive bayes classifier. In: IJCAI 2001 Workshop on Empirical Methods in Artificial Intelligence, vol. 3, pp. 41–46 (2001)
21. Salem, A., Zhang, Y., Humbert, M., Berrang, P., Fritz, M., Backes, M.: Ml-leaks: model and data independent membership inference attacks and defenses on machine learning models. arXiv preprint arXiv:1806.01246 (2018)
22. Vaidya, J., Clifton, C.: Privacy preserving naive bayes classifier for vertically partitioned data. In: Proceedings of the 2004 SIAM International Conference on Data Mining, pp. 522–526. SIAM (2004)
23. Vaidya, J., Shafiq, B., Basu, A., Hong, Y.: Differentially private naive bayes classification. In: 2013 IEEE/WIC/ACM International Joint Conferences on Web Intelligence (WI) and Intelligent Agent Technologies (IAT), vol. 1, pp. 571–576. IEEE (2013)
24. Wei, K., et al.: Federated learning with differential privacy: algorithms and performance analysis. IEEE Trans. Inf. For. Secur. **15**, 3454–3469 (2020). https://doi.org/10.1109/TIFS.2020.2988575
25. Yi, X., Zhang, Y.: Privacy-preserving naive bayes classification on distributed data via semi-trusted mixers. Inf. Syst. **34**(3), 371–380 (2009)
26. Zhang, H.: The optimality of naive bayes. Aa **1**(2), 3 (2004)
27. Zhu, L., Liu, Z., Han, S.: Deep leakage from gradients. Adv. Neural Inf. Process. Syst. **32** (2019)

Intrinsic Weaknesses of IDSs to Malicious Adversarial Attacks and Their Mitigation

Hassan Chaitou(✉), Thomas Robert, Jean Leneutre, and Laurent Pautet

LTCI, Télécom Paris, Institut Polytechnique de Paris, Paris, France
{hassan.chaitou,thomas.robert,jean.leneutre,
laurent.pautet}@telecom-paris.fr

Abstract. Intrusion Detection Systems (IDS) are essential tools to protect network security from malicious traffic. IDS have recently made significant advancements in their detection capabilities through deep learning algorithms compared to conventional approaches. However, these algorithms are vulnerable to meta-attacks, also known as adversarial evasion attacks, which are attacks that improve already existing attacks, specifically their ability to evade detection. Deep learning-based IDS, in particular, are particularly susceptible to adversarial evasion attacks that use Generative Adversarial Networks (GAN). Nonetheless, well-known strategies have been proposed to cope with this threat. However, these countermeasures lack robustness and predictability, and their performance can be either remarkable or poor. Such robustness issues have been identified even without adversarial evasion attacks, and mitigation strategies have been provided. This paper identifies and formalizes threats to the robustness of IDSs against adversarial evasion attacks. These threats are enabled by flaws in the dataset's structure and content rather than its representativeness. In addition, we propose a method for enhancing the performance of adversarial training by directing it to focus on the best evasion candidates samples within a dataset. We find that GAN adversarial attack evasion capabilities are significantly reduced when our method is used to strengthen the IDS.

Keywords: Adversarial machine learning · GAN · Intrusion detection system · Sensitivity analysis

1 Introduction

A network intrusion detection system (NIDS) plays an important role in protecting networks by monitoring the state of the network activity. A NIDS can be designed in two ways: signature-based IDS and machine learning (ML)-based IDS. In the first one, an expert identifies solutions to common problems by collecting a large database of signatures for well-known attacks, and then the IDS scans the network traffic to see whether it matches one of the attack signatures or not. This approach, however, has a number of downsides, including a large number of rules to handle, limited detection capabilities, and high maintenance

M. Van Sinderen et al. (Eds.): ICSBT/SECRYPT 2022, CCIS 1849, pp. 122–155, 2023.
https://doi.org/10.1007/978-3-031-45137-9_6

costs. Therefore, many researchers have focused on designing IDSs that rely on machine learning techniques to address the above problems (ML-based IDS). It is generally accepted that such IDSs perform better in detecting variations of known attacks and, in some cases, unknown attacks.

We focus on IDSs that monitor network activity by observing packets, events, or connections. As a result, whenever such observations are made, the IDS is expected to determine whether it is an attack or normal activity (its class). Such IDS have a parametric model that must be optimized to predict the class of the observed activity with the highest attack detection rate and the lowest false alarm rate.

This optimization process is divided into three stages: collecting field data, extracting features, cleaning and preprocessing them to make them usable by the model, and iteratively modifying model parameters to improve detection and false positive rates. The collected field data should contain labelled examples of both attacks and normal activities in a low-level representation that combines scalar and categorical values. The second step, network data analysis, consists of packet preparation and feature extraction up to the feature conversion to scalar types only (called preprocessing). Eventually, it converts the low-level representation of network activities into vectors of values known as "samples," a term borrowed from the general Machine Learning community. The last step is the actual training step, which aims to find the best model parameters for the highest detection rate and lowest false alarms based on the training data. Therefore, the quantity and quality of data used to train the parametric function are critical factors in determining IDS detection performance. Many works highlight the quality of datasets that may require to be sufficiently representative [13].

The studied system consists of two sides, the attacker and defender sides, with the attacker responsible for performing attacks and attempting to evade detection and the defender responsible for training and deploying an efficient IDS. In this context, an attacker can benefit from "evasion attack," a well-known approach to evade detection for IDSs. The evasion attack makes the above mentioned training pipeline vulnerable to adversarial samples [30]. Crafting adversarial attack samples consists of transforming attacks that are unaware of an IDS being used into attacks specifically designed to avoid the IDS while having a malicious impact. Such transformations are possible using Generative Adversarial Networks [9] among other generative approaches. On the other hand, a defender employs countermeasures against evasion attacks mainly by injecting adversarial samples into the IDS's training dataset. Consequently, the training pipeline is extended by this training dataset enhancement. Interestingly, the literature shows that such a dataset enhancement is typically based on the same method, namely "adversarial training." However, despite the fact that the method appears to be similar at first glance, in practice, the result of this enhancement can vary a lot in terms of countermeasure performances. In the literature, it has been hypothesized that this variation can be partly explained by how the defender and attacker define and use the extent to which attack can be altered [4].

In this work, we reuse and extend the dataset issues of regular training pipelines to analyze adversarial training ones on well-understood models [10] and datasets. Moreover, it allows us to understand why some approaches perform perfectly on some datasets but not on others or even exhibit rather unpredictable behavior on the same dataset.

Processes and criteria for improving and assessing the quality of training pipelines and the datasets on which they rely have been defined, according to [8]. Three criteria can be retained: i) If one wants to predict their class accurately, they should avoid underrepresented types of activities, ii) Train distinct binary models to separate pairs of classes if possible (e.g., normal type vs. attack type, for each attack class), iii) Avoid dataset issues with the same sample associated with different classes.

One example of the point iii issue is storing the incorrect class in the collected data. However, a more complicated situation arises when the dataset appears to contain the same sample associated with two distinct classes. It would result in a dead end in terms of determining whether or not a sample is an attack without impairing false alarms or detection capabilities.

To the best of our knowledge, such criteria are not taken into account when expanding the training dataset with examples of evasion attacks. Therefore, the following are our research objectives:

Question 1. Can the dataset consistency issue intuitively introduced above be relevant as it is for adversarial training datasets? If not, why not, and what should be done about it?

Question 2. Can consistency issues for adversarial training datasets be responsible for IDS performance issues against evasion attacks (qualitatively)?

Question 3. What are the potential solutions to consistency issues on adversarial training datasets?

Question 4. To what extent, quantitatively, do these issues really pose threats to IDS performance without or with countermeasures applied?

Section 2 describes the system architectures as well as the IDS regular training pipelines. Section 3 explains and formalizes the notion of the adversarial neighborhood of attack. Section 4 formally defines the main consequence of being able to generate adversarial samples that remain attacks without testing. Furthermore, it introduces the threats this situation entails and presents mitigation strategies. Section 5 presents the evaluation metrics besides the experimentation descriptions. Sections 6 and 7 present the experimental assessment of the threats we identified and the performance of the mitigation strategies.

This paper is an extension of the one published in the SECRYPT proceedings [5].

In [5], we only considered one adversarial neighborhood definition, assuming that a single perfect definition exists. This paper, on the other hand, assumes that each attack generator has its own definition of neighborhood. This is demonstrated by examining two datasets, the NSL-KDD, and the CIC-IDS2017, with three adversarial neighborhood definitions. Furthermore, this paper refined the measures on the best evasion attack candidate (BEAC) to demonstrate quantitatively that the BEAC set elements poses a severe threat to the IDS detection performance.

2 Systems Under Review and Regular Training Pipelines

This section recalls the system architecture described in this paper as well as the main steps in the IDS training pipeline. It recalls the vocabulary and formalizes the concepts needed to describe IDS training pipeline and the consistency issue mentioned above in its training dataset.

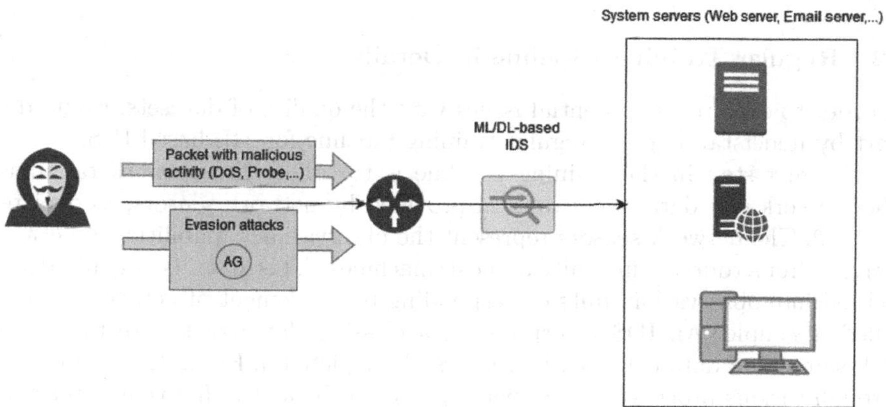

Fig. 1. Overview of the system architecture.

2.1 Systems Architecture

As shown in Fig. 1, an attacker is interested in sending to the system packets with malicious payload to bypass the defense mechanism (e.g., IDS) and ensure that the malicious payload has the intended impact on the targeted system behind the IDS. However, when the defense mechanism detects the malicious activity, it drops the attacker's packets.

In this case, the attacker can launch a meta-attack, which consists in modifying the given malicious activity detected by the IDS into an activity that can bypass the defense system. The authors of [21] propose a meta-attack approach that aims to modify a malicious activity so that it is different to the IDS leading it to consider it as a normal activity. This meta-attack is exactly an evasion attack. In order to automate evasion attacks, an "attack generator" (AG) is defined. It is a function, denoted *ag* that should select for an attack the best changes to apply. The result of those changes on the activity is usually called a mutation.

The defender, on the other hand, relies on ML-based IDS to protect its network from packets with malicious payloads and potentially evasion capabilities. Set of examples of normal and attack activities contains usually no example of evasion. Then an IDS train with such data cannot a priori detect the attack on which the meta-attack, the evasion attack, has been applied. In this situation, the defender must also employ an *ag* to generate several mutations of the malicious activities in order to have examples of evasion attacks. This dataset enhancement aims to improve the efficiency of IDS detection against attacks without and with evasion capabilities without compromising other important IDS performance metrics. For instance, it should not reduce the availability of the normal activity.

In the next subsection, we formalize and explain the different procedures and phases of the training pipeline in detail.

2.2 Regular Training Pipeline in Details

In order to explore the potential issues with the quality of datasets, we need to start by understanding the regular training pipeline for ML-based IDS.

The first step in the training pipeline is to collect the network raw data. The network raw data refers to data provided by network sensors, as depicted in Fig. 2. The network sensors represent the observation capabilities of network activity from routers, firewalls or host machines. This data is organized and merged into observation units corresponding to an element of network activity, called a sample. An IDS incorporating a classifier for attack detection is fed with samples of data collected by sensors. As depicted in Fig. 2, the sample goes through various processes before being processed by a classifier that determines for each sample whether it belongs to a normal or attack class.

Definition 1 (Raw Sample). *A* raw sample *is a tuple of* n *values respectively of types* T_1, ..., T_n. *The raw sample type* T_R *is* $T_R = T_1 \times ... \times T_n$.

The PCAP format is the type of raw sample usually used: it is detailed enough that the activity can even be replayed from the raw sample. Basically, raw samples are expected to be enough detailed to be able to decide whether a sample corresponds to normal activity or attack. Let L be the set of possible labels: $L = \{normal, attack\}$.

Definition 2 (Raw Labeled Sample and Dataset). *A* raw labeled sample *is a couple* (x, y) *where* $x \in T_r$ *and* $y \in L$. *A* raw labeled dataset *is a set of raw labeled samples.*

The raw sample type often relies on non-numeric types to capture metadata about packets or application behaviors. Therefore, the values of raw samples can be of very diverse types (e.g., binary, categorical, numeric, strings). It is extremely difficult to feed a classifier with such data without first transforming all these types into scalar normalized values. This step is called pre-processing. Let call *prep* the function that produces IDS scalar inputs from raw samples R.

Therefore, *prep* function takes elements of T_R and produces a vector of values q in $[0, 1]$, we now use T_P such that $T_P = [0, 1]^q$.

Definition 3 (Preprocessed Samples and Labeled Dataset). *For any raw sample x, $prep(x)$ is a* preprocessed sample, *and for any raw labeled dataset D, $prep(D) = \{\{(prep(x_i), y_i)|(x_i, y_i) \in D\}\}$, is the corresponding* preprocessed labeled dataset.

To apply *prep* to a labeled dataset, one has to apply it to the raw sample portion of each labeled sample. In the Machine Learning community, a dimension of a sample is called a feature in the feature space. A labeled sample is said to be an *attack sample* if its label is *attack*, and a *normal sample* if it is *normal*. Each labeled dataset can be split in two subsets respectively called *normal traffic* and *attack traffic*.

Definition 4 (Normal and Attack Traffic of D). *Given a labeled dataset D (raw or preprocessed), the* normal traffic *of D denoted $N(D)$, and the* attack traffic *of D denoted $A(D)$ are defined as follow:*

$$N(D) = \{(x_i, y_i)|(x_i, y_i) \in D, y_i = normal\}$$
$$A(D) = \{(x_i, y_i)|(x_i, y_i) \in D, y_i = attack\}$$

A labeled dataset is necessary when training a classifier, or defining its parameters; such a dataset is called a training dataset.

As stated in Sect. 1, the most important quality criteria are the absence of label issues on a sample and the balance in the proportion of sample types (i.e., to avoid under-representation of large sample classes).

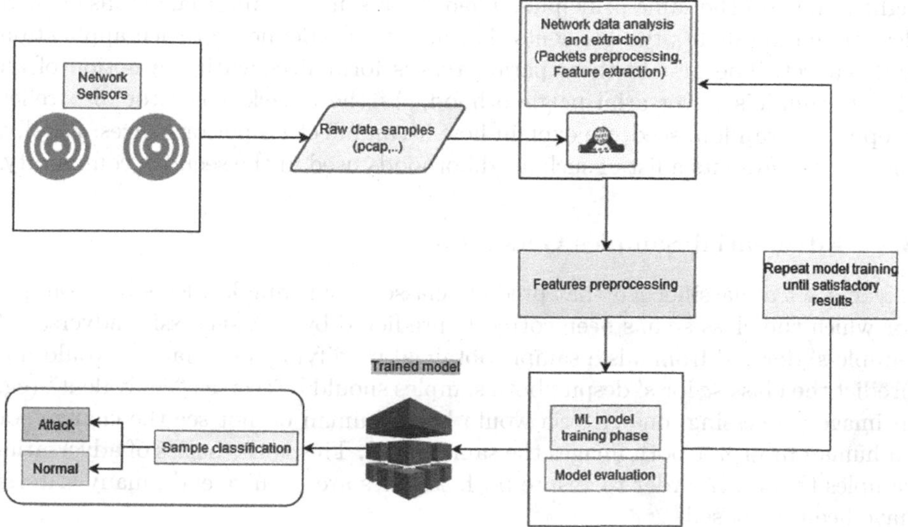

Fig. 2. Deployed architecture of classifier based IDS.

Datasets may contain problematic samples due to sample collection problems or too high-level observations. Beyond wrongly labelled samples, we point out another type of labelling issues that affect also the IDS.

Definition 5 (Contradictory Samples). *Two labelled samples* (x_1, y_1) *and* (x_2, y_2) *are* contradictory samples *if and only if (iff)* $x_1 = x_2$ *and* $y_1 \neq y_2$.

Such pairs of samples if present in a training dataset are problematic as they contradict each other.

Definition 6 (Contradictory Set of D). *The contradictory set of* D*, denoted* $CS(D)$ *is the set of all contradictory samples contained in* D.

A classifier is a parametric model that must be configured, and the training process is responsible for determining the appropriate parameters. Usually it relies on minimizing the gap between the label produced by the model (predicted one) and the label stored in the dataset. Yet, in case of contradictory samples, one can consider that there is no good answer for such samples. Indeed, the class predicted by the IDS contradicts at least one of the samples. In such a case, the IDS is always partly wrong.

The regular training pipeline is vulnerable to adversarial evasion attacks. Therefore, the following section shows how malicious adversarial samples can evade detection and how enriching the dataset with adversarial samples affects the IDS training pipeline.

3 Detailed Analysis of Attack Generators

This section explains how attack generators found in the literature appear at first sight to rely on the same principles. Then, it presents the internal details of their design and highlights two elements that are often redefined for each application and dataset. The first of these parameters is formalized with the notion of an attack sample's adversarial neighborhood. As the attack generator also relies deeply on a random seed, we explain how it can affect its performances. Finally, the section presents a list of such neighborhoods used in the security community.

3.1 Adversarial Samples Generator

Given a set a classifier *cla* that predicts classes from samples, let s be a sample for which the class sc has been correctly predicted by t. A successful adversarial sample s' derived from s is a sample obtained modifying s so that ids would not predict the class sc for s' despite both samples should be seen as "equivalent" (eg. in image processing, one criteria would be "a human do not see the change" or "a human interpret both images the same way"). This is the basics of adversarial samples theory. In order to ensure both samples are "equivalent", many criteria have been proposed.

The result of an evasion attack on sample is in practice an adversarial attack sample. Indeed, if the adversarial attack sample is successfully crafted, it will be not classified as an attack and thus evade the IDS. In the remainder of the paper, we reason about adversarial samples defined in T_p (the space of preprocessed samples) but only for attack samples.

A *malicious adversarial sample* ($MAdv$) is an adversarial sample derived only from attack samples. In the case of attack samples, the adversarial sample is considered "equivalent" if it yields the same consequences on the systems, ie. it has the same malicious impact. Malicious adversarial samples are basically a synonym of evasions attacks against IDSs built upon a classifier.

Let us now depict the usual generic approach followed to generate those samples. A function is used to represent this process. Its first input parameter is the sample to alter. For each input sample, many adversarial samples could be proposed. Then this function takes another input that helps exploring these alternatives. This second parameter is called a "noise" parameter as it has no particular meaning except to ensure that with the same function, one can obtain many adversarial samples for the same input sample.

Definition 7 (Adversarial Sample Generator). *An adversarial sample generator ag is a function with parameters (x,d) of type* (T_p) *(a sample) and* $[0, 1]^k$ *(a value used to explore possible changes) and returns* x' *a sample (a member of* T_p*)*

One has to recall that this function is intended to be used only on samples that correspond to attacks (e.g. only samples that labels would be *attack*). Recall that T_p corresponds to vectors of scalars for which $+$ and $-$ have the usual meaning, then the perturbation introduced by ag on x with z is $ag(x, z) - x$.

This function is almost never used only once, it is used to produce most often huge amount of adversarial samples. These samples are either used as means to assess the likelihood of generating a successful malicious adversarial sample. It can also be used as means to improve the training pipeline of the IDSs. We will discuss it later. Such a function is often dedicated to certain kinds of attack and normal activities, e.g. a dataset and thus incidentally an IDS. Let us explains the constraints and best practices when generating such sets.

3.2 Adversarial Sample Generation and Its Usage

In this subsection section, we discuss what are the objectives behind producing those sets and their properties.

Adversarial attack samples could be required either for training IDSs or assessing their performances. In the second case, the IDSs are tested against a large number of adversarial samples to capture the likelihood of success of these meta-attacks. Yet, the problem is the following: the attack generator can be applied several times to the same attack, and nothing guarantees that it will necessarily produce distinct adversarial samples. Yet, most of the time set of samples are considered as approximation of the distribution of possible samples. Therefore, counting how many times such samples evade detection is sufficient to estimate the likelihood of undetected attacks.

In the case many adversarial samples are generated for the same sample, it might be important to recall (i.e. store) how much time the same adversarial sample is produced (possible). For this reason, we consider generating bags of adversarial samples instead of simply sets. Picking at random an element from the bag would mimic the distribution of generated adversarial samples. To differentiate bags from sets, bags would be denoted with brackets. $[[1, 1, 2, 2, 3]]$ is thus the bag that contains 5 integers, twice 1 and twice 2.

We introduce a notation to denote bags corresponding to i adversarial samples generated for each attack sample of a dataset. Whenever an adversarial sample is generated, the noise input is assumed to be drawn at random in the set of noise values. The distribution of noise values picked that way is assumed to follow a uniform distribution.

Let ag be an attack generator, D a dataset made only of attack samples.

Definition 8 (Bags of Adversarial Samples of D). *We denote $Uniform$ (i, ag, D) a bag defined as follow*

$$Uniform(i, ag, D) = [[ag(a, z_j) | a \in D,\ 1 \leq j \leq i,\ z_j$$
$$uniform\ i.i.d. random\ variables\ over [0, 1]^k]]$$

Counting the occurrence of an element in such a bag for high values of i provide an approximation of the likelihood that this attack sample is actually produced if the noise element is picked actually at random. Notice that the set of possible images of ag for a fixed attack sample could be far smaller than the set of possible noise vectors (it is even expected).

This situation is illustrated in Fig. 3. For simplicity, we consider a simplified example of sample type with only three dimensions. The noise value is defined

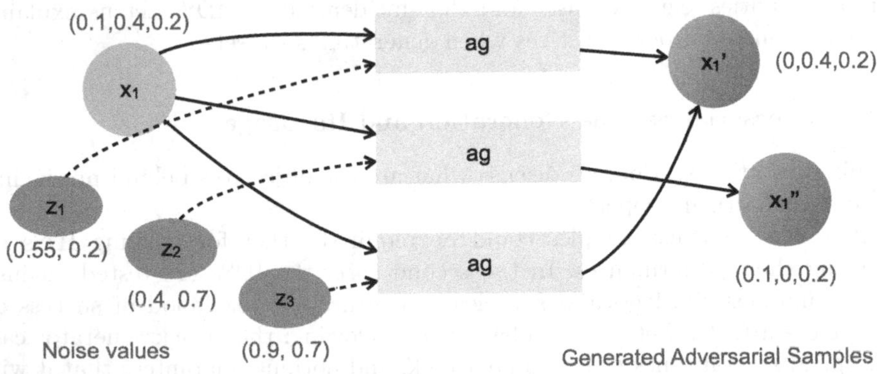

Fig. 3. Malicious adversarial samples generated for one attack and multiple noise values.

over $[0, 1]^2$ and the attack generator ag_s is defined as follows:

$$ag_s((a_1, a_2, a_3), (z_1, z_2)) = \begin{cases} (0, a_2, a_3) & if \quad z_1 > 0.5 \\ (a_1, 0, a_3) & if \quad z_2 < 0.5,\ z_1 \leq 0.5 \\ (a_1, a_2 + z_1, a_3) & otherwise \end{cases}$$

This function applied on the same sample but for different noise values can produce exactly the same adversarial example. The values $(0.55, 0.2)$ and $(0.9, 0.7)$ illustrate this claim: they lead to the same result on x as shown in the Fig. 3. In such a situation, if we compute $Uniform(100, ag_s, (0.1, 0.4, 0.2))$ it is very likely that we obtain more than 40 times $(0.1, 0, 0.2)$ because the probability for a noise value uniformly distributed to have $z_2 < 0.5$ is 0.5.

Deep neural network models are known to be vulnerable to $MAdvs$ [10]. Hopefully, efficient adversarial defense approaches have been proposed to prevent these attacks, and are surveyed in [24]. Adversarial training consist in adding sets of adversarial samples to the training dataset of an IDS.

Definition 9 (Adversarial Training Pipeline for IDSs). *The adversarial training of an IDS is a training pipeline that uses a training dataset containing malicious adversarial samples generated from an attack generator ag.*

Basically, if the attack generator is not available, one has first to train an IDS as defined previously and then propose a relevant attack generator for this IDS. Finally, a new IDS is trained using the first training dataset to which adversarial samples generated with ag are added (for instance using the $Uniform$ procedure). Adversarial training or its extensions remain the most effective approaches to improve the robustness of classifiers against $MAdvs$ [25]. The purpose of using ag is to inject samples into the training dataset to make the IDS robust compared to ag without having to execute anything on the real system. Otherwise, extending the dataset would be too expensive.

As said in Sect. 3.1, the adversarial attack samples need to remain "equivalent" as much as possible i.e. still entail a malicious impact on the system. Finding a good attack generator remains challenging mainly because the extent to which a sample can be modified remains hard to evaluate. Next section discusses this situation and highlights the role of the set of allowed sample modifications in the performances of attack generator.

3.3 Adversarial Neighborhood and a Catalog of Its Various Types

Adversarial sample generation is based on the assumption that an attack generator (AG) can only generate relevant adversarial attack samples. Section 7 highlights that it is possible to generate a large number of adversarial attack samples from a single attack sample. Hence, the question become what is the complete set of samples that can be obtained from an attack sample x through an attack generator. We introduce a notation to describe more easily this set. As this set can change for each attack, we need a function to designate for each attack this set.

Definition 10 (Adversarial Neighborhood of Attacks (ANA)). *An adversarial neighborhood of attacks ana is a function that returns for each attack sample x a set of sample denoted $ana(x)$ such that each element of $ana(x)$ is declared equivalent to x according to ana*

This notation facilitates the describe the possible outputs of an attack generator. Defining the adversarial neighborhood is the starting point of any attack generator design. However, choosing the neighborhood is always a very complex and challenging task in any constrained domain, specifically in the network security domain. As the ANA identifies to what extent attack sample can change and yet have a similar malicious impact on the system. It clearly means that the ANA depends on the attacks considered, in the kind of data that are collected on network activities.

This notion of neighborhood seems mostly related to cases where all the dimension of some subspace of the sample space $T_p = [0,1]^q$ can be freely modified.

Let review the different approaches:

- The first approach allow to change everything in sample as in [3] and [29]. Such a neighborhood is far from realistic as it can hardly guarantee the malicious impact of these samples. On the other hand, it requires no particular knowledge on attacks at first sight. Yet, it might generate sample that are no longer malicious.
- The second group of approaches rely on their knowledge of the practical backgrounds that accompanied the construction of the dataset (e.g., tools used to generate the attacks, the network heterogeneity in terms of devices and systems). The dataset designers define the neighborhood the subset of sample features (e.g. dimension) that can be modified as in [16].
- The third group of approach still aim to determine which dimension in the same can be modified and how. Statistical criteria such as SHAP [18], LIME [26] on sample features are used to define the sample feature that can be modified freely. Other approaches have been applied such as singular value decomposition (SVD) [14] in order to extracting the important features that can preserve the impact of an attack class during sampling generation as done also in [6,27,28], and [36].
- The last group of approaches relies on the domain experts. As cited in [11], and [31]. An expert analyzes the dataset to specify the features that can be modified for adversarial sample generation.

Many works focus on better exploring these ANAs as it can help to find successful malicious adversarial samples. Other studied how to improve the way noise is picked, or the attack generator built so that with less sample we can sufficiently improve the robustness of the defense mechanism [22]. The next section details the role of the ANA in creating contradictory samples with respect to a dataset containing both normal and attack samples (e.g. the training dataset of an IDS). Then, it explains how such samples can threaten the quality of an IDS trained with such a dataset, and how to mitigate those threats.

4 Contradictory Adversarial Sample, Threat and Mitigation

Attack generator are used on both sides, attack and defense. Thus, one has to be careful that their definition might be an issue for the defender either because it facilitates too much the task of the attacker to evade detection, or because it might impair the quality of the trained IDS on non malicious adversarial samples. This section presents the contribution that motivated this paper, it explains why the notion of contradictory sample in Sect. 2.2 needs first to be extended to capture the full consequences of choosing the ANA of an attack generator.

4.1 Revisiting the Labelling Issues for Adversarial Training Datasets

In previous sections we highlighted the importance for the defender to ensure a training pipeline of good quality and to have samples that are label error free, as much as possible. In particular, we highlighted the case of contradictory samples. Recall that the adversarial training process basically consists in adding to a dataset called original dataset OD a set of adversarial samples called AD (adversarial dataset), OD is assumed to contain both normal and attack samples. Conversely AD contains only malicious adversarial attack samples.

We identified the following issue: even if two labelled dataset OD and AD have separately no contradictory samples, their union $OD \cup AD$ can have some contradictory samples. Actually, the pairs of contradictory samples would involve a normal sample of OD and some attack sample of AD. From the defender point of view, this situation would be the worst as an attack adversarial sample could not be distinguished from normal samples present in the original training dataset. The question become, is it sufficient not to use these samples in adversarial training dataset. Our claim is that it is not sufficient. In order to explain why it is not sufficient, we extends the notion of contradictory set to capture potential contradictions: contradictions between normal samples, and possible adversarial samples.

Definition 11 (Extended Contradictory Set of OD). *Given an adversarial neighborhood ana, and a dataset OD, the Extended Contradictory set of OD with respect to the adversarial neighborhood ana is the set of all contradictory samples contained in $OD \cup ana(A(OD))$ and is noted $EC(ana, OD)$, more formally:*

$$EC(ana, OD) = \bigcup_{(x,normal)\in N(OD)} \{(x, normal), (x, attack) | (x, attack) \in ana(A(OD))\}$$

If this set is not empty it means that given the adversarial neighborhood ana, the content of OD make it possible to define an attack generator ag from ana, and an attack x such that $ag(x)$ is a sample that matches perfectly a normal sample from the training set OD. For Attacks samples from OD for which this is possible, it is thus very likely to be able to perform a successful evasion attack.

Indeed, an IDS trained on OD is trained with the normal sample from the extended contradictory set and would most likely not contradict the class of the training sample, e.g. normal.

Definition 12 (Best Evasion Attack Candidates (BEAC)). *Best evasion attack candidate set is the set of attack samples in OD whom adversarial neighborhood do include a normal sample from OD.*

$$BEAC(ana, OD) = ana^{-1}(N(OD)) \cap A(OD)\}$$

This notion could be seen as a clue to the attacker whose sample could best evade the IDS after applying the attack generator. It should be noted that to have a non empty BEAC set, the attacker must have a good knowledge of normal samples. Let now illustrate all these concepts on a simplified dataset.

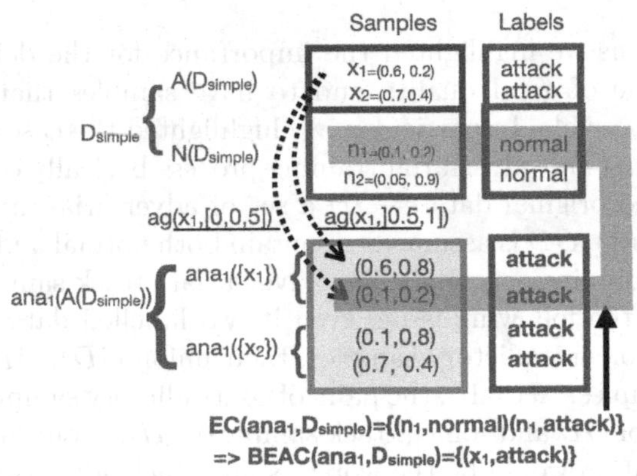

Fig. 4. Relation between ANA, $BEAC$ and EC.

Figure 4 depicts a simplified dataset D_{simple} with four elements including two labelled attack samples, $(x_1, attack)$ and $(x_2, attack)$, and two normal ones $(n_1, attack)$ and $(n_2, attack)$(the detailed values are provided later). The sample space is $[0, 1]^2$ and the noise space is $[0, 1]$. We consider ag defined as follow:

$$ag((a_1, a_2), z) = \begin{cases} (0.1, a_2) \text{ if } z \leq 0,5 \\ (a_1, 0.8) \text{ Otherwise} \end{cases}$$

We consider the following values for the samples: $x_1 = (0.6, 0.2)$, $x_2 = (0.7, 0.4)$, $n_1 = (0.1, 0.2)$, $n_2 = (0.05, 0.9)$. Let ana_1 be the neighborhood used for ag, then $ana_1(\{x_1\}) = \{(0.1, 0.2), (0, 6, 0.8)\}$, $ana_1(\{x_2\} = \{(0.1, 0.4), (0.7, 0.8)\}$. In this example, please notice that in fact n_1 belongs to $ana_1(\{x_1\})$. In this context, $EC(ana_1, D_{simple}) = \{(n_1, normal), (n_1, attack)\}$ an that the attack from which the adversarial sample n_1 can be obtained is x_1. Therefore, an IDS trained on D_{simple} has a high likelihood to predict the adversarial sample $ag(x_1, 0)$ as a normal sample (as it equals to n_1).

From the attacker's point of view, applying the attack generator on samples that are transformed into elements of $EC(ana1, D_{simple})$ could represent its best chance of success. In this case, the BEAC set is the singleton: $\{(x_1, attack)\}$. In this section, we have shown why the adversarial neighborhood of attack need to be known in order to anticipate for an IDS trained on a dataset the adversarial sample that if labelled attacks would contradicts normal sample from it training set. Ignoring such a situation is shown in the next section to be the source of several weaknesses for IDSs with or without adversarial training applied.

4.2 Threat to IDS Robustness Due to Misuse of Attack Generators

In this subsection, we investigate how the knowledge of the ANA of an Attack Generator should be considered with care. Otherwise, retraining an IDS would either not provide the expected robustness to evasion attacks, or impair the system availability due to higher false positive detection rates. Those two events are the major issues that need to be taken care of when refining an IDS.

In Sect. 3.3, we pointed out that several ANA have been considered for adversarial training. Moreover, in [23] authors insist on the fact that ANA definition could be difficult to capture in so call feature space (i.e. after preprocessing the raw observation of the system activity). In particular, they emphasize the difficulty of guaranteeing for ANA that the neighborhood contains only actual attacks, i.e. activities that produce a malicious impact.

Definition 13 (Impactful Neighborhood of Attacks). *An adversarial Neighborhood of attacks is said to be an Impactful Neighborhood of Attacks if it contains only samples for which a network activity could be observed in a case it yields a malicious impact on the system.*

A first issue is related to the difficulty to ensure that all the samples generated for adversarial training belong to some impactful neighborhoods of attacks. The first trivial case of such an issue can be found in the literature in early years of adversarial attack sample generation. This situation lead to a risk of generating adversarial samples labelled as attacks in the training process while they became simply normal sample after the attack sample is altered.

Definition 14 (Poisoning Threat (Thr1)). *If adversarial training is performed for an IDS using an AG for which it cannot be proved that $AG(w, z) \in INA(w)$, then this training procedure is said to poison the IDS training dataset.*

Intuitively this situation would raise the rate of false positive on the IDS side without any action of the attacker. The use of Attack Generator for adversarial training aims at not paying the cost of carrying out the network activity on an actual system to capture observations of this activity. Yet, a workaround of the first threat could be to "execute" the adversarial sample against an actual network. Yet, recall that the number of needed samples remain unclear. Hence, it can lead to unbearable overhead to perform this dataset extension.

Definition 15 (Testing Cost Threat (Thr2)). *An adversarial training process is said to be subject to the testing cost threat if the adversarial attack samples are tested against an actual network to determine whether they remain attacks or not.*

Both threats could be simply disabled using only impactful neighborhood when designing an attack generator for generating an adversarial training dataset.

Let now assume the defender only considers an impactful neighborhood. Hence, the neighborhood of each attack only contains attacks. Now assume that OD, the original dataset available to train the IDS, has a non empty Extended Contradictory set, $EC_{ANA}(OD) \neq \emptyset$. This means that in this dataset, the defender knows a normal sample n and an attack a so that the observation of normal behavior, n, cannot be distinguished from at least a contradictory sample of a. Samples such as the normal sample n that belong to $EC_{ANA}(OD)$ are a weakness in the dataset used to form the IDS.

Definition 16 (Confusing Normal Sample Threat (Thr3)). *An adversarial training dataset AD built from OD and neighborhood ana exhibits the confusing normal sample threat iff $N(AD) \cap EC(ana, OD) \neq \varnothing$*

Even if AT does not contain contradictory sample, it does offer the opportunity for the attacker to exploit the presence of "weak" normal samples that allow more efficient evasion attacks.

Finally the last threat is much more classic, attackers have a better evasion rate on underrepresented classes. Still, one would expect $BEAC$ to be poorly represented (otherwise the detector's performance would be poor and the IDS not deployed). Yet this particular class is even worse because it is a class for which escape is a priori easier.

Definition 17 (Best Evasion Attack Threat). *The* best evasion attack threat *corresponds to the situation where an attacker focuses on applying evasion attacks only for elements of $BEAC_{ANA}(OD)$ for an IDS trained on OD extended through adversarial training relying on neighborhood ANA.*

We now propose different mitigation strategies for these threats either based on fixing the ANA or the adversarial training pipeline.

4.3 Mitigation Strategy

We identified four threats to an efficient usage of adversarial training related to the adversarial neighborhood. Note that the first two threats cannot be mitigated; they represent situations in which adversarial training is either too costly or risky as it may significantly reduce the system's availability. Here are mitigation strategies to deal with the two last threats.

Definition 18 (Sample Removal). *This mitigation strategy consists in removing normal samples from D that belong to $EC(ana, D)$.*

This method is aimed at removing from training set the normal sample that are part of the extended contradictory set. Yet, the IDS might not have the forcefully be trained to output the attack class for such samples. In order to reduce the likelihood of evasion, we can change their label in D instead of removing them.

Definition 19 (Pessimistic Relabelling). *Relabel any normal sample from* $D \cap EC(ana, D)$ *as attacks.*

We now introduce mitigation approaches for the last threat. The selection of attack samples on which the attack generator is applied is called the *attack sampling.* The attack sampling is almost never discussed on the attack side and is assumed to be uniform on defense one. Yet, attackers that restrict themselves to $BEAC(ana, D)$ elements would be less likely to be detected as too few training samples are available to the IDS for these elements or because it use an attack generator that creates an element of $EC(ana, D)$. Our mitigation strategy would be to change the proportion of $BEAC(ana, D)$ elements when sampling $A(D)$ during adversarial training.

Definition 20 (Oversampling of $BEAC$). *This strategy consists in increasing the likelihood of generating* $MAdvs$ *from elements of* $BEAC$.

As the attacker might only apply evasion attack on BEAC set elements, the IDS need to be train in priority on this set. It thus need far more examples in this set because normal and malicious adversarial attack samples generated from this set can be very similar (and even equal if the first mitigation strategies are not applied).

First, the impact of confusing normal samples and best evasion attack candidates related threats need to be assessed on IDSs without mitigation. Secondly, it is also necessary to check to what extent the proposed mitigation approaches actually limit these threats. Next section details the experimentation campaign conducted to assess all these aspects on a dataset for which the ANA concept is defined.

5 Assessment Method and Architecture

This section presents the metrics and experiments used to asses both the threats identified previously and the effects of the proposed mitigation. It recall how GAN can be used as attack generator for a given neighborhood against IDSs. Finally, it details datasets targeted during our experiments.

5.1 Assessment Objectives and Selected Metrics

As said above, we are interested in assessing the impact of non empty extended contradictory set. A first step is to find metrics to capture the performance of evasion attacks and adversarial training. Two basics expected properties of the

IDS need to be measured: to what extent does the IDS detect actual attacks, and to what extent does it designate normal activities as attacks. The "abc" of classifier assessments relies on sets of labelled test samples called test datasets to compute the so called confusion matrix [35]. The confusion matrix indicates for each kind of labels (normal or attack) the output of the IDS on the samples of this kind. In our case, we have a binary classification with "positive" and "negative" classes (positive stands for detected attack, negative stands for detection normal activity). Hence, true positives (TP) are actual attacks that are detected, false negatives (FN) are undetected attacks, true negatives (TN) are normal activities considered as legit activities by the IDS and false positives (FP) are normal activities identified as attacks. Different metrics can be derived from this confusion matrix [35]. The table recalls the main metrics used here based on counts taken from a confusion matrix (TP,TN,FP,FN) and explain how it can use to assess the IDS (Table 1).

Table 1. Basic performance metrics and their description.

Metric Name	Formula	Intuition from risk management point of view
Recall, R	$R = \frac{TP}{TP+FN}$	Ratio of detected attacks, meaningful if all attacks are equivalent
Precision, P	$P = \frac{TP}{TP+FP}$	Ratio of samples signaled as attacks that are actual attacks, useful if detection handling is costly
Accuracy, A	$A = \frac{TP+TN}{TP+TN+FP+FN}$	Ratio of correctly classified samples by the IDS, can be misleading if normal samples are far more present in the test set than attack samples.
F1-score, $F1$	$F1 = \frac{R*P}{R+P}$	Combined assessment of precision and recall. A high value means almost no attack evaded the detection and also almost no false positives among samples classified as attacks

In the reminder, the notation for each metric is extended with the name of the dataset used as a test set, and the IDS it is submitted to when it is not obvious. Assume we compute the confusion matrix for the IDS $ids1$ using the test dataset TD then the recall would be denoted as $R(ids1, TD)$.

Additionally, metrics to assess how the evasion capability of an attack changed after applying an attack generator or IDS are required. Thus, we can compute the expectation ($\mathbb{E}$) of the recall, precision and other metrics on bags of adversarial samples generated through the $Uniform(i, ag, D)$ function.

We define Evasion Increase Rate for an IDS ids_1 and an attack generator ag and a set of attacks D as follows (for non null $R(ids_1, D)$):

$$EIR(ids_1, ag, D) = \mathbb{E}\left(\frac{R(ids_1, D) - R(ids_1, Uniform(1, ag, D))}{R(ids_1, D)}\right)$$

Hence, an EIR very close to 1 means the attack generator ag almost manages to make all attacks undetected by the IDS among those that were originally detected. A negative value means the attack generator makes it worse in terms of evasion, and a null value means it does not change anything in the average case.

The last metric helps to compare two IDSs against attacks generators. We introduce the evasion reduction rate that compares the EIR of two IDSs against two attack generators taking the same initial test dataset. Basically, it is used to see how two IDS work against the same type of evasion attacks.

The *evasion reduction rate (ERR)* compares EIR for the same attack generator but against different IDSs.

$$ERR(ids_2, ids_1, ag_2, ag_1, D) = 1 - \frac{EIR(ids_2, ag_2, D)}{EIR(ids_1, ag_1, D)}$$

Hence, assume ids_2 is a more robust than ids_1 against ag_1, $ERR(ids_2, ids_1, ag_1, ag_1, D)$ is expected to be strictly positive and as close as possible to 1. It is still important to check that the recall of both IDS is similar to avoid false conclusion : a more robust IDS with a significantly lower recall on D is not necessarily better. If the value is negative, it means the second IDS is strictly less robust. Now we need to explain how attack generators are obtained in our experiments and how we do use them to generate test sets and adversarial training datasets.

5.2 Adversarial Dataset Design Using Generative Adversarial Network (GAN)

In this section, we recall how one can obtain an attack generator using Generative Adversarial Networks (GAN). Then, we explain how we use it to generate the collection of adversarial samples used either for testing purpose of an IDS (mimicking an attack), or for adversarial training.

We assume a black-box training strategy for the GAN as it allows us to exploit it on both attacker and defender sides. Such generators are built to specifically target one IDS. The GAN is made of two components: the Generator and the Discriminator. The GAN-based attack generator targets one pre-trained IDS model and repeatedly updates the parameters of its components: the Generator and the Discriminator. We only consider neighborhoods that are subspaces (i.e. identified by a set of features that can be changed). The Generator only modifies the features of the attacks that are part of the selected ANA for the attack generator and generate $MAdvs$. The generator input is made of an attack sample concatenated with a random vector The Generator is trained to evade the detection from the Discriminator component. The Discriminator component concurrently is trained to match as much as possible the behavior of the IDS. This architecture aims at avoiding to have a Generator that cannot be progressively be optimized due to an IDS that is too efficient in terms of detection in the first step of the training.

Each component has its own loss function: Discriminator is penalized when it outputs a different class for a sample than the targeted IDS, and the generator is penalized when it generates adversarial samples that do not evade the Discriminator detection (ie. they are classified as attacks by the Discriminator). Thus, among the key parameters of the Generator and Discriminator, there is the number of update iterations called epochs. We consider GAN trained here either on 20, 100 or 1000 epochs which are typical values when training GAN to attack IDSs. A generator of type *GAN–N* would denote a generator trained in N epochs. As the Generator keeps changing during the training, we only retain the best Generator when tested against the target IDS (and not the Discriminator this time). This point is important to avoid oddities as the optimization process is not guaranteed to be monotonous in terms of performances of the Generator against the IDS.

Let us now detail how the datasets are named and built in our experiments. First, the amount of BEAC samples in a dataset of adversarial samples for a given attack generator depend only on the dataset and the neighborhood considered in the generator definition. As we want to see how this ratio affects training and testing, we will generate datasets of adversarial samples in two steps (assuming the generator is trained). Let q in general denote the desired ratio of desired adversarial samples directly derived from BEAC samples for a dataset D and attack generator ag. For simplicity, we assume q is a fraction (i/p) with i, p two integers.

Then, we define $AdvDataset(N, q, D, ag)$ a set of N samples drawn uniformly from $Uniform((p-i) * \lceil N/p \rceil, ag, A(D)) \cup Uniform(i * \lceil N/p \rceil, ag, A(D))$. This union of bags contains at least N elements, the proportions of adversarial samples derived from BEAC samples is in the average q, and all those samples are adversarial attack samples derived from D.

The adversarial training datsets consist of the union of the dataset OD, that needs to be extended, with a set of adversarial samples. This set is obtained applying *AdvDataset* on OD with a selected generator, a size parameter, and a ratio of BEAC elements (if omitted the ratio is assumed unchanged compared to the proportion of such element in OD). We focus in our experimentation only on adversarial training dataset sizes that are multiples of the size of the dataset they extend. Let *AdvTrainDateset* be the procedure applied to generate these datasets. Its parameters are OD, s, ag, and q such that:

- OD is the dataset to be extended.
- s defines the size of the set of adversarial sample to be added as a multiple of the size of OD (ie. s times the cardinal of the original dataset)
- ag is the attack generator used to produce the adversarial samples

- q is the rate of BEAC elements of OD used as seed to generate the adversarial samples (considering the ANA of ag).

The adversarial training datasets obtained by $AdvTrainDateset$ are built using the generated sample from $AdvDataset$.

We rely for dataset extension of OD using GANs specifically trained to attack IDSs trained on OD as it is. In addition to the above mentioned parameters, we need a parameter to tell the number of epochs during which the generator is trained. Moreover, there could be variability in GAN training performances because the training process rely on sampling uniformly the noise domain to generate adversarial samples. Hence, training the GAN could yield very distinct results. For each vector of parameters, we always train 50 attack generators of the same kind and use each of them to generate the collections of adversarial samples used as test sets. It provides us a mean to capture the average behavior the identified threats and mitigations. It gives us also a mean to determine how stable are our conclusions. Hence, when it is not specifically said the value depicted are the average value over experiments carried out with each of these 50 GANs. For adversarial datasets, we train attack generators as long as needed against an IDS trained on the original dataset so that they achieve an EIR higher than a threshold. If this threshold is not met, the process is fully restarted as it might be the hint that the Discriminator became too good too early. Since IDS training datasets are generally highly vulnerable to adversarial attack samples, we chose a very high threshold (0.99).

In an integrated process, we generate many artifacts given an IDS trained only on non adversarial samples and its training set.

Algorithm 1. *IDS* Adversarial training.

Input: OD (an original dataset), ids (an IDS trained on OD), s (extension size factor), q (rate of added adversarial sample obtained from $BEAC$ samples, ep the number of epochs to be considered (if 0, the threshold is applied);
Output: ag the attack generator targetting ids, at corresponding to $AdvTrainSet(s, ag, q)$, $idsat$ the IDS trained on ad;

procedure ADV-TRAIN(OD, ids, s, q)
  Train a GAN over ep epochs or as long as the threshold is not met if $ep = 0$ against ids. Identify the Generator with the best performances against ids and store it into ag.
  Apply $AdvTrainData(OD, s, ag, q)$ to obtain one adversarial training dataset, let ad be this dataset.
  train an IDS on ad and store it into $idsat$; {A}t the end of this process $idst$ contains the new ids, ag the attack generator use for this, and ad contains the adversarial training dataset.
end procedure

We explained the kind of dataset we need to generate and how we do obtain the related attack generator.

Let us now discuss the "original datasets" on which we focused, and what are theirs possible ANAs, and related BEAC rates. This will give us basic clues about the reality of the situation of a non-empty extended contradictory set.

5.3 Datasets in Use

This section describes the datasets used to evaluate the impact of adversarial neighborhoods on IDSs and attacks and discuss the neighborhood that can be found in the literature for these datasets.

NSL-KDD Dataset. To our knowledge, NSL-KDD is the only dataset that provides a clear definition of the ANA based on the dataset creator criteria (Sect. 3.3). Since it does not cover recent attacks, NSL-KDD is considered an out-of-date dataset. Many papers, however, used it and overlooked the threat identified in Sect. 4.2. Therefore, we assessed NSL-KDD because it provides a clear definition of $ana1$. The NSL-KDD attacks are classified as Denial of Service (DoS), User to Root (U2R), Root to Local (R2L), and Probe. Each record in the NSL-KDD training dataset has 41 features and class identifiers. For NSL-KDD, the concept of $ana1$ is defined by the concept of functional features: the dimension that maintains the attack malicious impact [16]. Hence, the ANA is obtained by changing the non-functional features of an attack class. NSL-KDD features are split into four groups: Intrinsic, Time-based, Content, and Host-based. Not surprisingly, the functional features are different for each attack category:

- DoS attacks: Intrinsic and Time-based
- U2R attacks: Intrinsic and Content
- R2L attacks: Intrinsic and Content
- Probe attacks: Intrinsic, Time-based and Host-based

We concentrate in this work on the normal, DoS, and probe classes because R2L and U2R have few samples. It should be noted that after searching for the BEAC set on the training dataset of NSL-KDD restricted to DoS and Probe attacks. We found that $BEAC(ana1, D)$ contains only DoS samples that represent 3.74% of DoS samples. In this dataset, the samples contain categorical attributes, such as protocol type or flags. As a result, we used the standard pre-processing approach on the dataset samples to obtain fully numerical attributes [17].

CIC-IDS2017 Dataset. As previously indicated, identifying the perfect neighborhood is very challenging. It might not even be unique conversely to NSL-KDD. In order to study this aspect, we selected CIC-IDS2017 [28], a dataset that is a good trade-off between a recent dataset and a mature one (one that is well understood).

CIC-IDS2017 contains fourteen types of attack traffic, including DoS and infiltration, along with normal traffic. Each sample of the dataset consists of more than 80 features. We found different definitions of neighborhood that can be considered as "relevant neighborhoods" for this dataset. It should be noted, however, that all of the neighborhoods defined in this dataset correspond to selecting a subspace of the feature space that can be freely modified. It means that to define these ANAs, we simply need to idetify which features can be freely modified. We identified two different ANAs. The first one is based on statistical criteria [27], while the second is based on expert knowledge [11].

- In [27], the authors of CIC-IDS2017 define *ana*2 by recognizing the most 28 relevant features associated with DoS attacks using the SVD approach. Their approach assume these features should remain as is. Hence, the adversarial neighborhood is provided by modifying all features except the 28 relevant ones.
- [11] follows security expert criteria and define *ana*3. They identified the relevant attack features as the one that cannot be modified by an attacker without losing the malicious impact of these network activities. This analysis results in the identification of 42 relevant features for DoS attacks. *ana*3 is obtained freely modifying the non relevant features again.

As done for the NSL-KDD dataset, we compute the proportion of $BEAC$ elements for each neighborhood. For the first definition of ANA it reachs 9.3% of DoS samples, while the $BEAC$ set in the second definition represents 5.2% of the DoS samples. The pre-processing approach to convert the value of the attributes in this dataset into fully numerical attributes is based on [7].

6 Assessing the Threats on IDS Training Pipeline

This section measures the threat level of identified issues in IDS training pipeline before and after adversarial training. We are especially interested in examining how well IDS performs on the non-empty BEAC set and whether or not this set is problematic for IDS detection performances before even considering adversarial training.

In our experiments, we train IDS on multiple datasets to test adversarial training with and without mitigations. We use the following notation to identify those IDSs: *ids–N–X–an–sr–opt* where *an*, *sr* and *opt* are optional variables.

- N denotes the name of the dataset. Mainly, *nsl* for NSL-KDD and *cic* for CIC-IDS2017.
- X denotes the size of dataset considered for training. (detailed later).

The parameter *an* specifies the type of adversarial neighborhood in use for a dataset. Mainly, *ana*1 for the NSL-KDD neighborhood, while *ana*2 and *ana*3 represent the statistical and expert neighborhoods for CIC-IDS2017, as described in Sect. 5.3. The parameter *sr* specifies the sampling rate used by $BEAC(an, X)$ if applied (not provided if unchanged). The *opt* parameter indicates whether the confusing normal samples are removed (noted as *wn* for without normal) or relabeled as attacks (noted as *na* for normal as an attack).

6.1 Assessment of Detection Performance of IDSs with Adversarial Training

This subsection examines how well regular adversarial training with different adversarial neighborhoods performs without using the proposed mitigation strategies.

NSL-KDD. As previously stated, probe and DoS attacks illustrate two distinct situations. When we compute the NSL-KDD BEAC set, we find that it contains no probe attack samples but only DoS samples. Thus, we train two IDSs, one for Probe and one for DoS attacks, and observe how they behave. The dataset to train the IDS to detect DoS attacks contains normal and DoS samples from the NSL-KDD training dataset noted as od_{DoS}. The second data set, denoted as od_{Pr}, contains normal and Probe samples only from the NSL-KDD training dataset.

We train two batches of 50 GANs, following the architecture of GAN–100 against ids–nsl–od_{Pr} and ids–nsl–od_{DoS}. We observe that evasion attacks reach an average EIR of above 0.99 for ids–nsl–od_{DoS} and is 0 for ids–nsl–od_{Pr}. These results suggest that our claim that the content of the BEAC set is correlated to the success of the evasion based on malicious adversarial samples is likely. Note that the trained IDSs have shown usual performances on non adversarial samples, e.g. as in [34], of ML-based IDSs. Hence, we have a 0.85 recall (ability to detect attacks) for $ids - od_{dos}$ on non adversarial samples. The next step is to understand how efficient is the adversarial training for different size factor parameters. Here, we test an adversarial training for size factors of 2, 5, and 10, leading to extended datasets for $at2$, $at3$, and $at4$. Each dataset is used to train an IDS without certain mitigations of the identified threats.

These IDSs have been tested against strong attack generators of type GAN–1000 to better understand their performances, and results are presented in Fig. 5. We notice that the risk of the adversarial evasion attacks drops significantly from 100% EIR on $ids - nsl - od$ to reach 9% EIR on a very costly IDS in terms of training, which is $ids - nsl - at_4 - ana1$. Adversarial training performs well but at the expense of scaling factors that are 5 or 10 times the size of the original dataset. Training an IDS on 10 times larger datasets, despite a linear effect on the training cost, might not be accepted as the training time also depends on the number of epochs(i.e. for large epochs parameter 10 times larger is perhaps too large). Note that applying adversarial training has not impaired the performance of $IDSs$ when no evasion attack is applied, as shown in the first three lines of Table 5.

CIC-IDS2017. The $ids - cic - od$ is trained to detect CIC-IDS2017 DoS samples and has a recall of 0.94 on non-adversarial samples, consistent with the literature [7]. However, a GAN–20 attack completely evaded IDS detection. We investigated the efficiency of enhanced CIC-IDS2017-based IDSs with adversarial training for a different size factor, namely on $at2$, $at3$, and $at4$, as we did for

IDSs trained on NSL-KDD. We also trained two groups of IDSs on the extended datasets by using two different adversarial neighborhoods *ana*2 and *ana*3 as noted in Sect. 5.3. After testing these two groups of IDSs against an attack generator of type *GAN*−100, the group of IDSs using *ana*2 systematically failed to detect the adversarial samples regardless the size of the adversarial training used. Note the IDSs in the *ana*3 group performed better against this type of attack, as depicted in Fig. 5. This result is consistent with our intuition that the larger is the ANA for adversarial sample generation the harder is the adversarial training and the larger is the BEAC set.

Even if the detection rate on non-adversarial samples is not degraded before and after adversarial training, as shown in the first three rows of table 2, it is clear that adversarial training is less efficient in CIC-IDS2017 than in NSL-KDD.

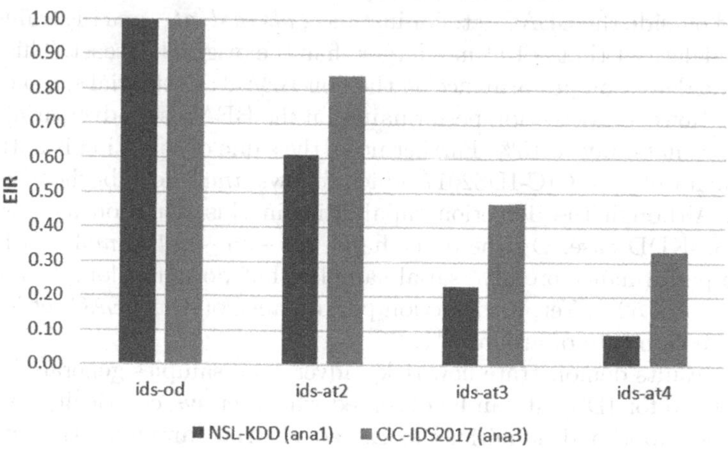

Fig. 5. The average EIR of $ids-at_2$, $ids-at_3$ and $ids-at_4$ for NSL-KDD and CIC-IDS2017.

Table 2. Performance metrics of idss for different adversarial training dataset based on CIC-IDS2017.

IDSs	Precision	Accuracy	F1 Score	Recall
ids−*cic*−*od*	95.3	94.7	94.3	94.0
ids−*cic*−*at*2−*ana*3	95.9	95.4	95.0	94.7
ids−*cic*−*at*4−*ana*3	96.7	96.2	96.0	95.8
ids−*cic*−*od*−*na*	96.9	94.9	96.3	97.7
ids−*cic*−*at*2−*ana*3−25	96.2	95.4	95.5	95.5

6.2 Assessing BEAC Set Threat on IDSs Without Mitigation

We need to determine whether the existence of a non-empty $BEAC$ set is problematic for the IDS detection performance.

IDS reinforced by adversarial training requires at least twice the size of the original dataset to have good detection performance against evasion attacks. This improvement comes at a very high cost in terms of computational training time, as training on larger datasets has a linear effect on the training cost, as illustrated in Fig. 5. However, comparing the detection performance of different sample categories within a dataset, while focusing on the BEAC set adversarial samples, and other adversarial samples, reveals that even the most expensive and robust IDSs are highly vulnerable to the BEAC set samples. Figure 3 depicts this observation on the IDSs trained with the NSL-KDD dataset. We observed a significant difference in detection performance between adversarial samples inside and outside the BEAC set. For instance, $ids\text{–}nsl\text{–}at_4\text{–}ana1$ is trained on an adversarial dataset that is 10 times larger than the original dataset. This IDS has a very good detection performance on the non-BEAC adversarial samples, with a R of 82%. However, detection performance on the BEAC set adversarial samples dropped dramatically to 15%. Furthermore, the same observation is noticed on a different dataset, the CIC-IDS2017 which follows $ana3$ neighborhood as shown in Fig. 4. Although the detection capabilities in this situation are lower than in the NSL-KDD case. On the other hand, $ids-cic-at4-ana3$ still has good detection performance on adversarial samples that do not belong to the BEAC set, with a R of 52%. Yet, its detection performance on the BEAC set is too low, with a detection rate of around 8%.

These results demonstrate how risky adversarial samples generated from the BEAC set are for IDSs. It can be observed whatever systematically considering different neighborhood definitions in the adversarial sampling strategy. Therefore, in the next section, we perform experiments to evaluate the mitigation proposed in Sect. 4.3 to improve the IDS detection against the adversarial sample generated from the BEAC set. The the detection performance on non-adversarial attacks or other evasion attacks that differ from the BEAC set are also assessed to check the overall performance are not impacted.

7 Assessing the Impact of the Mitigation Strategies

We want to evaluate the effectiveness of the proposed mitigation strategies (4.3). In particular, we have to assess the impact of various adversarial training sampling strategies on IDS detection capabilities on adversarial samples.

Table 3. Measurement of adversarial detection rate for BEAC and non-BEAC samples for various IDSs trained and tested on NSL-KDD.

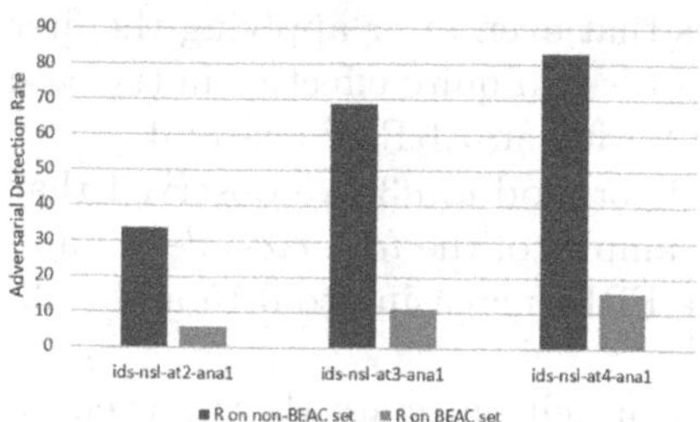

Table 4. Measurement of adversarial detection rate for BEAC and non-BEAC samples various idss trained and tested on CIC-IDS2017 with *ana*3.

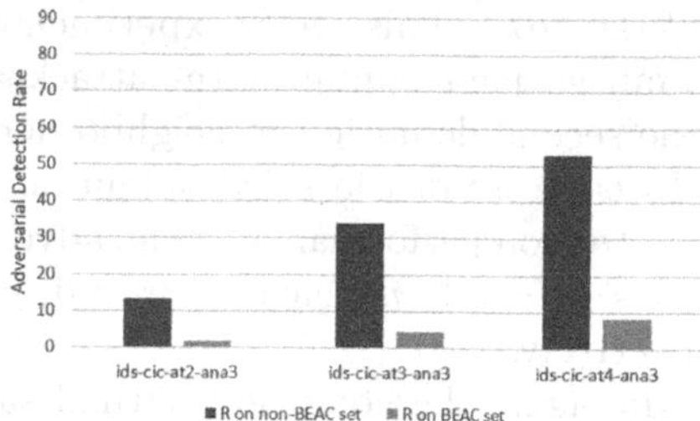

7.1 Confusing Samples Mitigation

This subsection evaluates the impact on performances when applying both regular and robust IDS of sample removal and sample pessimistic relabeling strategies defined in Sect. 4.3.

Effect on Regular IDS Performances. As pointed out, confusing samples can make it harder for the IDS to resist attack generators. We train two IDSs to see how the normal sample threat affects the resilience of regular IDSs. The first is called ($ids-nsl-od-wn$), and was trained on *od* without confusing normal samples using the sample removal mitigation. The second is $ids-nsl-od-na$, and was trained on *od*. We relabeled the confusing normal samples as attacks, as proposed in the sample pessimistic relabelling mitigation.

Table 5. Performance metrics of various ids models trained on NSL-KDD dataset.

IDSs	Precision	Accuracy	F1 score	Recall
$ids-nsl-od$	85.8	86.4	84.4	85.1
$ids-nsl-at2-ana1$	82.4	86.2	84.6	86.9
$ids-nsl-at4-ana1$	88.4	87.6	85.2	82.2
$ids-nsl-od-na$	88.1	87.9	85.7	83.4
$ids-nsl-at2-ana1-25$	87.6	87.3	84.9	82.5

These IDSs are not designed to be resilient to evasion attacks. Thus, we use the weaker attack generator. In the case of NSL-KDD, we primarily use the generator of type GAN–100, and in the case of CIC-IDS2017, we mainly use the generator of type GAN–20. Each attack generator was specifically trained against $ids-od$ and tested on $ids-od-wn$ and $ids-od-na$.

NSL-KDD: We observe in the case of NSL-KDD that the attacks still manage to evade *ids–nsl–od–wn* completely. However, the average ERR for *ids–nsl–od–na* is 0.5 in this case.

CIC-IDS2017: This set of experiments shows that even after applying the first two mitigation techniques, the attack generator is still quite effective in the case of the second definition of neighborhood *ana*2, with an ERR of nearly 0.

In the case of the third definition of neighborhood *ana*3, we observed that the detection performance of the adversarial samples of the *ids–cic–od–wn* and the $ids-cic–od-na$ have improved, with the ERR increasing to 0.15 and 0.12, respectively.

Managing the confusion normal samples can help mitigate threats even on weak IDSs. These findings are encouraging because relabeling is a low-cost adversarial training method. As a result, normal samples related to $EC(od)$ appear to be very useful for adversarial training.

Let now consider adversarial training with these mitigation strategies.

Effect on Robust IDS Performance. We examine the mitigation approaches for confusing samples combined with IDS reinforced by regular adversarial training. We assess the performance using $ids–at_2$, $ids–at_2–wn$, with sample removal mitigation and $ids-at_2-na$ using the sample pessimistic relabeling mitigation. This time, we use 50 *GAN*–1000 for NSL-KDD and *GAN*–100 for CIC-IDS2017 attack generators against each of these idss.

NSL-KDD: The first row in Table 6 summarizes the results of the case of IDSs trained with NSL-KDD. The ERR of the ids without mitigation but with adversarial training on at_2 remains low at 0.39. However, the first mitigation strategy, sample removal, performs significantly better this time. It increased the ERR by almost 50% to 0.57. Surprisingly, the relabelling strategy did not perform as expected, with a slight increase in ERR.

Table 6. ERR of *GAN* attacks on idss trained and tested on NSL-KDD and CIC-IDS2017 with *ana*3.

	ids-at2	ids-at2-wn	ids-at2-na
NSL-KDD (ana1)	0.39	0.57	0.43
CIC-IDS2017 (ana3)	0.16	0.36	0.33

CIC-IDS2017: When the first two mitigations were applied to *ids–cic–at*2*–ana*3, the ERR increased from 0.16 to approximately 0.36 on both IDSs. However, *ids–cic–at*2*–ana*2 appears to be very vulnerable to evasion attacks, with ERR nearly equal to zero on all tested idss.

The first two mitigations manage to close the gap between IDSs trained using adversarial training of scaling factor 2, i.e., 0.39, and scaling factor 5, 0.83 in the case of NSL-KDD by at least 50%. They also strengthen the IDSs' resistance to evasion attacks. However, we found that the larger the ANA space, the less effective the adversarial training, as in the case of $ids{-}cic{-}at2{-}ana2$. This limitation is due to the complexity of the sampling in the high dimensionality of the neighborhood. This issue is beyond the scope of this paper. Moreover, while those two mitigations perform well against evasion attacks, removing a portion of normal samples from the training dataset can impair IDS detection capabilities against regular attacks, especially if this proportion of normal confusion samples is large.

In the next subsections, we examine the effect of the oversampling strategies on the $BEAC$ set elements when generating the adversarial samples. We compare it to adversarial training approaches in which this rate is unchanged.

7.2 Adversarial Training on $BEAC$ Set

In this section, we examine adversarial training datasets formed by controlling the sampling rate of samples from the $BEAC$ set.

This set of experiments compares the effect of the last proposed mitigation to sample removal and sample relabeling. We consider $BEAC$ sampling rates of $\{0.25, 0.50, 0.75\}$. The sr parameter value is used to represent percentages. Therefore, $ids - at2 - 25$ represents an adversarial training on a dataset with a size factor of two and a sampling rate of 0.25. We use GAN–1000 on the NSL-KDD neighborhood and GAN–100 on the CIC-IDS2017 that follows $ana3$ neighborhood against idss trained with an adversarial training set of size factor of 2, e.g., $ids - at_2 - j$ family.

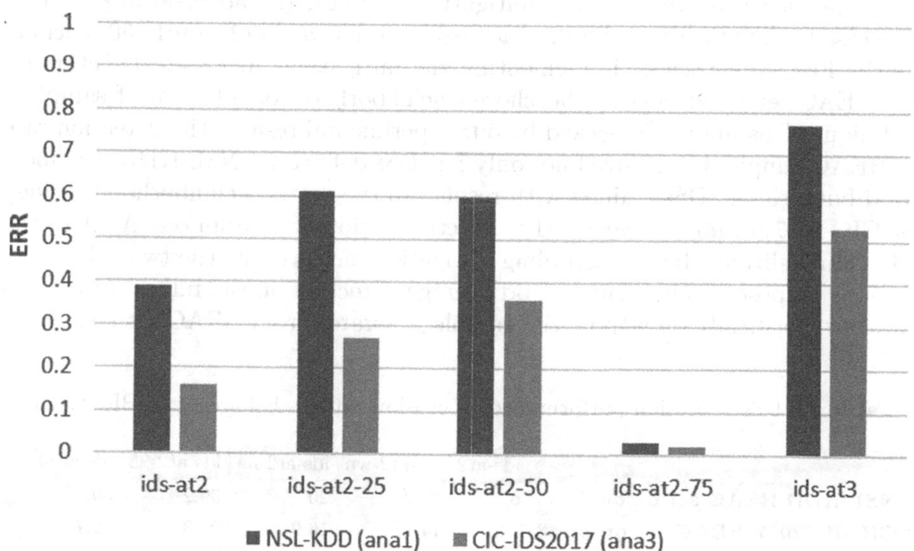

Fig. 6. Average ERR on 50 GAN against $ids - at_2 - j$ for various j trained and tested with NSL-KDD and CIC-IDS2017 with $ana3$.

The results of the experiments on idss trained on NSL-KDD and CIC-IDS2017 with *ana*3 are shown in Fig. 6. The results reveal that adversarial evasion attacks are much less effective in most of these idss than $ids-at_2$ but significantly more effective in $ids-at_2-75$. However, this situation is expected because a high sampling rate prevents the IDS from correctly detecting evasion attacks applied to attacks in $A(D) - BEAC(D)$. A sample rate of 25% to 50% seems similar for the NSL-KDD neighborhood, while the latter seems slightly better for CIC-IDS2017.

Furthermore, using oversampling of $BEAC$ mitigation narrows the margin with $ids-at_3$ in both neighborhoods by nearly dividing the difference in ERR by two.

7.3 Assessing the Effect of the Mitigations on BEAC Set

Section 6.2 demonstrated that IDSs are sensitive to evasion attacks from the BEAC set, even after adversarial training has increased overall detection performance on the whole population within the tested dataset.

Table 7 shows that the detection performance of IDS is improved drastically on evasion attacks that specifically belong to BEAC set after applying the proposed mitigations. For instance, in the case of IDSs that follow the NSL-KDD neighborhood, the results show that using the first two mitigations increase detection on BEAC by approximately 3 times compared to regular adversarial training, as the adversarial detection rate increases from 6% on *ids–nsl–at*2*–ana*1 to nearly 20% on *ids–nsl–at*2*–ana*1*–wn* and *ids–nsl–at*2*–ana*1*–na*. However, after applying the oversampling mitigation strategy, the adversarial detection rate rose by 5, with *ids–nsl–at*2*–ana*1–25 and *ids–nsl–at*2*–ana*1–50 reaching nearly 40%. Nonetheless, implementing the mitigations increases detection on the BEAC set regardless of the chosen neighborhood or adversarial sampling technique. This finding is backed by our experimental results: the detection rate on BEAC samples is improved not only for IDSs defined for NSL-KDD neighborhood but also for IDSs trained with respect to the second neighborhood defined for CIC-2017 (*ana*3). However, the detection ratio differs from one ANA to the other. In addition, the oversampling mitigation outperforms the two other mitigations proposed as it ensures good average detection on the full set of attacks but also specifically on adversarial sample generated from BEAC set elements.

Table 7. IDSs detection performance on evasion attacks belonging to BEAC set.

	ids-at2	ids-at2-wn	ids-at2-na	ids-at2-25	ids-at2-50
NSL-KDD BEAC set on *ana*1	6	20.2	20	39.2	39.5
CIC-IDS2017 BEAC set on *ana*3	1.9	14.1	16.9	26.3	32.7

8 Related Work

[8] proposes criteria for better dataset sampling strategies and the use of diversification approaches to improve the training of generic classifiers. However, they do not take into account the particularity of IDS as a security classifier or even the specificity of adversarial samples. With the recent advances in Machine Learning research, adversarial attacks have piqued the interest of researchers in a wide variety of domains. Several studies have focused on the sampling strategy of $MAdv$s in order to achieve a reasonable balance between IDS training performance and detection capabilities against adversarial evasion attacks.

In [3,29] and [19] generated $MAdv$s by applying the mutation on the entire set of features on the CIC-IDS2017 attack samples. While in [12], they generated $MAdv$s from NSL-KDD attack classes using two methods, either by mutating all the dimensions of attack samples or by mutating the 16 principal components obtained with Principal Component Analysis (PCA) as a dimensionality reduction technique. Other works follow the same methodology in generating adversarial samples, such as in [37] and in [1]. In all these works, there is no limit to the $MAdv$ sampling subspace because the adversarial generator is applied to the entire set of features in the feature space. However, not defining the adversarial neighborhood of the $MAdv$s can increase the likelihood of generating a $MAdv$ that successfully avoids IDS detection. But, the impact of those $MAdv$s on the actual systems is not assured because there are no constraints on the adversarial generator; thus the preservation of attack behaviors is not assured after the mutation process.

To the best of our knowledge, all approaches for the NSL-KDD dataset that take ANA into account define attributes that divide attack samples as functional or non-functional features based on the categorization given by [16]. Hence, the subspace of producing $MAdv$s is bounded by adjusting only the non-functional features of any attack class while preserving attack behavior by leaving the functional features unchanged, as in [17,38] and [32]. However, choosing the adversarial neighborhood for $MAdv$s generation is a very challenging task in any constrained domain, specifically in the network security domain. Furthermore, selecting ANA is critical for defining any adversarial sampling strategy because the subspace of sampling $MAdv$s depends on the selected adversarial neighborhood. This difficulty of defining ANA is reflected in the literature as many papers define different approximations of ANA even for the same attack class in the same dataset, as in CIC-IDS2017.

To our knowledge, the choice of ANA is typically performed through statistical criteria or throughout a domain expert analysis. According to [28], the authors use RandomForestRegressor to determine the optimal short feature set for each attack, which can then be used to detect those attacks. [20] and [36] use the [28] method to define ANA in order to craft $MAdv$s with GAN attacks generator. [27] defines ANA as a dimensional reduction technique based on singular value decomposition (SVD), which can provide insights into the relationship of the selected features after dimension reduction. The SVD can then be used to determine the most significant features for the adversarial neighborhood from the given feature set. [6] the authors rely on the Shapley Additive Explanations (SHAP) to identify ANA that preserves the attack's functionality during the adversarial sampling. Other works rely on other statistical criteria, such as in [2] and in [33]. Nevertheless, using statistical approaches to explore the adversarial neighborhood can suffer from problems, such as the disagreement problem [15], in which different statistical criteria end up selecting different functional features for the same type of attack inside the same dataset.

[11] offers systematic expert analysis to develop effective and efficient adversarial samples on the CIC-IDS2017. In their work, they proposed the idea of categorizing the features of this dataset into four groups, i.e., grouping flows based on whether they can be modified by an adversary and still yield correct flows. [31] relies on [11] work to present their own definition of ANA. While in [39], the authors introduce a MACGAN framework that is divided into two parts. In order to examine ANA, the initial part of MACGAN is used to analyze the attack based on the author's expertise. Then, in the second part, they use a GAN attack generator to bypass the IDS.

In this paper, we examine the quality of the extended dataset after $MAdv$s mutations. In addition, this paper aims to examine the threats linked to the generation process used in adversarial training. Furthermore, we propose a new strategy to improve the IDS performance of adversarial training by changing adversarial sampling strategies to account for confusing samples and $BEAC$ samples in two datasets, the NSL-KDD, and the CIC-IDS2017.

9 Conclusions

This paper examines how different adversarial sample generation approaches affect the quality of adversarial evasion attack samples. In particular, this paper focuses on how the newly generated samples can affect IDS' robustness performance and the quality of IDS's training pipeline. We revisited previous work on well-understood models and datasets. This assessment aids in defining the notion of adversarial neighborhood of an evasion attack sample (ANA), which helps to identify and formalize threats to the robustness of IDSs against adversarial evasion attacks. These threats are enabled by flaws in the structure and content of the dataset rather than its representativeness. We have demonstrated that even the most robust intrusion detection systems are vulnerable and perform poorly against a specific set of evasion adversarial attacks, the best evasion attack candidates samples (BEAC). In addition, we have developed a method to improve adversarial training performance by making it to focus on the BEAC set in the dataset. We found that this technique increases the detection of BEAC samples and the detection of IDS on all adversarial evasion attacks, regardless of the ANA used to generate the adversarial samples.

However, while the proposed mitigations improve the efficacy of adversarial training, this strategy has a limit. This drawback comes from the complexity of covering the full dimensions in the feature space when producing efficient adversarial samples (e.g., the limitation is severe when the dimensions of ANA are very close to the full dimensions in the feature space).

In future work, we will investigate the adversarial neighborhood of attacks in the problem space domain to determine how to overcome this limitation on proposed mitigations in the feature space domain [23].

Acknowledgements. This research is part of the chair CyberCNI.fr with support of the FEDER development fund of the Brittany region.

References

1. Alahmed, S., Alasad, Q., Hammood, M.M., Yuan, J.S., Alawad, M.: Mitigation of black-box attacks on intrusion detection systems-based ml. Computers **11**(7), 115 (2022)
2. Alhajjar, E., Maxwell, P., Bastian, N.: Adversarial machine learning in network intrusion detection systems. Expert Syst. Appl. **186**, 115782 (2021)
3. Ayub, M.A., Johnson, W.A., Talbert, D.A., Siraj, A.: Model evasion attack on intrusion detection systems using adversarial machine learning. In: 2020 54th Annual Conference on Information Sciences and Systems (CISS) (2020)
4. Backes, M., Manoharan, P., Grosse, K., Papernot, N.: Adversarial perturbations against deep neural networks for malware classification. CoRR (2016)
5. Chaitou., H., Robert., T., Leneutre., J., Pautet., L.: Threats to adversarial training for idss and mitigation. In: Proceedings of the 19th International Conference on Security and Cryptography - SECRYPT, pp. 226–236. INSTICC, SciTePress (2022)
6. Chauhan, R., Shah Heydari, S.: Polymorphic adversarial ddos attack on ids using gan. In: 2020 International Symposium on Networks, Computers and Communications (ISNCC) (2020)
7. Faker, O., Dogdu, E.: Intrusion detection using big data and deep learning techniques. In: Proceedings of the 2019 ACM Southeast Conference, SE 2019. ACM, Association for Computing Machinery (2019)
8. Gong, Z., Zhong, P., Hu, W.: Diversity in machine learning. IEEE Access **7**, 64323–64350 (2019)
9. Goodfellow, I., et al.: Generative adversarial nets. In: NIPS (2014)
10. Goodfellow, I.J., Shlens, J., Szegedy, C.: Explaining and harnessing adversarial examples (2015)
11. Hashemi, M.J., Cusack, G., Keller, E.: Towards evaluation of nidss in adversarial setting. In: Proceedings of the 3rd ACM CoNEXT Workshop on Big DAta, Machine Learning and Artificial Intelligence for Data Communication Networks, Big-DAMA 2019. Association for Computing Machinery (2019)
12. Khamis, R.A., Shafiq, M.O., Matrawy, A.: Investigating resistance of deep learning-based ids against adversaries using min-max optimization. In: ICC (2020)
13. Khraisat, A., Gondal, I., Vamplew, P., Kamruzzaman, J.: Survey of intrusion detection systems: techniques, datasets and challenges. Cybersecurity **2**, 1–22 (2019)
14. Klema, V., Laub, A.: The singular value decomposition: its computation and some applications. IEEE Trans. Autom. Control **25**(2), 164–176 (1980)
15. Krishna, S., et al.: The disagreement problem in explainable machine learning: a practitioner's perspective. arXiv preprint arXiv:2202.01602 (2022)
16. Lee, W., Stolfo, S.J.: A framework for constructing features and models for intrusion detection systems. ACM TISSEC **3**, 227–261 (2000)

17. Lin, Z., Shi, Y., Xue, Z.: IDSGAN: generative adversarial networks for attack generation against intrusion detection. arXiv e-prints (2018)
18. Lundberg, S.M., Lee, S.I.: A unified approach to interpreting model predictions. In: Proceedings of the 31st International Conference on Neural Information Processing Systems. Curran Associates Inc. (2017)
19. Martins, N., Cruz, J.M., Cruz, T., Abreu, P.H.: Analyzing the footprint of classifiers in adversarial denial of service contexts. In: Moura Oliveira, P., Novais, P., Reis, L.P. (eds.) EPIA 2019. LNCS (LNAI), vol. 11805, pp. 256–267. Springer, Cham (2019). https://doi.org/10.1007/978-3-030-30244-3_22
20. Msika, S., Quintero, A., Khomh, F.: Sigma: strengthening ids with gan and metaheuristics attacks (2019)
21. Papernot, N., Mcdaniel, P., Goodfellow, I.J., Jha, S., Celik, Z.B., Swami, A.: Practical black-box attacks against machine learning. In: ACM ASIACCS (2017)
22. Picot, M., Messina, F., Boudiaf, M., Labeau, F., Ayed, I.B., Piantanida, P.: Adversarial robustness via fisher-rao regularization. ArXiv (2021)
23. Pierazzi, F., Pendlebury, F., Cortellazzi, J., Cavallaro, L.: Intriguing properties of adversarial ml attacks in the problem space. In: 2020 IEEE Symposium on Security and Privacy (SP) (2020)
24. Qiu, S., Liu, Q., Zhou, S., Wu, C.: Review of artificial intelligence adversarial attack and defense technologies. Appl. Sci. **9**, 909 (2019)
25. Ren, K., Zheng, T., Qin, Z., Liu, X.: Adversarial attacks and defenses in deep learning. Engineering **6**, 346–360 (2020)
26. Ribeiro, M.T., Singh, S., Guestrin, C.: "why should i trust you?": explaining the predictions of any classifier. In: Proceedings of the 22nd ACM SIGKDD International Conference on Knowledge Discovery and Data Mining, KDD 2016. Association for Computing Machinery (2016)
27. Sharafaldin, I., Habibi Lashkari, A., Ghorbani, A.A.: A detailed analysis of the CICIDS2017 data set. In: Mori, P., Furnell, S., Camp, O. (eds.) ICISSP 2018. CCIS, vol. 977, pp. 172–188. Springer, Cham (2019). https://doi.org/10.1007/978-3-030-25109-3_9
28. Sharafaldin, I., Lashkari, A.H., Ghorbani, A.A.: Toward generating a new intrusion detection dataset and intrusion traffic characterization. In: ICISSP (2018)
29. Shu, D., Leslie, N.O., Kamhoua, C.A., Tucker, C.S.: Generative adversarial attacks against intrusion detection systems using active learning. In: Proceedings of the 2nd ACM Workshop on Wireless Security and Machine Learning, WiseML 2020. Association for Computing Machinery, New York (2020)
30. Szegedy, C., et al.: Intriguing properties of neural networks. In: ICLR (2014)
31. Teuffenbach, M., Piatkowska, E., Smith, P.: Subverting network intrusion detection: crafting adversarial examples accounting for domain-specific constraints. In: Holzinger, A., Kieseberg, P., Tjoa, A.M., Weippl, E. (eds.) CD-MAKE 2020. LNCS, vol. 12279, pp. 301–320. Springer, Cham (2020). https://doi.org/10.1007/978-3-030-57321-8_17
32. Usama, M., Asim, M., Latif, S., Qadir, J.: Generative adversarial networks for launching and thwarting adversarial attacks on network intrusion detection systems. In: IWCMC (2019)
33. Usama, M., Qayyum, A., Qadir, J., Al-Fuqaha, A.: Black-box adversarial machine learning attack on network traffic classification. In: 2019 15th International Wireless Communications & Mobile Computing Conference (IWCMC) (2019)
34. Vinayakumar, R., Alazab, M., Soman, K.P., Poornachandran, P., Al-Nemrat, A., Venkatraman, S.: Deep learning approach for intelligent intrusion detection system. IEEE Access **7**, 41525–41550 (2019)

35. Wang, Z.: Deep learning-based intrusion detection with adversaries. IEEE Access **6**, 38367–38384 (2018)
36. Qui, C.P.X., Quang, D.H., Duy, P.T., Hien, D.T.T., Pham, V.H.: Strengthening ids against evasion attacks with gan-based adversarial samples in sdn-enabled network. In: 2021 RIVF International Conference on Computing and Communication Technologies (RIVF) (2021)
37. Yang, K., Liu, J., Zhang, C., Fang, Y.: Adversarial examples against the deep learning based network intrusion detection systems. In: MILCOM 2018–2018 IEEE Military Communications Conference (MILCOM) (2018)
38. Zhao, S., Li, J., Wang, J., Zhang, Z., Zhu, L., Zhang, Y.: attackgan: adversarial attack against black-box ids using generative adversarial network. Procedia Comput. Sci. **187**, 128–133 (2021)
39. Zhong, Y., Zhu, Y., Wang, Z., Yin, X., Shi, X., Li, K.: An adversarial learning model for intrusion detection in real complex network environments. In: Yu, D., Dressler, F., Yu, J. (eds.) WASA 2020. LNCS, vol. 12384, pp. 794–806. Springer, Cham (2020). https://doi.org/10.1007/978-3-030-59016-1_65

Compressing Big OLAP Data Cubes in Big Data Analytics Systems: New Paradigms, a Reference Architecture, and Future Research Perspectives

Alfredo Cuzzocrea[1,2(✉)]

[1] iDEA Lab, University of Calabria, Rende, Italy
alfredo.cuzzocrea@unical.it
[2] Department of Computer Science, University of Paris City, Paris, France

Abstract. In the current *big data* era, *big data analytics systems* play a leading role due to their popularity in a wide collection of application scenarios, ranging from healthcare systems to e-science platforms, from social networks to smart cities, from intelligent transportation systems to graph analysis tools, and so forth. Among various proposals, *multidimensional big data analytics methodologies*, which basically are based on well-understood OLAP paradigms, are gaining the momentum due to their flexibility and expressiveness power. In this so-delineated scenario, *performance issues* clearly represent a significant obstacle to the effective impact of these methodologies in real-life settings. *Data compression techniques* indeed represent successful approaches to face-off performance drawbacks in big multidimensional data analytics systems. According to this main concept, the idea of *compressing big OLAP data cubes* is a natural proposal arising in this field. Inspired by this main framework, in this talk we focus the attention on the issue of effectively and efficiently supporting big OLAP data cube compression in modern big data analytics systems. In particular, we first report on some recent proposals in this field, and then introduce some effective and efficient approaches we proposed in the context of the investigated research area, tailored to well-known big data requirements. Future research perspectives are presented and discussed as well.

Keywords: Big data · Big data management · Big data analytics · Big multidimensional data analytics · OLAP · Big OLAP data cubes · Compression techniques for big OLAP data cubes · Big data analytics systems

A. Cuzzocrea—This research has been made in the context of the Excellence Chair in Big Data Management and Analytics at University of Paris City, Paris, France.

M. Van Sinderen et al. (Eds.): ICSBT/SECRYPT 2022, CCIS 1849, pp. 156–175, 2023.
https://doi.org/10.1007/978-3-031-45137-9_7

1 Introduction

OnLine Analytical Processing (OLAP) and *Business Intelligence* (BI) have conquered the scene of decision-making systems research for decades (e.g., [8,36]), thus defining a wide collection of models, techniques and algorithms whose main goal is that of effectively and efficiently *representing, querying and mining massive OLAP data cubes*. With the advent of the modern *Big Data* era (e.g., [23,28,53]), *Big OLAP Data Cubes* arise (e.g., [26,31,50]), thus posing novel challenges to be faced-off by the research community. Big OLAP Data Cubes are mainly processed over *Clouds*, due to tight high-performance computing requirements, thus opening the door to a large number of big data processing platforms, from both the academic and industrial world.

Coupled with the problem of big OLAP data cubes, the new research line falling under the term "*Multidimensional Big Data Analytics*" appeared (e.g., [6,17–19]), with an important impact over the research community. Basically, this novel paradigm purses the goal of engrafting the multidimensional analysis in the whole big data analytics process, as to magnify the expressive power and the retrieved accuracy in the (final) decision-making process.

As regards relevant research aspects related to this research, among several ones, one relevant is represented by *scalability issues*. Indeed, when applied to large big datasets, multidimensional big data analytics procedures terribly slow-down their execution performance, thus resulting in a real bottleneck for real-life applications and systems.

Following this main research challenge, recently a plethora of research proposals appeared in literature. This initiative founds its roots in decades of research in *database representation and query optimization* (e.g., [41]). In this area, many approaches have been proposed across years. In this paper, we specially focus on *data compression paradigms* (e.g., [16]), which has animated and is continuing to do so the database research community first and, again, the big data research community at now.

In the so-delineated context, the main research challenges again consist of the following issues: *(i)* effectively and efficiently representing Big OLAP Data Cubes over Cloud architectures; *(ii)* effectively and efficiently querying Big OLAP Data Cubes over Cloud architectures; *(iii)* effectively and efficiently mining Big OLAP Data Cubes over Cloud architectures. This paper will discuss these issues, provide overview on state-of-the-art proposals, and illustrate future research directions in this scientific context. In addition to this, a reference Cloud-based architecture is presented.

The paper is organized as follows. In Sect. 2, we focus the attention on traditional OLAP and BI Systems. Section 3 introduces the innovative *multidimensional big data analytics* metaphor. In Sect. 4, we report on a comprehensive related work analysis on both OLAP data and big data compression. In Sect. 5, a reference architecture for big OLAP data cubes over Clouds is described. As to integrate this architecture, Sect. 5 also provides solutions for supporting big OLAP data cube compression over Clouds. Section 6 contains future research directions in the investigated research field. Finally, in Sect. 7 we report conclusions and future work.

2 Traditional OLAP and BI Systems

OLAP and BI systems are technologies developed on top of the so-called *multidimensional model* [36]. *Multidimensional analysis* (e.g., [8]) is a paradigm that allows the development of very effective and easy-to-use systems. The underlying model introduces the concept of *multidimensional space* that founds on the concepts of *measures* (attributes of interest for the analysis) and *dimensions* (functional attributes on the basis of which the measures are accessed and explored). Based on the derived data multidimensional structures, OLAP and BI systems define a rich set of queries and operators capable of supporting a large number of perspectives of analysis, such as *range queries* (e.g., [40]), *top-k queries*, (e.g., [47]), *iceberg queries* (e.g., [39]), and so forth.

The multidimensional analysis model was initially born for relational data but, over the years, it has been extended to other types of data, including text, web, graph data, etc. This has originated a plethora of state-of-the-art applications.

In traditional OLAP and BI systems, the most challenging research problems can be identified in *scalability issues* (e.g., [10,29]). Summarizing, when large-scale *OLAP Data Cubes* are processed, query answering algorithms fail in keeping high-quality performance, thus conveying in relevant computational overheads. In order to deal with these challenges, one of the main research lines developed across years is represented by *data compression paradigms* (e.g., [25,30]). According to this general paradigm, OLAP data cubes are compressed, based on a given metrics such as space occupancy bound, so that the necessary time due to evaluating queries over the compressed representations is significantly reduced.

3 Multidimensional Big Data Analytics

Multidimensional big data analytics (e.g., [6,17–19]) is an emerging paradigm whose main goal is that of coupling multidimensional models with the main *Big Data Analytics Process*. The idea is *not* applying big data analytics over multidimensional data cubes, but *rather* embedding the multidimensional model directly into the big data analytics process itself.

Basically, dimensions and measures concepts must be directly embedded into the fundamental algorithms supporting big data analytics, in a native manner. For instance, dimensional attributes can be processed with *Machine Learning procedures* over Clouds, like in *MS Azure*, while measures can be processed with naïve *aggregation algorithms* specifically developed for big data (e.g., [60]). As a while, the multidimensional nature turns to the embedded into the native algorithms themselves, by discarding the solution of applying traditional algorithms for big data analytics, perhaps inspired by classical *Data Mining* and

Machine Learning libraries, over multidimensional data structures (like OLAP data cubes) directly.

This analytical paradigm superimposes a *shift* in the fundamental big data processing algorithms, with a specific orientation to high-volume big data repositories. On the other hand, conceptually, multidimensional analysis fits very well with big data analytics systems since the fundamental operator for the calculation of aggregates, i.e. *scanning* (e.g., [34]), is implemented *natively* in numerous platforms of big data analytics, also in the open source context (e.g., *Apache Spark*). Therefore, the multidimensional-paradigm/ big-data-analytics marriage is a perfect marriage to build powerful, flexible and scalable big data analytics systems. Last but not least, the model is perfect for a wide family of big data applications scenarios, ranging from smart cities to social network analysis, from bio-informatics to *e*-government, and so forth.

4 Related Work Analysis

Two main research areas are relevant to our research: (*i*) *OLAP data compression*, and (*ii*) *big data compression*. In the following, we provide a comprehensive overview on proposals falling in these areas, and that are relevant to our research.

4.1 OLAP Data Compression

The challenge of viewing multidimensional data cubes is examined in [27], in which a novel method for enabling sophisticated *OLAP visualization* of these data structures is presented. The proposed technique is based on the capability of producing "semantics-aware" compressed representations of *two-dimensional OLAP views* extracted from multidimensional data cubes via the so-called *OLAP dimension flattening process*. It is founded on very effective data compression solutions for two-dimensional data domains. Numerous experimental findings on various types of synthetic two-dimensional OLAP views clearly demonstrate the usefulness and efficiency of this method, even when compared to cutting-edge ideas.

An interesting strategy for providing approximate aggregate query responding in OLAP is presented in [12], which represents the most frequent application interfaces for a *Data Warehouse Server* (DWS), that is based on an analytical interpretation of multidimensional data and the well-known *least squares approximation* (LSA) method. Due to the extremely huge amount of multidimensional data contained in the underlying DWS, inefficient query response is the primary downside of *Decision Support Systems* (DSS). The most common and effective types of queries for these systems are aggregate ones since they enable a variety of analysis depending on the *multidimensionality* and *multi-resolution* of the data. As a result, offering quick responses to aggregate queries, if feasible, sacrificing accuracy for efficiency has emerged as a crucial criterion for enhancing the efficacy of DSS-based systems. The method proposed in [12] entails creating data synopses by interpreting the original data distributions as a set of discrete functions. These synopses, referred to as "$\Delta - Syn$", are created by approximating data with a set of *polynomial coefficients* and storing these coefficients in place of the original data. The number of disk accesses required to process the replies is decreased since queries are delivered on the compressed form.

An essential method for *assessing* and *forecasting* data with categorical variables is *logistic regression.* [58] explore the possibility of enabling online analytical processing (OLAP) of logistic regression analysis for multidimensional data in a data cube where it is expensive in terms of time and space to develop *logistic regression models* for each cell from the raw data. This study provide a unique data compression method that allows us to recreate logistic regression models to respond to any OLAP query without having to access the raw data. Therefore, is proposed a compression strategy based on a *first-order approximation* to the maximum likelihood estimating equations that condenses each base cell into a compact data block with all the information required to allow the aggregation of logistic regression models. There are presented aggregation equations for higher level logistic regression models to be derived from lower level component cells. By showing that the aggregate estimator deviates from the genuine model by a finite error that approaches zero as data size grows, it demonstrate that the compression is almost lossless. The findings demonstrate that OLAP of logistic regression in a data cube is doable using the suggested compression and aggregation approach. Additionally, it allows for the *real-time* logistic regression analysis of *stream data*, which is only capable of being scanned once and is not capable of being permanently stored. Experimental findings support these theoretical analysis and show how this technique may significantly reduce time and space expenses while maintaining a high level of modeling accuracy.

The primary shortcomings of mobile devices (limited storage, a tiny display screen, loss of WLAN connection, etc.) frequently conflict with the requirement of searching and browsing information collected from vast volumes of data that are available over the network. Data *summarizing* and *compression* play a major part in this application scenario since loss compressed data may be transferred more effectively than uncompressed data and stored effectively in portable devices (by adjusting the compression ratio). The system *Hand-OLAP* uses this technique to enable handheld devices to extract and browse compressed two-dimensional OLAP views derived from multidimensional data cubes stored on a remote OLAP server located on the wired network. [21], introduce a very effective multidimensional data cube compression technique. By utilizing the "naturally" *decentralized character* of such contexts, *Hand-OLAP* effectively and efficiently allows OLAP in mobile environments and also expands the potentialities of *Decision Support Systems.* The foundation of the system is the hypothesis that it may be more practical to generate a compressed OLAP view of the original multidimensional data cubes, store this view in the handheld device, and query it locally (offline), resulting in approximations that are suitable for OLAP applications.

In [14], a *brand-new top-down* compression method for data cubes is described and experimentally evaluated. This method takes into account the hitherto overlooked scenario in which numerous *Hierarchical Range Searches*

(HRQ), a particularly helpful class of OLAP searches, must be assessed simultaneously against the target data cube. Due to the fact that typical data cube compression methods only take into account one limitation (for example, a certain storage space bound), they are unsuccessful in this circumstance. The study's output entails the introduction of a novel *multiple-objective OLAP computational* paradigm and a *hierarchical multidimensional histogram*, the latter of which has the main advantage of effectively implementing an intermediate compression of the input data cube that can simultaneously accommodate a sizable family of HRQ that are distinct from one another in nature. A supplementary aspect of this study is a thorough experimental assessment of the performance of this method against benchmark and actual data cubes, as well as a comparison to cutting-edge histogram-based compression methods.

In [20], authors present and experimentally evaluates ECM-DS, a novel event-based *lossy compression paradigm* for effective and efficient OLAP over *data streams*. By utilizing the semantics of the reference application scenario to control the compression process by the "*degree of interestingness*" of events occurring in the target stream, the approach to compression approach differs significantly from conventional data stream compression techniques. In turn, this enhances the quality of complicated knowledge discovery tasks over data streams created on top of ECM-DS and implemented using ad-hoc *data stream mining* algorithms. This increases the quality of the approximate answers to OLAP queries over data streams that are finally obtained. Overall, the compression strategy we suggest in this research establishes the framework for a novel class of *intelligent applications* over data streams in which the knowledge about actual streams is integrated with and correlated to the knowledge about expired events that are considered crucial for the target OLAP analysis scenario. Last but not least, a thorough experimental evaluation across a number of kinds of data stream sets unequivocally demonstrates the advantages of the *event-based* data stream compression approach suggested in ECM-DS.

In [22], authors describe a novel OLAP *data cube compression strategy* that maintains the crucial innovation of depending on *R-tree* based partitions instead of more restrictive traditional sorts of partition, this research extends a *quad-tree* based *multi-resolution* approach for *two-dimensional* summary data. This significant innovation offers the useful advantages of (*i*) enabling end users to exploit the *semantics of data* and (*ii*) obtaining compressed representations of data cubes where more space can be invested to describe those ranges of multidimensional data for which they retain a higher level of interest. As a result, this paper represents a significant improvement over current methods. Experimental findings support the advantages of suggested strategy.

Authors in [44] describe performance of the main memory, especially in light of the so-called *memory wall*, is becoming a more crucial component of overall system performance. The *Hybrid Memory Cube* (HMC), which stacks DRAM on top of a logic die and connects them with dense, quick through silicon vias (TSVs), aims to break through this memory wall. The Hybrid Memory Cube exhibits a natural temperature range, with the warmest layers at the bottom and the coolest layers at the top, according to modeling done in *HotSpot*. Reduced performance and efficiency might be the result of high temperatures and temperature fluctuations inside a DRAM, especially when *Dynamic Thermal Management* (DTM) techniques are employed to cut DRAM bandwidth whenever temperature rises too high. The goal of this research is to use *data compression* to lower the maximum temperature and variation. The compression is carried out in the *on-chip memory controller*, and the compressed blocks are read/written in the hybrid memory cube using fewer bursts, which reduces power consumption. To lessen the heat gradient in the cube, the compressed blocks are only kept in the hotter banks. The HMC spent less time throttling when DTM schemes were utilized, resulting in a maximum speed gain of 14.2%, at an average of 2.8%, and a maximum temperature reduction of up to 6 °C.

[54] contains unique research on parallel and distributed computation of *low-rank* decomposition for huge tensors, a brief introduction to *Hadoop*, and a tutorial on *state-of-the-art* tensor decomposition as it applies to *big data analytics MapReduce*. It is suggested to use a unique architecture for the distributed and parallel computing of low-rank tensor decomposition, which is particularly well suited for large tensors. The new architecture is based on the concurrent processing of a collection of huge tensor replicas that have been randomly compressed and shrunk in size. Following independent decomposition of each duplicate, the results are combined using a *master linear equation* for each tensor mode. If the big tensor is of low rank and the system parameters are properly selected, then the rank-one elements of the big tensor will actually be recovered from the analysis of the *reduced-size* replicas. This method permits huge *parallelism* with guaranteed *identifiability* qualities. Additionally, the architecture provides memory/storage and *order-of-magnitude* complexity gains for a large tensor of rank F with the tensor and underlying latent factors do not need to be sparse, but they can be used to their advantage to increase memory, storage, and computational savings.

In [7], authors outline a method for effectively compressing *XML OLAP* cubes. They suggest a multidimensional snowflake cube schema as the fundamental physical arrangement. One XML fact document plus as many XML documents as there are members of the dimension hierarchy make up the cube at that point. In order to increase both query response time and compression ratio, the fundamental setup is purposefully rebuilt into two different methods by adding data redundancy. The cube's documents are combined into one XML document in the second configuration. In the third configuration, the entire XML referenced fragments are used in place of each reference between a fact and its dimensions or between its members. Authors use a novel compression method called *XCC* on the cube's three physical configurations. Both before and after compression, they illustrate how effective the third setup is. They also demonstrate how effective their compression method is when used with XML OLAP cubes.

4.2 Big Data Compression

An innovative application field in which Big Data Compression has a leading role is proposed by [43], in which big data must be collected for *advanced telemedicine applications* using wireless body area networks or internet of things platforms. These networks carry out a number of operations that use the most energy while sending massive amounts of data, which consumes the battery and needs regular battery replacement. Additionally, a sizable quantity of storage space would be needed to transfer and store the enormous data. Compressing the large amounts of data collected from the sensors before transmission solves the aforementioned issue by lowering power consumption and making better use of available storage. A *Hybrid Compression Algorithm* (HCA) based on *Rice-Golomb Coding* is suggested in this study. On ECG data from the physio-net ATM database and real-time data obtained from the ECG sensor, the effectiveness of the suggested compression strategy is evaluated. Both lossy and lossless compression are included in the suggested HCA. Utilizing *NI my-RIO* hardware and the *Lab-VIEW* graphical tool, the proposed compression technique is implemented in real-time. Following storage of the compressed data in the Google cloud, an analysis of storage space using the HCA reveals a reduction in storage space of 70% for 10 minutes of ECG data.

In the study [57], instead, authors looks at data compression that enables local updating and decoding at the same time. The primary outcome is an *all-encompassing compression* method for memory-less sources with the following characteristics. Contiguous fragments of the source can be recovered or updated by probing or modifying a number of *code-word bits* that is typically linear in the size of the fragment, and the overall encoding and decoding complexity is quasi-linear in the block length of the source. The rate can be made arbitrarily close to the entropy of the underlying source. For instance, a single message symbol's local decoding or updating can be carried out by probing or changing an average constant number of code-word bits. The latter section outperforms earlier best-known studies, which saw a *logarithmic* growth in local decodability or update efficiency with block length.

Authors in [38] suggest an ecological big data adaptive switching compression method based on a *1D convolutional neural network* (1D CNN) to address the large data transmission needs and high transmission power consumptions characteristic of micro-environment monitoring systems that are frequently used in *forest health* and *safety* applications. In order to verify that data samples apply to various compression dictionaries, the samples are first divided into two sets using a 1D CNN based on the samples' properties. The switching factor S is then established based on the classification outcomes, allowing for the adaptive attainment of sparse expression and data compression using the predetermined dictionary for the *discrete cosine transform* (DCT) and the *learning dictionary* (K-SVD). The sparse signal is then rebuilt via the *orthogonal matching pursuit* (OMP) method. We experiment with four different types of data: *air temperature* (AT), *air humidity* (AH), *soil temperature* (ST), and *soil humidity* (SH) in order to assess the viability and robustness of the suggested method. According to the findings, the suggested method outperforms K-SVD and DCT dictionaries for all data samples with fewer sparse errors, smaller reconstruction errors, and larger compression ratios at various levels of sparsity.The reconstructed signal closely resembles the original signal when sparsity K is 16, in particular. In addition, when compared to uncompressed data transfer, the suggested solution consumes 79.90% less power. In comparison to using only K-SVD or DCT dictionary, the adaptive switching compression approach based on 1D CNN has higher reconstruction accuracy and uses less power.

[42] reports that big data is now a common phenomenon across almost all academic fields, from engineering to science. The utilization of such data for statistical and machine learning model fitting, which might result in high computational and storage costs, is a significant problem. Model fitting on a well chosen subset of the data is one approach. The literature has put forth a number of data reduction techniques, from random sub-sampling to strategies based on the best experimental designs. Such reduction strategies, however, may not be appropriate when the objective is to learn the underlying input-output relationship because they do not utilize the output's information. To achieve this, authors suggest the *supercompress supervised data compression technique*, which integrates output information by sampling data from regions most crucial for simulating the ideal input-output connection. The fact that *supercompress* is non- parametric, i.e. the compression technique doesn't rely on parametric modeling assumptions between inputs and outputs-is a benefit of the technique. The suggested strategy is hence resistant to a variety of modeling options. Authors use simulations and a predictive modeling application for taxi cabs to show how *supercompress* is superior to other data reduction techniques.

Big Data Compression, moreover, occupies a very important place in the the modern era according to a recent study proposed by [49] due to the fact that photos and videos are the main types of digital data that are produced and communicated. A lot of computer resources, such as *storage* and *bandwidth*, are needed to store and communicate such a large number of photographs. Therefore, compressing and saving the image data instead of storing it in its original form saves a lot of resources. The process of *image compression* involves deleting as much redundant information from an image as feasible and keeping only the *non-redundant* information. A distributed environment with a *map-reduce paradigm* employing the *Hadoop* distributed file system and *Apache Spark* is utilized to compress and decompress such huge image data. Additionally, the infrastructure as a service cloud environment provided by *Microsoft Azure* is utilized. With the use of a self-created huge image collection, various setups including a single system, $1+4$ *node cluster*, $1+15$ *node cluster*, and $1+18$ *node cluster* cloud infrastructure are utilized to provide time comparisons between different setups. More than 100 million (109,670,400) images are compressed and decompressed on these four self-built clusters, and the execution times are compared with those of two well-known image compression techniques: *Lempel-Ziv-Welch* (LZW) and *Huffman coding*. LZW and Huffman coding are examples of lossless picture compression methods. The Huffman coding merely eliminates coding redundancy, but LZW eliminates both spatial and coding redundancies. These two compression methods-LZW and Huffman-are merely stand-ins; any other compression method for huge image data may be used in their place. In order to verify that the compression and decompression processes for each technique are exactly the same regardless of the number of systems employed, distributed or not, we have used compression ratios, *average root mean square error* (ARMSE), and *average peak signal* to noise ratios in our work.

In [51], authors describe today's environment in which photos and videos are mostly used to create and distribute digital data. Such a high number of photographs require a lot of computer resources, such as storage and bandwidth, to store and transport. In order to reduce space, the image data could be compressed instead of being stored in its original form. The method of image compression involves deleting as much redundant information from an image as is practical and keeping only the non-redundant information. The classic JPEG compression method is used in this research to process large amounts of image data in a distributed context using the *map-reduce paradigm*. This method is used to demonstrate the time comparisons between both setups using a self-created huge image dataset in both a serial and parallel mode with varying worker counts. More than one *Lakh* (121, 856) photos are compressed and decompressed in this, and the execution times for three alternative setups a single system, *Map-Reduce* (MR) with two workers, and MR with four workers are compared. Using a single system and MR with 4 people, compression on more than one million (1, 096, 704) images is also completed. Two performance measurements, such as *Compression Ratio* (CR) and *Peak Signal to Noise Ratio* (PSNR), are employed to assess the effectiveness of the JPEG approach.

In [59], authors describe the issue related to *WebGIS-based RIA* data files, the sizes of individual data files have steadily increased, creating problems like poor WebGIS-based RIA data compression, transmission, and rendering efficiency due to complex visualization systems. In this paper, a technical approach based on WebGIS is suggested for the effective transmission and presentation of meteorological big data. The suggested approach takes into account distributed data compression and transmission on the server side as well as distributed queries and page rendering on the browser side. It is based on open-source technology such as *HTML5* and *Mapbox GL*. With a 90% compression ratio and data recovery accuracy to two decimal places, a high-low 8-bit compression method is designed to condense a 100 megabyte (MB) file into a megabyte-scale file. Pyramid tile cutting, concurrent domain name request processing, and texture rendering are all combined in another portion of the design. According to experimental results, this method can transfer and display grid files up to 100 MB in milliseconds and support multi-terminal service applications by creating a grid data visualization mode for big data and technology centers, which could be used as a model by other sectors.

Instead, in [3] author analyzes how data is being gathered from a wide range of sources at an astounding rate, and the amount of data is growing tremendously in recent years as a result of the *Internet of Things* (IoT) entering our lives and the quickly rising number of digital applications. It is possible to collect huge volumes of data thanks to social networks, cloud computing and data analysis. The idea of big data has now developed into a crucial subject in many industries. Big data poses a severe danger to the security of a person's sensitive information because it is extremely complex to store and evaluate. The author explains the problems with big data privacy and security and offers a new security model based on *blockchain technology* as a fix. The *Blockchain-based Special Key Security Model* (BSKM) is the name of the suggested model. The three components of information security (*confidentiality, integrity, and availability*) for big data are proposed, implemented, and integrated by BSKM. The read, write, update, and delete actions on a database with actual data are established with this proposed model in a more realistic and adaptable manner. There was a framework in this study that could guarantee both secrecy and integrity at the same time, and all independent blockchain transactions were used for read, write, update, and delete operations. It has been demonstrated what kind of authorization and access control can be built between which processes and which users by taking a distinctive key for all the blockchain transaction operations conducted on the huge data. Therefore, data confidentiality, data integrity, and data consistency were guaranteed for all transactions, in contrast to earlier experiments found in published literature. An experimental analysis of the proposed BSKM model's use has also been done to compare the findings. Additionally, this study has demonstrated the value and effectiveness of the path compression technique. This outcome has been demonstrated by experimental investigations that modeled massive data, and it also offers hope for future research.

Authors in [46] analyze the behavior of *high-performance computing platforms* (HPC), scientific simulations can produce a lot of floating-point data each run. Floating-point compressors are frequently used to reduce the data volume and alleviate the data storage bottleneck. Lossy compressors, like *SZ* and *ZFP*, can aggressively reduce data volume while keeping the usefulness of the data. This is in contrast to lossless compressors. However, it is nearly impossible to achieve a reduction ratio of more than two orders of magnitude without significantly affecting the data. The *autoencoder technique* in deep learning has demonstrated excellent potential for data compression, particularly with images. However, it is questionable whether the autoencoder can provide a comparable performance on scientific data. In this work, authors perform a thorough investigation-for the first time-on the use of autoencoders to compress actual scientific data, and reporting several significant findings. To minimize floating point data, the authors implemented a prototype *autoencoder-based compression algorithm*. Research shows that further fine-tuning is needed for the *out-of-the-box* approach in order to attain high compression ratios and acceptable error boundaries. The evaluation results prove that the custom autoencoder beats *SZ* and *ZFP* in terms of compression ratios for the majority of the test datasets by up to 4X and 50X, respectively. Future optimizations for using autoencoders to compress scientific data can be guided by these practices and the lessons we have learned from this effort.

In [35], authors address the issue of use of IoT devices and sensors results in the production of a significant number of time series. *Time series compression* is frequently used to lower storage costs and transportation expenses. Most *cutting-edge methods* today concentrate on *single-variate time series*. Because of this, the challenge of compressing0 *multivariate time series* (MTS) remains a crucial yet difficult problem. The correlations between variables are not taken into account by conventional MTS compression methods, which treat each variable separately. In order to compress MTS and increase its compression ratio, a unique MTS prediction approach is proposed in this study. The technique, which is based on the *prediction-quantization-entropy framework*, may extract the spatial and temporal correlation across various variables to produce a more accurate prediction and improve the *lossy compression* performance of MTS. To extract the temporal properties of all variables within the length of the window, a *Convolutional Neural Network* (CNN) is used. The image classification algorithm then extracts the spatial features from the changed data once the CNN-generated features have been converted. Spatio-temporal properties are used to make predictions. The AR *autoregressive* linear model is incorporated simultaneously with the suggested network to increase the robustness of the model. Experimental findings show that, in the majority of circumstances, this approach can increase MTS's prediction accuracy and compression performance.

5 A Reference Architecture for Big OLAP Data Cubes Over Clouds

When OLAP data cubes must be processed and managed on top of Cloud architectures, which are essentially *distributed* in nature, they convey in the so-called big OLAP data cubes. Since these data structures tend to easily become massive in size (e.g., [11]), they cannot be naturally processed and managed via centralized architectures and, even traditional experiences devoted to achieve effective and efficient distributed representations of such structures (e.g., [2]) fail. The reason of that is the need for different approaches in multidimensional data representation over Clouds, thus realizing a real research innovation. To be convinced of this, focus on traditional MOLAP-based representation of OLAP data cubes (e.g., [8]). According to this approach, OLAP data cubes are represented as *multidimensional arrays*, which, of course, are very hard to be implemented on tops of distributed (data) repositories, especially for their *indexing data structures requirements* (e.g., [33]). On the other hand, as regards distributed aggregates computing, it should be noted that some aggregate operators are suitable to be computed according to this model (e.g., SUM, COUNT) whereas some others are not (e.g., AVG).

Following this main conceptual and methodological motivation, we propose an innovative mechanism for representing big OLAP data cubes over Clouds, which is inspired by previous research experiences in the context of *in-memory database management* (e.g., [37]). According to this mechanism, big OLAP data cubes are first *partitioned in columns* and, then, these columns are *distributed across Cloud nodes* of the reference (Cloud) architecture. This Cloud-based, column-based representation model is fully compliant with modern big data processing platforms. For instance, consider the case of integration with Apache Spark: it is worthy to notice that, here, one whole (OLAP) column or partitions of it can be easily processed by ad-hoc Apache Spark libraries, even according to a full in-memory processing schema (e.g., for evaluating the COUNT aggregate of the elements of the column that satisfy a given filtering condition). This contributes to increase the performance of the entire big data framework. Figure 1 shows our reference architecture for big OLAP data cubes over Clouds.

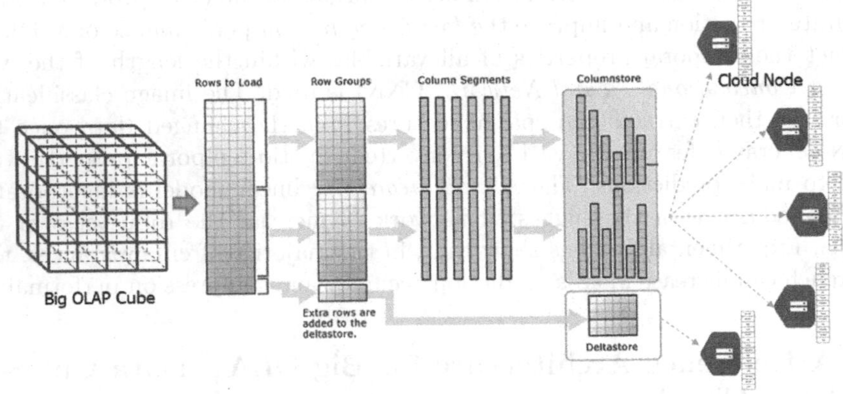

Fig. 1. A Reference Architecture for Big OLAP Data Cubes over Clouds.

Despite the proposed reference architecture, big OLAP data cubes over Clouds can still pose severe limitations for what regards their accessing, querying and mining phases (e.g., [52,56]). Therefore, we propose to further enrich our reference architecture via well-understood *data compression paradigms* (e.g., [42]). Data compression allows us to effectively and efficiently achieve a significant speed-up while ensuring the *accuracy* of the underlying analytical process (e.g., [1]). Data compression has been applied in the specific context of OLAP data cube compression (e.g., [13]), with alternate fortune. Here, we propose to still follow this general paradigm, and make use of data compression methods to further enhance the computational capabilities of our reference architecture for big OLAP data cubes over Clouds.

As shown in Fig. 2, after the columns derived from the column-based representation of the input big OLAP data cube are distributed over the Cloud nodes of the target architecture, they are compressed in order to gain into a more efficient data representation, still compliant with the goals of the target multidimensional big data analytics process, where decimal precision is not mandatory (e.g., [15]). The compressed representations of columns are obtained via ad-hoc *compression algorithms* specifically tailored to multidimensional (i.e., OLAP) data (e.g., [7]). Then, the compressed columns are delivered on top of ad-hoc

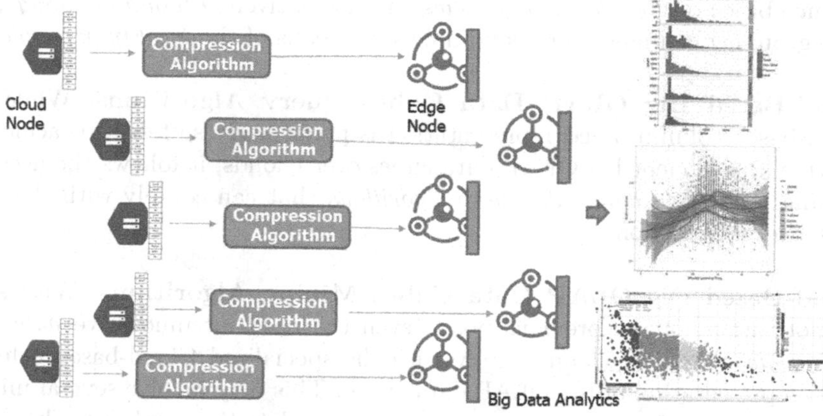

Fig. 2. Big OLAP Data Cube Compression over Clouds.

edge nodes of the overall Cloud architecture, as to achieve a proper and original *big data architecture*, particularity devised for big OLAP cata cubes over Clouds. It should be noticed that this approach follows some recent paradigms appeared in literature recently (e.g., [32,48]). The final (multidimensional) big data analytics processing is, therefore, issued on the compressed columns, being the latter scheme perfectly suitable for a large number of real-life big data applications. To become convinced of this, it suffices to consider application scenarios such as social network analysis, massive graph data processing, scientific and statistical distributed data repositories, and so forth.

How to compress multidimensional data columns? This is a critical question in our investigated context. While in literature there exist a plethora of proposals in the data compression research area, in our specific application scenario, we seek for data compression techniques particularly suitable to multidimensional and OLAP data, since the latter expose specific characteristics (e.g., [29]). This is an open question of our research, which deserves future investigations.

6 Multidimensional Big Data Analytics: Future Research Directions

From the analysis of fundamental concepts of the general multidimensional big data analytics framework, several interesting future research directions derive. In the following, we report and briefly discuss the most relevant ones.

Cloud-Based Big OLAP Data Cubes Distribution Algorithms. After the target big OLAP data cube is split into columns, how these columns should be distributed over the reference Cloud architecture? This is a critical question that must be addressed. Indeed, several *policies* can be devised here, for instance based on *load balancing issues*, or, alternatively, *column grouping goals* (e.g., grouping columns over Cloud nodes by means of the *locality principle*).

Cloud-Based Big OLAP Data Cubes Query Algorithms. While the Cloud-based column-based representation is particularly suitable for achieving effective and efficient big OLAP data cubes over Clouds, it follows the need for devising innovative *data cube query algorithms* that can comply with this specialized representation.

Cloud-Based Big OLAP Data Cubes Mining Algorithms. With similar motivations of the previous point, even the need for innovative *data cube mining algorithms* that can comply with the specialized Cloud-based column-based representation of big OLAP data cubes. This may involve several mining libraries, such as *frequent pattern mining*, *outlier detection*, and so forth.

Extending Multidimensional Big Data Analytics Over Cloud-Based Big OLAP Data Cubes via Artificial Intelligence Paradigms. Nowadays, *Artificial Intelligence* (AI) is (re-)gaining the scene of research, both in the industrial and the academic settings. It is therefore a natural consequence to think on how to extend the general multidimensional big data analytics over Cloud-based Big OLAP data cubes via engrafting novel methodologies inherited from the AI world. For instance, *explainability* turns to play a key role in our investigated context, due to the fact that *big data understanding* is a major challenge in multidimensional big data analytics.

Privacy-Preserving Cloud-Based Big OLAP Data Cubes Computation Algorithms. How to compute Cloud-based column-based big OLAP data cubes in a *privacy-preserving manner*? This question is critical at both the theoretical side but also the pragmatic side, being relevant for a wide number of applications (e.g., healthcare analytics, epidemiological analytics, and so forth). Also, privacy issues are directly related to *security issues*, so that the complexity of the problem gets worse.

Integration with Modern Big Data Processing Platforms. Last but not least, the integration of multidimensional big data analytics paradigms with well-known modern big data processing platforms, such as *Hadoop* and *MS Azure*, will specifically play a first-class role, even due to the need for *standardization* of the proposed paradigms.

7 Conclusions and Future Work

Inspired from traditional OLAP and BI systems, this paper has explored their evolution towards Cloud systems and, particularly, an innovative conceptual framework defined as multidimensional big data analytics. Also, we proposed a reference architecture for supporting this framework via Cloud-based column-based big OLAP data cubes, enriched by compression paradigms. Future work is mainly devoted to make our general framework more and more compliant with emerging research challenges dictated by modern big data trends (e.g., [4,5,9,24,45,55]).

Acknowledgments. This research is supported by the ICSC National Research Centre for High Performance Computing, Big Data and Quantum Computing within the NextGenerationEU program (Project Code: PNRR CN00000013).

References

1. Ainsworth, M., Tugluk, O., Whitney, B., Klasky, S.: Multilevel techniques for compression and reduction of scientific data-quantitative control of accuracy in derived quantities. SIAM J. Sci. Comput. **41**(4), A2146–A2171 (2019)
2. Akinde, M.O., Böhlen, M.H., Johnson, T., Lakshmanan, L.V.S., Srivastava, D.: Efficient OLAP query processing in distributed data warehouses. Inf. Syst. **28**(1–2), 111–135 (2003)
3. Bakir, Ç.: New blockchain based special keys security model with path compression algorithm for big data. IEEE Access **10**, 94738–94753 (2022)
4. Balbin, P.P.F., Barker, J.C.R., Leung, C.K., Tran, M., Wall, R.P., Cuzzocrea, A.: Predictive analytics on open big data for supporting smart transportation services. Procedia Comput. Sci. **176**, 3009–3018 (2020)
5. Bellatreche, L., Cuzzocrea, A., Benkrid, S.: *F&A*: a methodology for effectively and efficiently designing parallel relational data warehouses on heterogenous database clusters. In: Bach Pedersen, T., Mohania, M.K., Tjoa, A.M. (eds.) DaWaK 2010. LNCS, vol. 6263, pp. 89–104. Springer, Heidelberg (2010). https://doi.org/10.1007/978-3-642-15105-7_8
6. Bochicchio, M.A., Cuzzocrea, A., Vaira, L.: A big data analytics framework for supporting multidimensional mining over big healthcare data. In: 15th IEEE International Conference on Machine Learning and Applications, ICMLA 2016, Anaheim, CA, USA, 18–20 December 2016, pp. 508–513. IEEE Computer Society (2016)
7. Boukraâ, D., Bouchoukh, M.A., Boussaïd, O.: Efficient compression and storage of XML OLAP cubes. Int. J. Data Warehous. Min. **11**(3), 1–25 (2015)
8. Chaudhuri, S., Dayal, U.: An overview of data warehousing and OLAP technology. SIGMOD Rec. **26**(1), 65–74 (1997)
9. Coronato, A., Cuzzocrea, A.: An innovative risk assessment methodology for medical information systems. IEEE Trans. Knowl. Data Eng. **34**(7), 3095–3110 (2022)
10. Cuzzocrea, A.: Overcoming limitations of approximate query answering in OLAP. In: Desai, B.C., Vossen, G. (eds.) Ninth International Database Engineering and Applications Symposium (IDEAS 2005), Montreal, Canada, 25–27 July 2005, pp. 200–209. IEEE Computer Society (2005)
11. Cuzzocrea, A.: Accuracy control in compressed multidimensional data cubes for quality of answer-based OLAP tools. In: 18th International Conference on Scientific and Statistical Database Management, SSDBM 2006, Vienna, Austria, 3–5 July 2006, Proceedings, pp. 301–310. IEEE Computer Society (2006)
12. Cuzzocrea, A.: Improving range-sum query evaluation on data cubes via polynomial approximation. Data Knowl. Eng. **56**(2), 85–121 (2006)

13. Cuzzocrea, A.: OLAP data cube compression techniques: a ten-year-long history. In: Kim, T., Lee, Y., Kang, B.-H., Slezak, D. (eds.) FGIT 2010. LNCS, vol. 6485, pp. 751–754. Springer, Heidelberg (2010). https://doi.org/10.1007/978-3-642-17569-5_74
14. Cuzzocrea, A.: A top-down approach for compressing data cubes under the simultaneous evaluation of multiple hierarchical range queries. J. Intell. Inf. Syst. **34**(3), 305–343 (2010)
15. Cuzzocrea, A.: Aggregation and multidimensional analysis of big data for large-scale scientific applications: models, issues, analytics, and beyond. In: Gupta, A., Rathbun, S.L. (eds.) Proceedings of the 27th International Conference on Scientific and Statistical Database Management, SSDBM 2015, La Jolla, CA, USA, 29 June–1 July 2015, pp. 23:1–23:6. ACM (2015)
16. Cuzzocrea, A.: Big data compression paradigms for supporting efficient and scalable data-intensive iot frameworks. In: Leung, C.K., Kim, J., Kim, Y., Geller, J., Choi, W., Park, Y. (eds.) Proceedings of the Sixth International Conference on Emerging Databases: Technologies, Applications, and Theory, EDB 2016, Jeju Island, Republic of Korea, 17–19 October 2016, pp. 67–71. ACM (2016)
17. Cuzzocrea, A.: OLAPing big social data: multidimensional big data analytics over big social data repositories. In: ICCBDC 2020: 2020 4th International Conference on Cloud and Big Data Computing, Virtual United Kingdom, August 2020, pp. 15–19. ACM (2020)
18. Cuzzocrea, A.: Multidimensional big data analytics over big web knowledge bases: models, issues, research trends, and a reference architecture. In: Eighth IEEE International Conference on Multimedia Big Data, BigMM 2022, Naples, Italy, 5–7 December 2022, pp. 1–6. IEEE (2022)
19. Cuzzocrea, A., Bringas, P.G.: CORE-BCD-mAI: a composite framework for representing, querying, and analyzing big clinical data by means of multidimensional AI tools. In: Bringas, P.G., et al. (eds.) Hybrid Artificial Intelligent Systems - 17th International Conference, HAIS 2022, Salamanca, Spain, 5–7 September 2022, Proceedings. Lecture Notes in Computer Science, vol. 13469, pp. 175–185. Springer, Heidelberg (2022). https://doi.org/10.1007/978-3-031-15471-3_16
20. Cuzzocrea, A., Chakravarthy, S.: Event-based lossy compression for effective and efficient OLAP over data streams. Data Knowl. Eng. **69**(7), 678–708 (2010)
21. Cuzzocrea, A., Furfaro, F., Saccà, D.: Enabling OLAP in mobile environments via intelligent data cube compression techniques. J. Intell. Inf. Syst. **33**(2), 95–143 (2009)
22. Cuzzocrea, A., Leung, C.K.: Efficiently compressing OLAP data cubes via R-tree based recursive partitions. In: Chen, L., Felfernig, A., Liu, J., Ras, Z.W. (eds.) ISMIS 2012. LNCS (LNAI), vol. 7661, pp. 455–465. Springer, Heidelberg (2012). https://doi.org/10.1007/978-3-642-34624-8_51
23. Cuzzocrea, A., Leung, C.K., MacKinnon, R.K.: Mining constrained frequent itemsets from distributed uncertain data. Future Gener. Comput. Syst. **37**, 117–126 (2014)
24. Cuzzocrea, A., Martinelli, F., Mercaldo, F., Vercelli, G.V.: Tor traffic analysis and detection via machine learning techniques. In: Nie, J., et al. (eds.) 2017 IEEE International Conference on Big Data (IEEE BigData 2017), Boston, MA, USA, 11–14 December 2017, pp. 4474–4480. IEEE Computer Society (2017)
25. Cuzzocrea, A., Matrangolo, U.: Analytical synopses for approximate query answering in OLAP environments. In: Galindo, F., Takizawa, M., Traunmüller, R. (eds.) DEXA 2004. LNCS, vol. 3180, pp. 359–370. Springer, Heidelberg (2004). https://doi.org/10.1007/978-3-540-30075-5_35

26. Cuzzocrea, A., Moussa, R., Laabidi, A.: Taming size and cardinality of OLAP data cubes over big data. In: Calì, A., Wood, P., Martin, N., Poulovassilis, A. (eds.) BICOD 2017. LNCS, vol. 10365, pp. 113–125. Springer, Cham (2017). https://doi.org/10.1007/978-3-319-60795-5_12
27. Cuzzocrea, A., Saccà, D., Serafino, P.: A hierarchy-driven compression technique for advanced OLAP visualization of multidimensional data cubes. In: Tjoa, A.M., Trujillo, J. (eds.) DaWaK 2006. LNCS, vol. 4081, pp. 106–119. Springer, Heidelberg (2006). https://doi.org/10.1007/11823728_11
28. Cuzzocrea, A., Saccà, D., Ullman, J.D.: Big data: a research agenda. In: Desai, B.C., Larriba-Pey, J.L., Bernardino, J. (eds.) 17th International Database Engineering & Applications Symposium, IDEAS 2013, Barcelona, Spain, 09–11 October 2013, pp. 198–203. ACM (2013)
29. Cuzzocrea, A., Serafino, P.: LCS-hist: taming massive high-dimensional data cube compression. In: Kersten, M.L., Novikov, B., Teubner, J., Polutin, V., Manegold, S. (eds.) EDBT 2009, 12th International Conference on Extending Database Technology, Saint Petersburg, Russia, 24–26 March 2009, Proceedings. ACM International Conference Proceeding Series, vol. 360, pp. 768–779. ACM (2009)
30. Cuzzocrea, A., Wang, W.: Approximate range-sum query answering on data cubes with probabilistic guarantees. J. Intell. Inf. Syst. **28**(2), 161–197 (2007)
31. Dehdouh, K., Boussaid, O., Bentayeb, F.: Big data warehouse: building columnar nosql OLAP cubes. Int. J. Decis. Supp. Syst. Technol. **12**(1), 1–24 (2020)
32. Dehne, F.K.H.A., Kong, Q., Rau-Chaplin, A., Zaboli, H., Zhou, R.: A distributed tree data structure for real-time OLAP on cloud architectures. In: Hu, X., et al. (eds.) 2013 IEEE International Conference on Big Data (IEEE BigData 2013), Santa Clara, CA, USA, 6–9 October 2013, pp. 499–505. IEEE Computer Society (2013)
33. Dehne, F.K.H.A., Kong, Q., Rau-Chaplin, A., Zaboli, H., Zhou, R.: Scalable real-time OLAP on cloud architectures. J. Parallel Distrib. Comput. **79–80**, 31–41 (2015)
34. Djenouri, Y., Djenouri, D., Lin, J.C., Belhadi, A.: Frequent itemset mining in big data with effective single scan algorithms. IEEE Access **6**, 68013–68026 (2018)
35. Feng, H., Ma, R., Yan, L., Ma, Z.: Spatiotemporal prediction based on feature classification for multivariate floating-point time series lossy compression. Big Data Res. **32**, 100377 (2023)
36. Gray, J., et al.: Data cube: a relational aggregation operator generalizing group-by, cross-tab, and sub totals. Data Min. Knowl. Discov. **1**(1), 29–53 (1997)
37. Gupta, M.K., Verma, V., Verma, M.S.: In-memory database systems - a paradigm shift. CoRR abs/1402.1258 (2014)
38. Han, Q., Liu, L., Zhao, Y., Zhao, Y.: Ecological big data adaptive compression method combining 1d convolutional neural network and switching idea. IEEE Access **8**, 20270–20278 (2020)
39. He, B., Hsiao, H., Liu, Z., Huang, Y., Chen, Y.: Efficient iceberg query evaluation using compressed bitmap index. IEEE Trans. Knowl. Data Eng. **24**(9), 1570–1583 (2012)
40. Ho, C., Agrawal, R., Megiddo, N., Srikant, R.: Range queries in OLAP data cubes. In: Peckham, J. (ed.) SIGMOD 1997, Proceedings ACM SIGMOD International Conference on Management of Data, Tucson, Arizona, USA, 13–15 May 1997, pp. 73–88. ACM Press (1997)
41. Jarke, M., Koch, J.: Query optimization in database systems. ACM Comput. Surv. **16**(2), 111–152 (1984)

42. Joseph, V.R., Mak, S.: Supervised compression of big data. Stat. Anal. Data Min. **14**(3), 217–229 (2021)
43. Kalaivani, S., Tharini, C., Saranya, K., Priyanka, K.: Design and implementation of hybrid compression algorithm for personal health care big data applications. Wirel. Pers. Commun. **113**(1), 599–615 (2020)
44. Khurshid, M.J., Lipasti, M.H.: Data compression for thermal mitigation in the hybrid memory cube. In: 2013 IEEE 31st International Conference on Computer Design, ICCD 2013, Asheville, NC, USA, 6–9 October 2013, pp. 185–192. IEEE Computer Society (2013)
45. Leung, C.K., Cuzzocrea, A., Mai, J.J., Deng, D., Jiang, F.: Personalized deepinf: enhanced social influence prediction with deep learning and transfer learning. In: Baru, C.K., et al. (eds.) 2019 IEEE International Conference on Big Data (IEEE BigData), Los Angeles, CA, USA, 9–12 December 2019, pp. 2871–2880. IEEE (2019)
46. Liu, T., Wang, J., Liu, Q., Alibhai, S., Lu, T., He, X.: High-ratio lossy compression: exploring the autoencoder to compress scientific data. IEEE Trans. Big Data **9**(1), 22–36 (2023)
47. Mamoulis, N., Bakiras, S., Kalnis, P.: Evaluation of top-k OLAP queries using aggregate R-trees. In: Bauzer Medeiros, C., Egenhofer, M.J., Bertino, E. (eds.) SSTD 2005. LNCS, vol. 3633, pp. 236–253. Springer, Heidelberg (2005). https://doi.org/10.1007/11535331_14
48. Nakabasami, K., Amagasa, T., Shaikh, S.A., Gass, F., Kitagawa, H.: An architecture for stream OLAP exploiting SPE and OLAP engine. In: 2015 IEEE International Conference on Big Data (IEEE BigData 2015), Santa Clara, CA, USA, 29 October–1 November 2015, pp. 319–326. IEEE Computer Society (2015)
49. Netalkar, R.K., Barman, H., Subba, R., Preetam, K.V., Undi, S.N.R.: Distributed compression and decompression for big image data: LZW and huffman coding. J. Electron. Imaging **30**(5), 053015 (2021)
50. Ordonez, C., Chen, Z., Cuzzocrea, A., García-García, J.: An intelligent visual big data analytics framework for supporting interactive exploration and visualization of big OLAP cubes. In: Banissi, E., et al. (eds.) 24th International Conference on Information Visualisation, IV 2020, Melbourne, Australia, 7–11 September 2020, pp. 421–427. IEEE (2020)
51. Raju, U.S.N., Barman, H., Netalkar, R.K., Kumar, S., Kumar, H.: Distributed JPEG compression and decompression for big image data using map-reduce paradigm. J. Mobile Multimedia **18**(6), 1513–1540 (2022)
52. Ramdane, Y., Boussaid, O., Boukraâ, D., Kabachi, N., Bentayeb, F.: Building a novel physical design of a distributed big data warehouse over a hadoop cluster to enhance OLAP cube query performance. Parallel Comput. **111**, 102918 (2022)
53. Sagiroglu, S., Sinanc, D.: Big data: a review. In: Fox, G.C., Smari, W.W. (eds.) 2013 International Conference on Collaboration Technologies and Systems, CTS 2013, San Diego, CA, USA, 20–24 May 2013, pp. 42–47. IEEE (2013)
54. Sidiropoulos, N.D., Papalexakis, E.E., Faloutsos, C.: Parallel randomly compressed cubes?: a scalable distributed architecture for big tensor decomposition. IEEE Signal Process. Mag. **31**(5), 57–70 (2014)
55. Song, J., Guo, C., Wang, Z., Zhang, Y., Yu, G., Pierson, J.: Haolap: a hadoop based OLAP system for big data. J. Syst. Softw. **102**, 167–181 (2015)
56. Tardío, R., Maté, A., Trujillo, J.: Beyond tpc-ds, a benchmark for big data OLAP systems (bdolap-bench). Future Gener. Comput. Syst. **132**, 136–151 (2022)
57. Vatedka, S., Tchamkerten, A.: Local decode and update for big data compression. IEEE Trans. Inf. Theory **66**(9), 5790–5805 (2020)

58. Xi, R., Lin, N., Chen, Y.: Compression and aggregation for logistic regression analysis in data cubes. IEEE Trans. Knowl. Data Eng. **21**(4), 479–492 (2009)
59. Yang, H., et al.: Quick compression and transmission of meteorological big data in complicated visualization systems. Complexity **2022**, 6860915:1–6860915:9 (2022)
60. Yun, X., Wu, G., Zhang, G., Li, K., Wang, S.: Fastraq: a fast approach to range-aggregate queries in big data environments. IEEE Trans. Cloud Comput. **3**(2), 206–218 (2015)

Author Index

M. Van Sinderen et al. (Eds.): ICSBT/SECRYPT 2022, CCIS 1849, p. 177, 2023.
https://doi.org/10.1007/978-3-031-45137-9

Printed in the United States
by Baker & Taylor Publisher Services